THE HOLY AND THE PROFANE

THE HOLY
and the Profane

EVOLUTION
OF JEWISH FOLKWAYS

Theodor H. Gaster

WILLIAM MORROW AND COMPANY, INC.
New York   1980

TO JOYCE AND SAVILLE COHEN

Library of Congress Catalog Card Number 80-80324

ISBN 0-688-01795-9
ISBN 0-688-06795-6 pbk.

Printed in the United States of America

2   3   4   5   6   7   8   9   10

CONTENTS

FOREWORD ix
NOTE TO THE SECOND EDITION xvii

I
Blessed Event

1   BE FRUITFUL AND MULTIPLY 3
2   THE PANGS OF EVE 9
3   A TIME TO BE BORN 16
4   THE WILES OF LILITH 18
5   DAYS OF PERIL 29
6   NAMES AND NICKNAMES 33
7   THE TREE OF LIFE 39

II
Childhood

1   THE COVENANT OF ABRAHAM 45
    The Rite of Circumcision

2   COMING OF AGE   66
    The Ceremony of Bar Mitzvah

III
Betrothal

1   TROTH AND RING   81
    Exchange of Gifts
    Spinnholz

IV
Marriage

1   WEDLOCK   93
    A Time to Embrace
    Bride and Groom
    Bride's Adorning
    Tresses and Wigs
    Swords and Daggers
    Torches
2   THE WEDDING CEREMONY: 111
    a. HUPPAH: *The Bridal Canopy*
    b. KETUBAH: *The Marriage Contract*
    c. *The Seven Blessings*
    d. *The Cup of Betrothal*
    e. *Smashing the Glass*

    Rice, Nuts and Confetti
    Insult and Ribaldry
    Round and Round

3 THE TWO COVENANTS 126
An Ancient Hebrew Wedding
"Children Under the Mantle"

V
Death

1 LAST RITES 137
2 LAST JOURNEY 142
3 A TIME TO MOURN 149
4 THE FOLKLORE OF DEATH: 156
  a. *Removal of Feather Pillows*
  b. *Opening Windows*
  c. *Closing the Eyes*
  d. *Closing the Mouth*
  e. *Rending of Garments*
  f. *Graveclothes free of Knots*
  g. *Laying the Dead upon the Floor*
  h. *Taharah*
  i. *White for the Dead*
  j. *Lamps*
  k. *Interment without Coffin*
  l. *Earth of the Holy Land*
  m. *Objects in the Coffin*
  n. *"Passports" for the Dead*
  o. *Speedy Burial*
  p. *Pallbearers walk Barefoot*
  q. *Pouring out Water*
  r. *Overturning Chairs and breaking Pots*
  s. *Halting the Cortege*
  t. *Circuits around the Dead*
  u. *Earth on the Coffin*
  v. *Mourners wash their Hands*
  w. *Plucking of grass and throwing of Dust*
  x. *Funeral Meats*
5 THE HOUSE OF LIFE 179
6 COMMEMORATION 182
Jahrzeit and Yizkor

VI
The Dietary Laws

"Clean and Unclean" 199
"The Blood is the Life"
"The Sinew that Shrinks"
Meat and Milk

VII
The Shield of David

SHIELD OF DAVID AND SEAL OF SOLOMON 217
EPILOGUE 223
REFERENCES AND NOTES 225
INDEX 251

FOREWORD

For nearly two thousand years the Jews have lived not as a single compact community in a land of their own but as a series of communities scattered over the face of the earth. Their daily life has therefore consisted in a fusion, now conscious and now unconscious, between their ancient Hebraic heritage and the cultures of their various and diverse neighbors.

Jewish folkways are a reflex of this situation. By and large, they are simply general folkways which the Jews happen to have picked up and which they have ingeniously adapted to the spirit of their own traditional teachings.

There is perforce no uniformity about them. Although, to be sure, there are many customs and beliefs which, by

virtue of constant migration, have now become common
to all Jews everywhere, there are just as many others that
have remained confined to particular lands and areas.
Those, for instance, that are commonplace among the
mountain Jews of the Caucasus are, as likely as not, utterly unknown to their brethren in Europe; while the daily
life of the mellahs of North Africa is very different from
that of a Polish ghetto. Consequently, it is both unsafe
and unsound, in speaking of popular usages, to say roundly
that "the Jews" in toto do or believe this or that, and
it must be clearly understood that the expression, "Jewish
folkways" is but an over-all, comprehensive term covering what is in fact a manifold, heterogeneous diversity.
Indeed, if there is one thing that the study of these folkways brings home especially, it is that Jewish life is, and
always has been, a sea fed by many rivers.

Nowhere, perhaps, is the extent of this diversity more
evident than in the multiplicity of Jewish dialects spoken
(and written) in different parts of the world. There is a
Judaeo-German (Yiddish) and a Judaeo-Spanish (La-
dino), a Judaeo-Greek and a Judaeo-Italian, a Judaeo-
Arabic and a Judaeo-Persian, each representing a fusion
between the language of a particular environment and a
commonly inherited Hebrew idiom.

Or take, as a further illustration, the multifariousness
of the Jewish cuisine. *Blintzes, gefillte fish* and *pirogen,*
favorite dishes among the mainly Ashkenazic Jews of the
United States, are virtually unknown to their Sephardic
and Oriental brethren. Conversely, who on Houston
Street has ever heard of such Purim delicacies as *kesami,
molyatot* and *itinyan,* once so common among the Jews of
Italy? Truly, as the sages observed, the manna of the
wilderness tastes different to every man that eats it!

The Jews were not mere "copycats" and did not borrow mechanically. The characteristic trait of Jewish folklore is a genius for infusing into originally "alien" material a new and more spiritual meaning and significance born of their own distinctive heritage and tradition. By deft and ingenious reinterpretation they sought always to convert the popular customs and superstitions of their neighbors into instruments for expressing their own message and for fulfilling, in daily practice and usage, their fundamental commitment to serve as the witnesses of God among men.

The process went back, indeed, to the very dawn of their history, that is, to the Bible; for scholars have had little difficulty in showing that many of the legends recounted in the earlier chapters of Genesis, or incidentally referred to by the prophets and poets, really hark back to the pagan lore current in Palestine and the neighboring countries even before the advent of Israel. The story of the Flood, for example, is related in substantially the same form in the far earlier Babylonian epic of Gilgamesh and was probably designed originally to account for the annual flooding of the Euphrates valley. In that version, too, we have the sparing of the righteous man, the construction of the ark, the dispatch of the birds, and the eventual sacrifice of thanksgiving. Similarly, the legend of the Tower of Babel, "with its top in heaven," very probably originated in a popular tale designed to account for the great stepped temple (*ziggurat*) of Babylon; while when the Psalmist speaks (Ps. 74: 13-14) of Jehovah's primeval combat with Leviathan, or when Job exclaims (7:12), "Am I sea or dragon, that Thou shouldst set watch over me?" they are alluding to a Canaanite myth which has been rediscovered, during the past twenty-five years, on clay tablets unearthed in North

Syria. Indeed, Isaiah's description of that monster (27:1) as "the slant serpent . . . the tortuous serpent," reproduces the very words of the more ancient pagan text!

Again, the familiar tale of the temptation of Joseph by Potiphar's wife has its earlier counterpart in an Egyptian story told in a papyrus of the thirteenth century B.C.E.; while an entire section of the Book of Proverbs has been traced to the Egyptian maxims of Amen-em-ope.

Even the Psalms—so distinctive an expression of the Israelite genius—draw heavily on earlier models. It has been pointed out, for example, that Psalm 93, with its reference to Jehovah's becoming king, dominating the seas and rivers, dispensing his sure decrees and occupying his palace of beauty, is in all likelihood a mere reworking or adaptation of a Canaanite hymn based on a recently recovered myth which relates how the god Baal attained sovereignty and was installed in a sumptuous palace by virtue of the fact that he engaged and vanquished the truculent Lord of the Sea and Streams. So, too, when "the sons of the mighty" are bidden, in Psalm 29, to "ascribe unto Jehovah glory and strength," it is not difficult to recognize the same process, for the fact is that the Hebrew words translated as "sons of the mighty" really mean "lesser gods," and this is the standard expression used in Canaanite texts to refer to the minor members of the pantheon.

Sometimes, to be sure, the indebtedness of the Hebrews to their neighbors is apparent only in an implicit allusion, a mere turn of speech embodying a tidbit of traditional mythology. A case in point is the prophet Habakkuk's statement (3:5) that when Jehovah goes on the warpath, "Pestilence stalketh before Him, and plague goeth forth at His feet"; for the word rendered "plague" is really the name of the Canaanite plague-god, Resheph, and the allusion is to the ancient belief that when gods walked abroad they were flanked by two celestial attendants. In the Babylonian story of the Flood, for example, it is said expressly that when the storm-god appeared on the horizon, he was escorted by two servitors, and in the Iliad we read similarly that Apollo and Ares were accompanied by the two demons Fear and Terror.

An even more striking illustration is afforded by the familiar passage in the Book of Genesis (3:24) which states that after the expulsion of Adam and Eve, cherubim were posted eastward of Eden "to keep the way to the tree of life." Throughout the centuries, these cherubim have been portrayed as nightgowned angels—a conception which is, in fact, utterly foreign to the ancient Semitic mind. In reality, as we now know from Mesopotamian sources, they were simply griffins, like those which the Babylonians and Assyrians placed at the doors of their houses, so that what confronts us is but another relic of primitive myth, analogous to the widespread motif of the dragon guarding the pot of gold.

Nor is it only in the field of literature that such indebtedness obtains. Scholars have shown also that the seasonal festivals of Israel were patterned largely upon earlier pagan institutions. Take, for example, the Feast of Unleavened Bread. Although this was given an historical *raison d'être* as the memorial of a crucial incident in Israel's past, the existence of similar practices elsewhere strongly suggests that the ban on fermented food was originally nothing more than a precautionary measure designed to insure that the communal meal eaten ceremonially by kinsmen at the season of harvest should leave no untoward effects; while the signing of the lintel with blood is paralleled in many parts of the world and was therefore scarcely an innovation; nor was it, in fact, conditioned by the particular circumstances by which it is validated in the Scriptural narrative.

In the same way, too, the popular celebration of Purim, with its burning of Haman in effigy, its election of a "Purim rabbi," and its burlesque mummeries, has undoubtedly drawn largely on the contemporaneous Carnival and Shrovetide ceremonies of the Christian year—themselves, in turn, derived from pagan prototypes. There, too, it is customary to burn the spirit of the past year, or the noxious and malevolent demons, to appoint a temporary "bishop of fools," and to stage guisings and miracle plays.

The devices by which the "pagan" material was "made kosher" are often as piquant as they are ingenious. The parade example is, of course, the way in which the letters N G H S on the four sides of the Chanukah *trendl* were converted from their original meaning of *Nichts* (nothing), *Ganz* (all), *Halb* (half) and *Stell* (put) game of chance to the initials of the Hebrew motto, *Nes Gadol Hayah Sham,* "a great miracle occurred there"—referring to the victory of the Maccabees and to the legend that, when the Temple was rededicated, oil which was really sufficient only for one day miraculously lasted for eight. But this by no means stands alone. Hermes, the inventor of the lyre, was transmogrified into the angel Hermesiel, leader of the heavenly choir, and this celestial being was in turn identified with David, "the sweet singer of Israel," who was believed to be still playing his harp before the throne of God. The vine of Bacchus, a common theme of pagan art, became the vine of Israel which God transplanted from Egypt and which "sent out her branches unto the sea, and her shoots unto the river" (see Ps. 80:9-14). Similarly, too, because the pagans had a traditional book of magic named for one of their ancient magicians, *The Sword of Dardanos,* a Hebrew work of the same character had perforce to be called *The Sword of Moses.*

Nowhere, perhaps, is the absorption of foreign elements by Judaism more strikingly brought out than in the decorations of synagogues, tombstones, and catacombs during the Graeco-Roman age. Discoveries made during the past twenty-five years have revealed that these very commonly include representations of pagan gods and goddesses and of figures and scenes drawn from pagan mythology. In the ancient synagogue at Chorazin, for example, there are pictures of centaurs and of the mace of Heracles; at Sheikh Abreiq, there is an Amazon and two Psyches; at Capernaum there is a frieze depicting six Cupids; at Jaffa, there is a typically Dionysiac design of a vine and a tiger; while elsewhere there are representations of Helios, the sun-god, of Leto and (on an amulet) of Hecate. These latter, no doubt, are extreme cases, for there is as yet no definite proof—though the theory has indeed been advanced—that the Jews attached to these pagan designs any deeper spiritual interpretations of their own, that is, that they were ever anything more than mere mechanical imitations of a contemporary convention. Nevertheless, even on this cruder level, they illustrate in striking fashion the constant tendency of Israel to accommodate "the beauties of Japhet in the tents of Shem."

The following pages seek to show how this process of adoption and adaptation has manifested itself in Jewish custom throughout the ages. For reasons of space, the discussion is limited to folkways and is not extended to folklore in general. Nothing is said, therefore, about Jewish costume, songs, music, folktales and the like, although the same broad principle is no less evident in those spheres. It is hoped, however, that within these necessary restrictions the reader will find ample demonstration of the basic truth that if—as is so often asserted—the Jews have been the middlemen of the world, they have been at the same time the middlemen of God.

T.H.G.

NOTE TO THE SECOND EDITION

This book was originally published twenty-five years ago. In issuing this new edition I have found it necessary only to make two or three slight corrections and to take care of a few misprints. There is, however, one important point on which a further word might be said.

Many traditionally minded Jews seem to believe that to trace the outward form of a religious custom or institution to its pagan antecedents or to align it with a common non-Jewish usage is to detract from its value and authority. It should therefore be stressed that what is important in religion is not the outward form but the inward and symbolic significance which comes to be attached to it in the course of the ages. Religion is essentially an expression of personal concern, but a living concern may nevertheless express itself in an antique idiom. The best analogue is language. We still employ in common speech such terms as *melancholy, trivial* and the like, although these no longer bear their original meanings of black-biled or connected with a place where three roads meet, but the fact that they can be traced etymologically to such meanings in no way invalidates our present use of them. Similarly, the Hebrew Bible is still written in an alphabet which derives from pre-Israelite script. Such development is, indeed, part of the process of revelation. "The light groweth brighter and brighter until the full day" (Proverbs 4.18).

T.H.G.

July 1979.

Blessed Event

I

1

BE FRUITFUL
AND MULTIPLY

It is written in the Scriptures that when the first human
child was born, its mother exclaimed, "I have gotten a
man with the help of the Lord" (Gen. 4:1); and, by an
inspired insight, the Jewish sages read into these words an
intimation that God in fact participates as a third parent
in every act of procreation.[1] Nevertheless, the broad
masses of Jews have never been averse to recruiting less
exalted aids to the propagation of the species, and
throughout the ages it has been firmly believed that a
woman can induce conception by absorbing special properties from plants and animals.

She can eat the root of mandrake, or wash her face and
hands in water mixed with the sap of an apple tree. She
can drink a decoction of leaves of vervain, or, if she de-

sire male offspring, she can eat a cock complete with comb and gizzard, or drink water in which the ashes of a burnt hare have been poured. Alternatively, she can transfer to herself the fertility of a fruit tree by burying at its foot a bowl filled with menstrual blood; and, if she remain barren after nine months of marriage, she can render herself receptive to pregnancy by crawling under the belly of a pregnant mare.

She can also exploit the properties of human beings— both living and dead. She will do well, for example, merely to touch a woman who is already with child, or to stroke the limbs of a bride or bridegroom, or to swallow the foreskin of a newly circumcised infant. More drastically, she can apply to her own person the water or soap with which a corpse has been washed, thereby transferring to her womb some of the life which has departed from the dead![2]

Most of these recipes are by no means exclusively Jewish, but represent general usages which the Jews have picked up from their Gentile neighbors. Mandrake, for instance, is regarded throughout the world as a peculiarly potent magical drug, by virtue of the fact that its root so strikingly resembles the human form; and, though the specific use of it as an aphrodisiac is indeed mentioned in the Bible (Gen. 30:14 ff.; S. of S. 7:14) as being common among the Hebrews, it was (and still is) equally familiar to other peoples.[3] Many scholars believe that this was the plant that Circe brewed in order to lure her lovers to their doom,[4] and in several parts of Europe it is considered both propitious and effective to place it under a bridal bed.[5] Moreover, the Greeks sometimes called the goddess of love, "Aphrodite of the Mandrake."[6]

Similarly, vervain is prescribed specifically both by

Pliny the Elder and by the medieval physician, Albertus
Magnus, as a remedy against barrenness; [7] while the Mas-
koki Indians of Alabama still use it as a sovereign cure for
sicknesses of women.[8] Among the Romans, it was held
sacred to Venus,[9] and in Germany, sprigs of vervain were
commonly placed in the hands of brides as a charm to ensure offspring.[10]

The hare, too, on account of its pronounced philopro-
genitive tendencies, is everywhere a favorite animal in
popular recipes to promote fertility. Pliny says expressly
that the eating of it helps to remove barrenness,[11] and in
many parts of Europe, its flesh is pulverized and decocted
to the same end.[12] Moreover, in ancient Greek usage, the
hare was used especially in sacrifices to Aphrodite; [13] while
in the Middle Ages, wedding rings were often embellished
with representations of this animal! [14]

Finally, the practice of crawling under a pregnant mare
is likewise paralleled elsewhere, the explanation being that
since a mare gestates for *ten* months, a woman who has
not yet conceived after nine may by this means absorb
something of its "fertility." [15]

Side by side with these more universal measures, however, there are others which are indeed of more specifically
Jewish character.

Pregnancy may be induced, for instance, by the mere
sight of the ritual knife used for circumcision, or by drinking from a bowl of water placed under the so-called "chair
of Elijah" * during the performance of that ceremony.[16]
Similarly, just as the Mohammedans attach special virtue
to the water of the sacred spring (Zemzem) at Mecca, or
Christians to that of the river Jordan in which Jesus was

. . . . .

* See below, p. 56.

baptized, or Hindus to that of the Ganges, so Jewish women in the Orient will seek to promote conception by drinking of the water in which the priests have washed their hands before blessing the congregation on the Day of Atonement.[17] Indeed, in Syria they are wont to bring rose water into the synagogue for this purpose on the preceding eve.

Sometimes, too, usages that have been borrowed "from the outside" have been given a peculiarly Jewish twist. The precious stone, ruby, for instance, is credited in many parts of the world with the special power of promoting conception.[18] Among the Jews, however, the peculiar explanation is given that the name of the stone resembles that of Reuben, the eldest son of Jacob, who helped his mother, Leah, to induce conception by supplying her with love apples or mandrakes (Gen. 30:14 ff.). Similarly, the very common use of willow leaves as a means to the same end is "validated" by the fact that the letters of the Hebrew word for *willow,* when taken in their numerical values, add up to the same total as those which compose the word for *seed!* On the same basis, too, the belief that pregnancy can be induced by eating the intestines of a hare —a belief widespread in European folklore—is endorsed on the grounds that in Hebrew the expression, "stomach of a hare" is numerologically equivalent to the Biblical phrase, "Be delivered and bear a male" (Lev. 12:2)!* Finally, the very common use of amulets in the shape of the open hand—what Mohammedans call "the hand of Fatima"—is "rationalized" by the fact that the five fingers at once suggest the numerical value of the Hebrew

. . . . .

* I confess that I do not understand how this computation works out. In numerology, however, the widest license is permitted, and the desired result can often be "rigged" by special devices.

letter *H* (*heh*), a common abbreviation for the Ineffable
Name of God (*YHVH*)!

Just as important as the ensurement of conception is
the prevention of miscarriage. Every year, at the conclusion of the most solemn service of the Day of Atonement, the high priest used to pray in the Temple that the
ensuing twelvemonth might be one in which "no woman
shall miscarry the fruit of her womb."[19] During subsequent centuries, however, popular usage both in the Orient
and in Europe has not disdained to supplement Divine
providence with more mundane "assists."

Of all the measures that have been adopted, none, perhaps, is more interesting or more widespread than that
of supplying expectant mothers with a so-called eaglestone
(*aetites*) which they wear round their necks or carry upon
their persons as a protective amulet. The object in question is a ferruginous pebble, usually found in streams,
which, when rattled, reveals the presence of a smaller
stone within it. It therefore serves as a very natural symbol of pregnancy.[20]

Here again, the practice is by no means exclusively
Jewish. Plutarch tells us that it was common also among
the ancient Romans, and it is duly described by both
Pliny and Dioscorides.[21] Among the Arabs, the stone is
known specifically as "the stone of birth," and some
scholars believe that it is mentioned also in the medical
texts of the Babylonians and Assyrians.[22] In Germany and
Italy, it is not uncommon to bind it on the left hip of a
pregnant woman,[23] and in medieval England, such a stone
was preserved in Durham Cathedral as a religious treasure.[24]

Not the least intriguing feature of the eaglestone is how
it got its name. Says a seventeenth-century English anti-

quary, drawing his information from Pliny and other
earlier writers: "The eagles, being mindful of the security of their young, are wont in the building of their nests
ever to make up their structures with these stones, by this
means hoping to secure their young from the annoyance
of serpents." [25] Moreover, it is alleged, there are always
two such stones in the nest, one male and the other female;
if they are missing, the birds cannot reproduce!

2

THE PANGS OF EVE

In pain shalt thou bring forth children
GENESIS 3:16

The actual moment of birth is regarded everywhere as a peculiarly "critical" occasion, and in the idiom of primitive thought, this means that it is a time when demons are especially rampant. Although such an attitude is, of course, foreign to Western thought, it is still very much alive in Oriental countries, and Jewish folklore knows several ways of averting or foiling those evil powers.

A piece of iron can be placed in the woman's bed or under her pillow. Once again, this is not specifically and distinctively Jewish. Mohammed's mother is said likewise to have had a piece of iron bound upon her hand at the time of his birth;[1] while in the rural areas of Germany, it is still common practice to put a bar of iron under the bed or in the cradle.[2] Among the Kols of India, mother and child are protected from demons by keeping a piece of iron boiling in an earthenware pot;[3] while the Toradjas of Indonesia make a point of laying the infant on a slab of iron on the seventh day after its birth.[4]

The custom is based on the widespread belief that demons, being essentially children of the Stone Age, are naturally apprehensive of the "newfangled" metal. Thus, when an Arab encounters a sandstorm, he fancies that he has met with a *jinn,* or demon, and at once cries out, "Iron! Iron!"[5] while in an ancient Aramaic incantation, the sorcerer declares expressly that he is fortified against the demons by means of *iron* armor and an *iron* headpiece.[6] Similarly, when a Hindu visits a sick friend, he carries a piece of iron to protect himself from the devils of disease.[7] To the same sphere of ideas belongs also, of course, the familiar notion that an iron horseshoe hung over a door averts evil and brings luck, and in some parts of England, a red-hot iron poker is plunged into the churn to prevent witches from interfering with the making of butter.[8]

Bronze, steel, and other hard metals likewise forfend the princes of darkness. In Sweden, for example, a woman has to carry an object made of steel when she first sets foot out of doors after bearing a child,[9] and in Finland, a piece of steel is tucked under the pillow as a guarantee against nightmare.[10] In line with this general belief, it is common in many parts of the world to *hang a bronze or steel sword over the head of a woman in childbirth.* This practice, too, once enjoyed considerable popularity among German and East European Jews. Indeed, it is not without significance, that in the pictures of childbed scenes included in Kirchner's celebrated *Jüdisches Ceremoniel,* published in 1726, a sword is displayed prominently beside the bed!

Here, to be sure, other ideas also enter into the picture,

for it is a worldwide and ancient notion that demons can be scared away by the mere sight of a drawn sword. Odysseus, says Homer, kept the spirits of the dead at bay by sitting with a drawn sword until he was ready for their approach,[11] and with this we may compare the modern Welsh superstition that the "little folk" vanish as soon as a sword is unsheathed.[12] Similarly, ancient Christian amulets are very often embellished with pictures of saints drawing their swords against grisly demons, and among the Mandaeans of Iraq, devils are said to be routed by the lance or spear of a hero named Qatros. So common, indeed, was this notion that compendia of spells and magical formulae were sometimes known as the "swords" of this or that hero or wizard. Such, for instance, was the *Sword of Dardanos,* mentioned occasionally in Greek and Coptic sources; while one of the oldest Jewish collections of charms is entitled *The Sword of Moses* !

Sometimes—as among the Jews of Hungary—the place of the sword is taken by an ordinary *knife.*[13] This has a particularly interesting parallel in the Danish custom of laying a knife at the bottom of a rowboat in order to protect its passengers from Nökhe, the mischievous spirit of the rivers.[14]

Another method of discomfiting the powers of evil is to *kindle a light,* since such powers can operate only under cover of darkness. This method is mentioned already in the Talmud,[15] and has abundant parallels all over the world. In ancient Rome, for example, it was believed that a taper lit in honor of the goddess Candelifera kept away noxious spirits from a woman in labor;[16] while even at the present day, it is not unusual, in Catholic countries, to place beside her bed a candle or oil lamp that has previously been blessed. The Parsis of India likewise make a point of keeping the room well lit at a birth,[17] and the Hindus light fires on such an occasion for the express purpose of keeping demons at bay.[18] In Teutonic folklore, it is believed that the continuous burning of a candle prevents elves and pixies from carrying off a newborn child and substituting a changeling.[19]

Devils and child-stealing warlocks can also be thwarted by *laying some of the husband's garments on the woman's bed.* They serve as a decoy: the demon jumps into them instead of entering the body of mother or child. The Jews would appear to have picked up this custom from the Germans, but it is current also in several other parts of the world, as, for instance, in Guatemala and among the Watubelas of Malaya.[20] In Southern China the extra precaution is taken of pinning to the clothes a written amulet.[21] The basic idea is likewise expressed in the singular usage of the Minahassans of Indonesia, who seek to divert disease from a sick man by dressing a dummy in his raiment.[22]

A variation of this custom, common among German peasants, is that whereby a woman is required to wear her husband's coat from the time of the delivery of her child until she is "churched," i.e. ceremonially purified forty days later. Here the idea is to fool the demon into mistaking his intended victim for her husband and thereby letting her alone.[23]

To prevent the fetus from being removed by demons, the mother's body is *sometimes bound with ribbons or threads,* and these are thought to be even more effective if they happen to be red. The Talmud tells us, however, that the ancient rabbis drew a nice distinction between winding the threads around the throat and tying them around the fingers. The former, it was ruled, was a mere harmless superstition, whereas the latter constituted a definite imitation of pagan practice—possibly, of the Roman sacral fillets—and was therefore forbidden.[24] The use of red is inspired, of course, by the fairly universal notion that this is an especially protective color. In the Babylonian *Epic of Creation,* for example, it is related that the god Marduk smeared red ocher on his lips before engaging in battle against the dragon Tiamat;[25] while to this day, Ashanti mourners bedaub themselves with the same substance as a safeguard against the hovering demons of death.[26] Even closer parallels are the custom of the Kaffir women of South Africa to smear themselves with red clay after giving birth,[27] or that of the Tupis of Brazil whereby the godfather of a child paints it red soon after it has been delivered.[28] Moreover, only sixty years ago, it was recorded of an English country woman that, while she was in labor, her thighs were bound with red skeins! [29]

Even more potent as a measure of protection is the use of *salt.* The prophet Ezekiel alludes (16:4) to the ancient Hebrew custom of rubbing children with salt as soon as the navel string had been cut, and this usage is mentioned also in the Talmud [30] and by Saint Jerome as standard procedure among Jews.[31] Here, once more, parallels are not hard to find. According to Galen (130-ca. 200 C.E.), newborn babes were similarly "salted" among the ancient Greeks,[32] and the custom obtains today not only in the Balkans [33] but also among the Todas of Southern India.[34] The Arabs protect their children from the evil eye by placing salt in their hands on the eve of the seventh day after birth; the following morning, the midwife or some other woman strews it about the house, crying, "Salt in the eye of all who look with envy!" [35] The Germans used

to put salt under a child's tongue as soon as it was delivered,[36] and in medieval Sweden, the same thing was
done when the infant was baptized.[37] Lao and Siamese
women "wash" with salt after childbirth as a means of
defending their persons from demons,[38] and in the northern counties of England, it is customary to tuck a small
bag of salt into baby's clothing on its first outing.[39] As
late as 1946, a couple was arraigned at Trowbridge, Wilt-
shire, for burning salt over a child in order to stop its
hysterical crying. The father attributed the cries to witchcraft, and pleaded in defense that "he felt he had to coun-
teract the evil influences that were around." [40] The basis
of such practices lies—in the words of an old writer—in
the belief that witches and warlocks "like their master,
the Devil, abhor salt as the emblem of immortality."

Somewhat analogous to the use of salt is that of *honey*
or *oil*, which are likewise regarded in many cultures as
symbols of life, health, and regeneration.[41] The Hebrew
word for "educate" (viz. *ḥ-n-k*) means properly "to do
something to the palate," and the original significance is
suggested by the Arab practice of smearing date juice on
the gums and palates of children immediately after birth.[42]
John Calvin (1509-64) states that the Jews of his day
used to make a similar application of honey; while in
more recent times, their coreligionists in Galicia were
accustomed, before a child was first suckled, to place part
of a honeycomb in its cradle.[43] But the custom is not exclusively Semitic. The Greek poet, Apollonius of Rhodes
(b. 295 B.C.E.) says that the lips of Dionysus were
smeared with honey at his birth, and this usage survives
in modern Greece as a protection against evil spirits.[44]
The same thing is done by the Hindus as soon as the
umbilical cord has been severed; [45] while among the Mo-

hammedans of the Punjab, the most honored male member of the family applies *ghatti,* made of honey, to the
mouth of the newborn.[46] Nor is it without significance that
an Egyptian charm of the thirteenth century B.C.E. prescribes honey as a means of keeping away the child-stealing witch.[47]

It is possible also to obtain protection by *having a scroll
of the Law carried to the door of the lying-in chamber,*
though the sages insist that it must be brought no nearer,
lest it come to be regarded as an instrument of magic
rather than a mere symbol of Divine providence;[48] as
Maimonides puts it: "The words of the Law are for the
health of the soul, not of the body." In the same way, it is
the custom in Scotland to keep an open Bible near a newborn babe during the first week of its life or at the ceremony of baptism;[49] while in Italy, the somewhat analogous usage prevails of placing on the bosom of a woman in
labor slips of paper containing accounts of miracles performed by Anna, mother of the Virgin Mary.[50]

3

A TIME TO BE BORN

Special importance is attached in popular belief to the day and hour of birth, for the entry of a child into the world is by no means fortuitous but preordained, and the circumstance and condition of nature at the time of his arrival are therefore regarded as decisive for his destiny. Familiar to everyone is the Scottish rhyme:

Monday's child is fair of face,
Tuesday's child is full of grace,
Wednesday's child is full of woe,
And Thursday's child has far to go.
Friday's child is loving and giving,
And Saturday's child has to work for a living.
But the bairn that is born on the Sabbath day
Is bonny and lucky and wise and gay;

and similar compositions (though with no agreement as to the qualities attributed to each day) are to be found among most European peoples.

The earlier Jewish counterpart, recorded in the Talmud in the name of the famous third-century rabbi, Joshua ben Levi,[1] states that a child born on Sunday will be resplendent as the sun, and all his deeds will be in the open; on Monday, sickly as the pale moon, likewise fickle in his fortunes, and addicted to dark deeds; on Tuesday, wealthy; on Wednesday, wise and retentive; on Thursday, generous and benevolent; on Friday, pious; and on Saturday, free from harm and hurt.

In characteristic Jewish fashion, the qualities are related to the story of Creation. Monday's child will be "double-minded" because on that day the upper and lower waters were divided; Tuesday's will be wealthy and lusty, since on that day the lush verdure of the fields was created and commanded to engender. Wednesday's will be "bright" because the luminaries were then brought into being. Thursday's will be generous and lavish because on Thursday, the waters were ordered to "teem"; Friday's will be pious, because on Friday man was created in the image of God; and the Sabbath child will be immune to harm and hurt because the sabbath was the day which God especially blessed and hallowed.

Here again, therefore, Judaism has effected a marriage between the current superstitions of its neighbors and its own sacred tradition.

4

THE WILES OF LILITH

Aroint thee, witch, aroint thee!

All of the fears and hazards of childbirth are concentrated, in Jewish lore, in the dread figure of Lilith, the phantom hag who seizes newborn babes and kills or injures their mothers.[1]

Lilith is really a composite of two characters: the Child-stealing Witch and the Dream-Girl.

The Child-stealing Witch has been known and feared in almost every part of the world for more than three thousand years, and infinite indeed have been (and are) her wiles and disguises. In ancient Egypt, for example, her favorite trick was to slip into a house under cover of darkness, pretending to be a friendly visitor or well-wisher, but carefully keeping her face averted to prevent detection;[2] while in modern Italy she has been known to gain access to her victim by posing as a midwife.[3] To the Babylonians and Assyrians she usually appeared as a hideous monster, with the head of a lion, the body of a woman and the feet of a bird, who came riding on an ass, brandishing a serpent in either hand and suckling at her breasts a black hound and a pig.[4] Among the Greeks, her customary form was that of a screech owl or bat, but she was also familiar as "Dame Donkey-legs" (*Onoskelis*), and sometimes—to add to the horror—it was whispered that one of her feet was made out of cow dung![5]

The Arabs know her as a goggle-eyed demon whose one foot is that of an ass, and whose other is that of an ostrich;[6] the Germans, as a sharp-nosed, scrawny harridan;[7] while in an ancient Aramaic spell, she is described as a kind of harpy who perches on rooftops ready to pounce on newborn babes.[8]

Nor are these her only disguises. A Canaanite magical plaque of the eighth century B.C.E. portrays her as a vixen, with the legs of a child protruding from her jaws;[9] while ancient Greek nurses used to scare their unruly charges with threats of the Bogey-wolf (*Mormolukeion*) who would come and carry them off;[10] and a seventeenth-century French writer[11] puts into the mouth of a magician the claim that he teaches witches "to take the form of wolves and eat children"![11a]

Quite different is the Dream-Girl. This is a glamorous, voluptuous sylph who consorts with men in their sleep and who is, *au fond*, nothing but a personification of the images and fantasies that people sexual dreams. She is, in fact, the creature of whom Faust is warned:

Beware of her fair hair! for she excels
All women in the magic of her locks;

And when she winds them round a young man's neck,
She will not ever set him free again.*

At first, the two characters were quite distinct; indeed, in its original Babylonian usage, the name Lilith meant no more than "female spirit" (or "wraith"), and she was sharply distinguished from Lamashtu, the child-stealing witch. In course of time, however, the point struck home that the Dream-Girl must be, after all, a singularly frustrated and embittered creature, seeing that her congress with men never in fact issues in procreation. Accordingly, she came to be represented as a perpetually disappointed woman who is perforce jealous and envious of all mothers, and from this it was, of course, but a short step to identify her with the spiteful and remorseless Child-stealing Witch.

The transition was sometimes embodied in an appropriate legend. Among the Greeks, for instance, the child-stealing witch Lamia was popularly identified as a clandestine mistress of Zeus whose offspring had been cruelly put to death by his indignant wife, Hera, and who, in retaliation, assailed the newborn children of men.[12] Similarly, on the island of Lesbos, the familiar Ghoul, or Vampire, was transformed into a young woman named Gello who had died childless and who sought posthumously to relieve her disappointment by coming as a phantom and emptying cradles.[13]

In the same vein, Jewish folklore asserts that Lilith was the first wife of Adam, fashioned, like him, out of the dust

• • • • •

* Goethe, *Faust*, Part I, Walpurgisnacht:

> Nimm dich in acht vor ihren schönen Haaren;
> Vor diesem Schmuck, mit dem sie einzig prangt.
> Wenn sie damit den jungen Mann erlangt,
> So lässt sie ihn so bald nicht wieder fahren.

Shelley's translation.

of the earth. Quarreling with her mate, however, she one day pronounced the Ineffable Name of God and was thereby transported immediately into the air and flew away. Adam thereupon complained to God, and God sent three angels in search for her and to bring her back. They overtook her at the Red Sea, and when she revealed to them that she was bent on destroying any progeny that might be born to Adam by a second wife, or (if that initial attempt failed) to any of his descendants, they threatened straightway to drown her. Begging for mercy, she struck a bargain with them: from that day forth she would never enter a house where the names of the angels were written up or repeated. Moreover, in compensation for the children that she might still succeed in carrying off, a thousand demons that might otherwise assail mankind would be put to death by God every day.[14]

The simplest and most popular safeguard against Lilith is to hang up in the lying-in chamber a written or printed Hebrew amulet, known in Western countries as the *Kimpezettl*—a Yiddish corruption of the German *kindbettzettel*, i.e. "childbirth-label." In its usual form—common since the sixteenth century—it bears the following legend:

Adam and Eve: Lilith, avaunt!
Sinoi, Sinsinoi, and S-m-n-g-l-f.

Once upon a time, the prophet Elijah was walking along the road when he encountered the wicked Lilith accompanied by all her gang.

"Whither away, foul creature," he demanded, "thou and all thy foul gang?"

"Sir," she replied, "I am off to the house of Mistress X who is expecting a child. I am going to plunge her into the sleep of death, take away her babe, suck its blood, drain its marrow* and seal up its flesh."

"Nay," cried the prophet, "By the curse of God thou shalt be restrained and turned to dumb stone!"

"Not that!" implored the hag, "For God's sake, release me from that curse, and I will flee; and I will swear unto thee in the name of Jehovah, God of the armies of Israel,† to forgo my intent against yon woman and her child. Moreover, whenever in future men recite my names, or I see them written up, neither I nor my gang shall have power to harm or hurt. And these be my names: ‡

> *Lilith, Abitr Abito, Amorfo,*
> *Kkods, Ikpodo, Ayylo, Ptrota,*
> *Abnukta, Strina, Kle Ptuza,*
> *Tltoi Pritsâ."*

On the face of it, this would appear to be as distinctively Jewish a creation as one could expect to find anywhere. In point of fact, however, it is simply a Jewish adaptation of an amulet that once enjoyed wide popularity throughout the Near and Middle East and that still survives in various parts of those areas and in the Balkans. In Abyssinia, for example, expectant mothers often carry upon their persons an ancient amuletic scroll in which virtually the same story is related in virtually the same words but with the difference that the hero is there not the prophet Elijah but a certain Saint Sisinnius—whoever he may have been*

. . . . .

* In Shakespeare's *Macbeth* (Act I, Sc. 3, l. 18), one of the witches declares: "I will drain him dry as hay"; and in *King Richard the Third* (Act III, Sc. 4, ll. 69-70), Gloucester exclaims: "See how I am bewitch'd; behold, mine arm / Is, like a blasted sapling, wither'd up."

† Cf. I Samuel 17: 45.

‡ There are many variations, and the sequence is not always the same.

* According to one view, he is to be identified with a Syrian saint of the third century whose sense of virtue was so great that he put his own sister to death when he suspected that she had consorted with the Devil! Another view maintains, however, that the legend is really of Manichaean origin, and that the person intended is Sisinnius who succeeded to the

—and the villain is not Lilith but a human beldam named Werzeliya, who has killed his first-born son.[15] A similar scroll is also worn by pregnant women in Armenia. It is known as "St. Cyprian's Scroll" because it also contains prayers attributed to that saint.[16] The story is there told as follows: †

When Saint Sisinnius was descending from Mount Sinai,* he met with [the demon] Abiahu.† Behold, his eyes were flaming, and his teeth were like unto a camel's.

Upon seeing him, St. Sisinnius said unto him: "Whence art thou come, and whither are thou going, thou foul one and unclean?"

And the foul one said: "I am going to enter the bosoms of women and to strangle their babes."

Then St. Sisinnius bound him with chains of iron,‡ and said: "We will not let thee go, except thou swear to do no harm."

So [the demon] swore by the many-eyed cherubim and by the six-winged seraphim and by the Lord Who sitteth enthroned upon them; and then he was released.

(The demon swore further, saying:) "Whenever [a woman] calls on the Kind and Merciful One (and says): IN THE NAME OF THE FATHER AND OF THE SON AND OF THE HOLY GHOST and IN THE NAME OF SAINT SI-SINNIUS—we* will not enter her house nor injure her babes.

---

leadership of that sect, in the third century, after the death of its founder, Mani. The Christians, it is supposed, promptly transformed the heathen champion into his later, more "respectable" namesake!

† See (Mrs.) J. S. Wingate, "The Scroll of Cyprian: an Armenian Family Amulet," in *Folk-Lore*, XLI (1930), 169.87. Mrs. Wingate's translation is here reproduced with a few slight changes designed to bring out more clearly the structure of the text.

* This, it may be suggested, is an ignorant distortion of an original: *When Saint Sisinnius was out walking with Saint Sinoe.* For in all of the sister versions of the tale, he indeed has a companion variously named as Sinoe, Silas and Synedorus; and even in this version, he subsequently observes, "*We* will not let thee go."

† In some versions of the *kimpezettl*, Abi(a)hu is indeed given as one of the names of Lilith.

‡ Concerning the use of iron, see above, pp. 9 ff.

* Obviously, in the original version of the tale, the saint encountered the demon *together with her companions,* as in the *kimpezettl*.

"Accordingly," [they now declare] "we will not go nigh unto
yon Mistress N.N., the handmaid of God, for a whole year before
she gives birth."

[Here follows a list of demonic names]

Wheresoever this text be displayed, thou shalt be driven away,
(O demon) and restrained!

In a Greek version, the same champion, accompanied
by his brother, Synidorus, is represented as doing battle
with a hag named Gylou (i.e. the Ghoul, Vampire) on behalf of his stricken sister, Meletia; [17] while in a Slavonic
version, the saint is called Sisoe, and his adversary is the
Devil. [18]

There is even an English version—hitherto overlooked,
for the following recipe against nightmare is cited by various Elizabethan writers: [19]

Take a flint stone that hath a hole of his own kind,† and hang it
over him, and write in a bill—

Saint George, our Lady's knight,
He walked by day, so he did by night,
Until he her* found;
He her beat and he her bound,
Till truly her troth she him plight
That she would not come within the night,
There as† Saint George, our Lady's knight,
Named was thrice.

And hang this scripture over him and let him alone.

Moreover, another form of the charm is to be found
in no less familiar a work than Shakespeare's *King*

• • • • •

† A Suffolk superstition, surviving into the nineteenth century, maintained
that a perforated stone placed under the foot of the bed would prevent
nightmare. See *Notes and Queries*, First Series, iv (1851), 53.
* i.e. the lilith.
† i.e. wherever.

Lear! [20] The hero of the legend is there Saint Withold
(a corruption of St. Vitalis), and the charm runs as follows:

Saint Withold footed thrice the [w]old;
He met the night-mare and her nine-fold;
   Bid her alight
   And her troth plight;
And aroint thee, witch, aroint thee! [20a]

That the *kimpezettl* is related directly to the Christian
form of the legend, and is not a mere general parallel to
it, is at least suggested, if not actually proved, by the curious resemblance between the name Sisinnius and the second word of the mysterious superscription: *Sinoi, Sin-
sinoi and S-m-n-g-l-f.* For this there would seem to be two
possible explanations. Either (a) the Jewish version was
copied mechanically and subsequently garbled; or (b) the
original hero of the story was identified by the Christians
with the obscure Saint Sisinnius simply in order to account
—at least partially—for a traditional magical formula the
real meaning of which had long been forgotten but which
has survived fortuitously in the Jewish version.

The charm evidently reached the Jews through a Byzantine source, for the various aliases of Lilith turn out, on
closer examination, to be nothing but distortions of familiar *Greek* names or epithets of demons! Ikpodo and
Ayylo, for example, are simply Okypete, "Swift-flying," *
and Aello, "Stormwind"—the names of the two harpies of
Classical mythology.[21] Strina is a corruption (through the
similarity of the Hebrew letters *g* and *n*) of Striga—the
Greek *strix,* "screech owl," the regular name of the child-

• • • • •
* Cf. Hesiod, *Theogony,* 267. To be sure, Ikpodo actually represents a
variant form, Okypode, "Swift-foot," but this alternative is indeed recorded
by the mythographer, Apollodorus (*Bibl.,* I, ix, 21).

stealing witch.† Similarly, Amorfō is the Greek *amorphos,* "unshapely, ugly"; Kkods is *kakoeidēs,* "of evil appearance"; Ptrota is *pterōtē,* "winged one"; Abnukta is *epinuktios,* "nocturnal"; and Klê Ptuza is *kleptousa,* "female thief," i.e. kidnapper! ‡

In identifying the hero of the story with Elijah, the Jews were treading a well-worn path. In a Coptic version, he is somewhat similarly transformed into the archangel Michael; [22] while in England, as we have seen, he assumed the character of Saint George, the patron saint of that country, or of Withold, i.e. St. Vitalis. Moreover, there was a special reason for the choice of the prophet: Elijah is regarded in Jewish lore as the patron of the rite of circumcision and hence as the special protector of male children during the week preceding that ceremony. Moreover, was it not Elijah that in fact revived the widow's son when "his sickness was so sore, that there was no breath left in him" (I Kings, 17:17)?

The legend of Lilith and the prophet is usually accompanied on the *kimpezettl* by the text of the One Hundred and Twenty-first Psalm ("I will lift up mine eyes unto the hills"), which is deemed especially appropriate on account of the significant words (v. 6): *"The sun shall not smite thee by day, neither the moon by night."* Indeed, the entire charm is sometimes known for this reason as a *Shir ha-Ma'alos,* which is Hebrew for "Song of Degrees." This, too, is not without parallel in Gentile usage. A rare and curious tract against "gross points of Popery," printed at Edinburgh toward the end of the reign of Queen Elizabeth, denounces the practice of "the church-

. . . . .

† Cf. the Italian *strega* and the Tyrolese *Streggele,* "witch."

‡ With the exception of *Amorfo* from *amorphos,* these identifications are here made for the first time.

ing of women with this psalm, *that the sun and moon shall not burn them!"* [23]

But it is not only by means of the *kimpezettl* that the assaults of Lilith can be averted. There are also two other effective methods of dealing with her.

She can be trapped under an inverted bowl, in the interior of which an appropriate formula has been written.[24] Ancient clay bowls designed for such use and inscribed with texts in Aramaic, Syriac and Mandaean, have been found in some profusion in Mesopotamia. Exactly how old they are is disputed, but they would appear to date between the sixth and ninth centuries of the current era.

Again, the beldam can be served with a bill of divorcement duly drawn up in the legal form prescribed by rabbinic authority. The following, for example, is a specimen of such a document inscribed on one of the bowls which we have just described: [25]

On such-and-such day of such-and-such year of such-and-such era of the world, I, N.N., renounced, parted from thee and put thee away, thou Lilith, thou Lilith of the desert, thou hag, thou ghoul. Though thy shapes and forms be never so many,* naked art thou sent forth, unclad,† with hair disheveled, streaming down your back. Thou art hereby apprised, thou whose mother is Terror and whose father is Terror-and-Quaking,‡ that thou art to depart and harass N.N. no more in his house. . . .

         . . . . .

* Literally, the three of you, the four of you, the five of you.
† Faithless wives, when divorced, were stripped. There seem to be allusions to this in Ezekiel (16:37-39) and Hosea (2:5). Tacitus (*Germania,* ch. 19) says the same custom obtained among the ancient Germans.
‡ In the original, Palḥan and Palaḥdad. These names are subtly chosen. On the surface, they look like normal Babylonian names meaning respectively "worshiper" and "worshiper of the god Hadad." But the word *palah,* which in Babylonian means "worship," in Hebrew and Aramaic

The bill of divorcement hath come down to us from heaven. . . .
Rabbi Joshua ben Perahyah hath declared:
A bill of divorcement hath come for thee across the sea. . . .
Thy bill of divorce and thy writ of separation have been conveyed
by holy angels, by the fiery hosts that are in the spheres, by the
charioteers of the Divine Presence that minister in His service, by
the Holy Creatures§ that worship before His throne and that travel
through fire and water, by the Legions of I-AM-THAT-I-AM.‖

---

means "terror, fear," while the element—*dad* which would ordinarily
be taken for an abbreviated form of "Adad," suggests at the same time
the Aramaic *dud* to "tremble."
§ Cf. Ezekiel 1:5 ff.
‖ Cf. Exodus 3:14.

5

DAYS OF PERIL

The demons of childbirth do not vanish automatically at the moment of delivery. Until the mother has fully recovered her strength—that is, until she is her "old self" again—she continues to be exposed to their assaults; she may succumb to puerperal fever, her milk may dry up, or she may suffer "complications." In this precarious state, she is a potential menace to her neighbors—a "typhoid Mary"—for she may unwittingly communicate to them the demoniacal influences which hover about her own person. Accordingly, it is the custom among many peoples to regard her as "unclean" and to keep her strictly isolated for a prescribed period. The latter usually lasts for forty days (i.e. a quarantine), forty being considered a round number marking a "span" or "term." * Such, for instance, was the practice of the ancient Greeks,[1] as it still is of their modern descendants;[2] and such too—to cite but a few representative examples—is the practice of the Mohammedans,[3] the Parsis,[4] and the Chi'ang on the western border of China.[5] The ancient Egyptians, however, deemed a new mother "impure" for only fourteen days;[6] and in modern Germany she is sometimes known as a *Sechswöchnerin*—that is, literally, a "six-weeker." [7] At the end of the prescribed period she has (or had), in all cases, to be ritually purged.

The ancient Hebrew version of this practice is described in the twelfth chapter of the Book of Leviticus. A woman, we read, is to be regarded as "unclean" for forty days after the birth of a male, and for eighty after that of a female. During this period she is not to be permitted to come into contact with any sacred object nor to enter the sanctuary, and at the end of it, she is to undergo a ceremony of "purgation" by presenting herself to a priest at the door of the "tent of meeting," bringing with her a yearling lamb * for a burnt offering and a young pigeon, or a turtledove, for a sin-offering.

The rite is portrayed as a purely hygienic measure. Its purpose, we are informed, is to cleanse the woman "from the fountain of her blood." The presence of the *sin*-offering, however—let alone the analogy of similar procedures elsewhere—makes it plain that it is simply a transmogrification of an earlier, more primitive practice and

· · · · ·

* Compare, in the Bible, the *forty* days during which the flood was upon the earth (Gen. 7:17); the *forty* days and nights which Moses spent on Mount Sinai; and the *forty* years' wandering of the Israelites through the wilderness.

* If she cannot afford a lamb, she may substitute two turtledoves or two young pigeons.

that the "impurity" was originally not so much physical uncleanness as demoniacal contagion.

The ancient sages were much exercised to explain why the period of contamination was twice as long for a girl as for a boy. A common view, sponsored by such redoubtable authorities as Abraham ibn Ezra (1104-1167) and Isaac Abravanel (1437-1508), and based on a statement of Aristotle, was that the fetus of a male develops in forty days, but that of a female only in ninety. Others, such as the illustrious Nahmanides (1194-c. 1270), gave as the reason the quite suppositious fact that the female embryo is moister than the male, so that the womb requires longer to get cleansed, and in support of this opinion it was pointed out that Hippocrates himself (c. 460-c. 357 B.C.E.) prescribes thirty days' purification after a male birth, but forty-two after that of a female! Others again preferred a less medical reason: Adam, they said—on the basis of an old legend—had been forty days old when God placed him in Eden, but it had taken a further forty days to produce Eve! [8]

Equally puzzling to the sages was the mention of a *sin-offering* in the ceremony of purification. The Mishnah came very near to the true explanation when it pointed out that this was not really a sin-offering in the strict sense, but simply an instrument of decontamination, and it is, indeed, in that sense that the equivalent of the Hebrew term is actually employed in early ritualistic inscriptions from South Arabia. This interpretation, however, did not command universal assent. The disciples of the famous Simeon ben Yohai, for instance, contended that the sin-offering was designed to expiate the tendency of most women in labor to curse their husbands and resolve, Never again! Alternatively, it was claimed that the offering made amends for any ritual impurity accidentally occasioned in childbed, or—even more fancifully—that it atoned for the sin of Eve in tempting Adam! [9]

When the Temple was destroyed in 70 C.E., this ceremony of puerperal decontamination naturally fell into abeyance. Christianity, however, revived it in the service of the "churching of women" after delivery. In the current Anglican ritual no date is set for this ceremony but in the Eastern Church it is laid down specifically that it must take place on the fortieth day after childbirth. Moreover, its derivation from the Old Testament usage is shown clearly by the fact that in the Prayer Book of 1549 it is entitled expressly "The Order of the *Purification* of Women," and the primitive idea of decontamination from uncleanliness actually survives in popular custom, for in many English churches special "churching pews" used to be set aside for the new mothers.[10]

From the Church the Jews in turn borrowed back the ancient usage, and it is now customary among those of "orthodox" persuasion for the mother to visit the synagogue and render thanks before the open Ark of the Law. The form of service is, however, of very recent compilation and is, in the main, an imitation of the Christian liturgy,[11] featuring especially Psalm 116:

The pangs of death encompassed me,
    and the straits of Sheol* came upon me,
    yea, I came upon pain and distress.
But I called on the name of the Lord:
    'O Lord deliver my soul!'

. . . .

Be tranquil again, O my soul,
    for the Lord hath dealt kindly with thee;
For Thou hast snatched my soul from death,
    mine eyes from tears,
    my feet from stumbling.

. . . . .

* That is, the netherworld.

6

NAMES AND
NICKNAMES

Among the ancient Hebrews, as the Bible abundantly
attests, children were named as soon as they were born.[1]
In the case of males, however, the custom later developed
of announcing the name only on the occasion of circumcision
(cf. Lu. 1:59; 2:21), and this is today the standard Jewish practice.* In the same way, the Greeks named children
on the seventh or tenth day after birth;[2] the Romans
named boys on the ninth day, and girls on the eighth;[3]

• • • • •

* Among the Jews of Corfu, however, the child is named at a special
feast called Mire, held on the third day after birth. This is a pure imitation of Greek belief. The word Mire is a distortion of the Greek *Moirai*,
"Fates," for it is believed that on this occasion the three Fates come and
pronounce the child's destiny.

while in Christian usage, the name is, of course, bestowed only at baptism.

Although the fact is nowhere expressly stated in ancient sources, the custom is based on the widespread popular and primitive belief that a person's name is not merely an appellation but part and parcel of his essential being or "self." In magic, for instance, one of the most effective ways of controlling a demon is to gain knowledge of his name.† The converse, however, is equally true, and for this reason it is considered imprudent to let an infant's name be divulged during those critical days after birth when the demons are still hovering about it. In Ceylon, for example, the father whispers it into the child's ear, and it is known to none but himself and the official astrologer, a formal public name being conferred only at puberty.[4] In several parts of Abyssinia, the birthname is likewise concealed,[5] and the same custom prevails also in Guiana;[6] while even in nineteenth-century England, it was not uncommon to keep it a close secret until the child had been duly "hanselled" by the rite of baptism.[7] Alternatively—as in Thailand and Cambodia—a deliberately unpleasant nickname,[8] or—as in the Cyclades—a deliberately ominous one (e.g. Iron Dragon)* is bestowed on the infant at birth in order to render it repellent to evil spirits, and this is replaced by a genuine one only when the child is considered old enough to fend for itself.†[9]

. . . . .

† See above, p. 22.
* On the power of iron to forfend demons, see above, pp. 9 ff.
† Analogous is the worldwide custom of changing a person's name as a means—so to speak—of changing his identity at a time of critical illness or when he is *in extremis*. In Borneo, for instance, this is the regular method of confounding demons when a child falls sick, and the same thing is done also by the Mongols and the Laplanders and, in fact, by several other peoples. This, too, has its counterpart in Jewish usage. Indeed, it is actually recommended in the Talmud (Rosh Hashanah,

Since the time of the Exile it has been customary among
Jews to name children for their grandparents, or for other
kinsmen, or even for distinguished persons of the remoter
past.* The custom is well attested, for instance, among
the Jewish population of the military colony at Elephantine, in Egypt, during the fourth century B.C.E.,† and the
Prologue to the Book of Ecclesiasticus (in the Apocry-
pha) informs us that the work was edited and translated
into Greek by "Jesus of like name with him." The same
system likewise marks the genealogy of the high priestly
family between 332 and 165 B.C.E.; while, for several centuries, descendants of the illustrious Hillel (fl. 30 B.C.E.-
10 C.E.) were named for their grandfathers.[10]

This practice—which the Jews appear to have borrowed from their neighbors ‡—reflects the widespread
primitive notion that the tender "personality" of a newborn babe can be protected from demonic assault by being
"screened" or "covered," as it were, by that of an older
or distinguished individual—an end which is accomplished
by conferring upon it the same name.* This process, however, often comes up against the contrary notion that by
giving his name to another, a man automatically dimin-

---

chap. 1), and Jewish prayer books of the traditional type sometimes include a formula for the occasion. The Arabs, for their part, often seek
to accomplish the same purpose by giving a sickly child the name of a
wild and ferocious animal (Chas. Doughty, *Arabia Deserta*, i, 329).
* The practice is unknown to the Old Testament.
† These Jews also called children by the same names as their fathers.
‡ It was common in antiquity among both the Indians and the Greeks,
and it can be abundantly documented also in Semitic inscriptions of the
Graeco-Roman age. The Jews of Palestine seem to have borrowed it
somewhat later than their brethren in the Diaspora. See G. B. Gray,
Studies in Hebrew Proper Names (1896), 3 ff.
* By the same reasoning, several primitive peoples adopt the converse
practice of making the parents of a child "take over" its personality by
themselves adopting its name. See Ernest Crawley, *The Mystic Rose*,
Second edition (1927), ii, 188 ff.

ishes or curtails his own personality and "self." Accordingly, it is common practice to avoid naming a child for
a living parent. This, for instance, is a standard taboo
among the Ainos of Japan,[11] in parts of Germany,[12] among
the modern Greeks,[13] and in the Northern Countries of
England.[14] Similarly, there is often a marked aversion to
naming a child for a grandparent unless the latter is dead.
Both customs have been the general rule among Jews at
least since the thirteenth century. The Ashkenazim, or
German-Polish Jews, have, however, been less rigorous
about it than their Sephardic, or Spanish-Portuguese
brethren, and have not infrequently permitted infants to
bear the same names as living parents. Here again, ambiv-
alence of attitude comes into play, for side by side with
the notion that a transference of name involves a diminu-
tion of vitality there exists also the very prevalent and
compelling idea that to pass on one's name to one's offspring is, in fact, to be "born anew" and thus to perpet-
uate one's own being. Indeed, in several of the Semitic
languages, "name" is a common synonym for "poster-
ity." [15]

Besides his Hebrew name which is used for religious
purposes among his own brethren, every Western Jew
usually possesses also a secular name in the vernacular
language, and it is by this name that he is known to the
community at large. Among German-speaking Jews, the
latter is conferred on the fourth sabbath after birth at
a curious home ceremony called *Hollekreisch*.[16]

The invited guests, boys in the event of a male birth,
and girls in that of a female, range themselves in a circle
around the cradle. They then lift the baby thrice in the
air, calling out each time *Holle Kreisch*. Sometimes, however, the actual lifting is done by the congregational pre-

centor (Hebrew, *ḥazzan*) and in that case he usually recites appropriate verses from the Bible.

This picturesque ceremony is borrowed directly from Gentile usage. It has been commonly interpreted as taken from a German custom of exorcising Holle (or Frau Holle), a grisly witch who was believed to attack infants. In fact, however, the puzzling term *Hollekreisch* is simply a corruption of the French words, *Haut la crèche*, "Up with the cradle!"

But why is the child lifted in the air? Here we have a lingering survival of the idea that newborn children must be delivered not only from their mother's wombs but also from that of Mother Earth. It is customary, in fact, among many peoples to place a child on the ground (sometimes, on the hearth) immediately after birth and then ceremonially to lift it therefrom.[17] In Hungary, for instance, it is common among the peasantry to smear the child's hands and face with blood and to place it on the floor until the placenta has been removed.[18] At Brieg, in Silesia, it used to be deposited forthwith on the ground,[19] and in Switzerland, this was done before it received baptism.*[20] In ancient Rome, fathers acknowledge the paternity of their children by "lifting" them,[21] and among the Tupis of Brazil it is the rule to this day that the godfather must pick the infant up from the ground, cut the navel string and paint its body with demon-averting ocher.[22] In England, the custom survives in attenuated form in the belief that a newborn child must be carried *upstairs* before it is carried downstairs.[23]

• • • • •

---

* To be sure, the true meaning of the custom has long since been forgotten. The Silesians say that the child thereby "absorbs strength from the earth," and the Swiss that it "learns humility"!

Illuminating also is the fact that alike in German as in Swedish popular parlance, a midwife is often known expressly as an "earth-mother" (*Erdmutter, Gördegumma*).[24] Moreover, the belief that children issue from the earth finds expression not only in ritual and popular idiom but also in legend. Many German cities boast neighboring springs whence the divine midwife is said to extract the newborn. To the east of Brunswick, for example, there are the well-known Godebrunnen, concerning which this story is told, and near the Kunibertskirche in Cologne there is a spring where the little ones are said to sit awaiting birth. Even more significantly, in the Meissner district of Germany, there is an expanse of water actually known as Frau Holle's Lake, whence the newborn are thought to emerge.[25]

It may be remarked, finally, that the custom of lifting a child from the ground shortly after birth has its direct counterpart in that of depositing the dead there at the moment of, or shortly after, their demise.* The symbolism is in both cases the same: naked, man comes from the womb of Mother Earth, and naked, he returns thither.

. . . . .

* See below, pp. 138, 163 f.

7

THE TREE OF LIFE

The righteous shall flourish like the palm tree.
PSALM 92:12

It was formerly a common Jewish custom to plant a tree at the birth of a child, a cedar for a boy, and a pine for a girl. When a couple married, their respective trees were cut down and used in the construction of the *huppah,* or bridal bower.

The custom is mentioned already in the Talmud,[1] but it is probable that the Jews of later generations did not so much inherit it by unbroken tradition as adopt it anew from their Gentile neighbors, for the fact is that, throughout the ages, it has enjoyed widespread popularity in all parts of Europe and Asia. A few examples must suffice.

In Switzerland, it is the practice to plant an apple tree at the birth of a boy, and a nut tree at that of a girl.[2]

In Sweden, an addition to the family is frequently

marked by the planting of a tree of destiny (*värd-trad*) in his or her honor.[3]

From Germany comes the familiar story that on the day Goethe was born, his grandfather promptly planted a pear tree in his garden at Frankfort;[4] while a legend from the Aar Valley tells of a father who was so incensed at finding his son a wastrel that he disowned him by cutting down the tree which he had planted at the latter's birth.[5]

Nor, indeed, is the custom unknown in more remote parts of the world. Missionaries have attested its prevalence in Java,[6] Amboina,[7] Guinea,[8] the Fiji Islands,[9] the Solomons[10] and New Zealand;[11] while on the Malacca Peninsula there is a special semisacred enclosure in which birth-trees are set up.[12]

The practice is inspired by the idea that the life and destiny of the newborn child are bound up in some mystic fashion with that of the tree. If the latter flourishes, so too will the child, but if it withers or fails to put forth shoots in due season, this is a sure sign that the child faces death or disaster. This idea—itself but one form of what folklorists call the concept of the life-token—is a favorite theme of folktale and legend.

An ancient Egyptian tale relates, for example, that when two brothers parted company, the younger mystically attached his heart to a pine tree, advising the elder that if he should meet with death, the tree would immediately die.[13]

Similarly, in a story from Madagascar, the hero, when setting out on his adventures, plants some *aruns* and plantain trees and informs his parents that "if these wilt, it will be a sign that I am sick; if they wither, that I am dead";[14] while in the Kalmuk legend of Siddhi Kur, six youths who go forth simultaneously to seek their fortunes each plant a tree the flowering or fading of which will apprise his family how he is faring; [15] and in a Scottish tale from Argyllshire, three trees serve as tokens of the fate and fortune of a fisherman's three sons. [16]

Ancient Roman literature likewise furnishes some arresting instances of this belief. Sabinus, the father of Vespasian, we are told, learned that his newborn son would become a Caesar when he saw that an oak tree in his garden suddenly put forth an exceptionally strong branch, [17] and when a laurel sprang up in the house and overshadowed a *malus Persica* or peach tree growing beside it, the father of Alexander Severus was informed by the soothsayers that his son was destined to conquer the Persians. [18]

The motif recurs also in the Scandinavian Eddas. Atli is warned that his child has been slain by seeing in a dream that the tree which he had planted at the latter's birth has suddenly become damaged. [19]

Lastly, there is an echo of the idea even in the Bible. For in the Book of Daniel (4:7 ff.), Nebuchadnezzar learns of his impending doom by dreaming of a mighty tree which, though "its height reached to heaven" and though "it could be sighted in every part of the earth," was nevertheless ordered by an angel to be felled.

A variation on the same theme may be recognized in the practice of planting a tree to symbolize the prosperity of a king and the stability of his reign. Such a tree formerly existed in the palace of the Emperor of China, [20] and in Uganda, the life of the sovereign is similarly bound up with that of a tree. [21] Analogous too is the custom observed in the Nile Valley of planting a tree at a wedding to symbolize the future fortune of the bride. [22]

II

Childhood

1

THE COVENANT
OF ABRAHAM

The Rite of Circumcision

*My covenant shall be in your flesh
for an everlasting covenant.*
GENESIS 17:13

On the eighth day after birth, every male child born of
Jewish parents is expected to undergo the rite of circumcision. Otherwise he cannot be regarded as a Jew; in the
words of Scripture, "his soul is cut off from his people."

According to the Bible (Gen. 17:10-14), the rite was
instituted at the time of Abraham, and it is the outward
sign of the covenant that was concluded between God and
the patriarch and that remains binding upon the latter's
offspring "throughout their generations." Actually, it is
yet another example of the Jewish genius for infusing
new, spiritual meanings into general popular usages. For
the fact is that circumcision was, and still is, an extremely

widespread practice from one end of the world to the
other; and even the Biblical account in no way implies
that it was "invented" by the Hebrews. That account is
concerned only with the how and why of its adoption in
Israel, not with its ultimate origin.

Herodotus, the "father of History," tells us explicitly
that circumcision was the common custom among the
ancient Egyptians,[1] and his words are borne out not only
by a graphic account of the rite in an inscription of the
twenty-third century B.C.E.,[2] but also by a portrayal of the
operation on a wall-painting at Thebes [3] and by the fact
that the Egyptian hieroglyphic sign for "phallus" depicts
it circumcised. The same authority states also that the
custom prevailed likewise among the Ethiopians, the
Phoenicians, the Colchians, and the "Syrians" of Palestine.[4]

Similarly, anthropologists and missionaries have reported that circumcision or some analogous operation is
standard procedure at the present day among primitive
tribes (of widely different race) in all parts of Africa, as
well as in India, Indonesia, the Philippines, Oceania and
Australia. It likewise enjoys widespread popularity among
American Indians.[5] Indeed, it is related by one observer
that the Tlingits and Eskimos in the remote north of the
continent came to adopt the practice only because they did
not want to feel inferior to their neighbors, all of whom
were circumcised! [6]

Lastly, circumcision is universal among Mohammedans,
and in the case of the Arabs, it is held by many scholars
that this is a direct survival of early Semitic usage rather
than a mere borrowing from the Jews.[7]

The operation is seldom performed, as among the Jews,
directly after birth. Usually, it takes place between the
fourth and seventh year, or (especially in Africa) at

puberty or immediately before marriage, the latter two stages of life often coinciding.*

Not infrequently, too, a form of circumcision (or incision) is performed also on girls as a premarital procedure. Thus, in Baroda and in Bombay, female circumcision is said to reduce sensuality,[8] and among certain tribes in the Sindo Province of India, to ease confinement.[9] In Baluchistan, young women are often subjected to the operation on the bridal night;[10] while among the Masai, those who have reached puberty are circumcised at the same time as the males, and marriages follow as soon as the latter's wounds have healed.[11]

The original purpose of circumcision has been widely debated, and no agreement on the subject has yet been reached.[12]

Certain theories, *e.g.* that it is a modified form of ritual castration, or a substitute for the sacrifice of one's entire person to a deity, or a device for prolonging and enhancing sexual pleasure, may be dismissed at once as lacking any solid basis or, indeed, any vestige of probability. Who can believe, for instance, that even at the most primitive level of civilization, the relation of a living god to a living people ever consisted in a demand that the latter should deliberately prevent its own perpetuation or commit mass suicide?

Equally untenable is the theory that the original purpose of circumcision was to provide a distinctive tribal mark and that it is therefore, *au fond,* of the same order as tattooing or cicatrization, by which devices many primitive peoples establish a method of recognizing their kins-

. . . . .

* From the fact that Ishmael is said to have been circumcised *at thirteen years of age* (Gen. 17:25) many scholars have concluded that circumcision at puberty was also the more ancient custom among the Hebrews.

men at sight. The fatal objection to this view is that most primitives happen to keep their genitals covered, so that the alleged sign would in fact be invisible!

The most plausible theory is, on the whole, that circumcision was originally designed to prevent or correct any untoward condition of the sexual organs that might threaten to interfere with the propagation of the species. Such a condition might be either magical or physical.

Magically, by the common device of sacrificing a part for the sake of the whole, the operation would have "hanselled" the genital members against the perils and hazards thought to be inherent in first intercourse—as, indeed, in all things done for the first time. It would have been, in fact, of the same order as the sacrifice of firstlings or first fruits to a god or demon in order to protect the rest of the herd or crop from disaster.

Physically, it would have been a purely medical procedure, and this finds excellent illustration from current medical practice. For modern physicians commonly recommend it as a remedial measure in cases of phimosis— that is, the obstruction of the phallic orifice by an overgrowth of the foreskin—and an analogous operation is frequently prescribed for females.

On this hypothesis, we can at once understand why circumcision is so often performed on females as well as males, and likewise why it usually takes place at puberty or just before marriage. Puberty is sexual ripening; marriage is sexual consummation. Either, therefore—and very frequently they coincide—would be an appropriate moment for a measure designed to ease procreation. Nor, indeed, is the alternative system of performing the operation at birth or in early childhood in any way irreconcilable with this view, for even today in cases where remedial circumcision is recommended, it is commonly advised that it be performed as soon as possible after delivery, or at least in early infancy, while the organs are still supple.

On this basis, too, it becomes immediately clear why the Hebrew word for "bridegroom" (viz. ḥatan) derives from a root meaning "to circumcise"; * why, in Lahore, the ceremony of circumcision is called a "wedding"; [13] why, in Mohammedan countries, it is frequently known as "purification," [14] a term which possesses at once both a magical and a physical connotation; why it is often combined among primitive peoples with the imparting of sex instruction; [15] and, finally, why, in West Africa and elsewhere, native women refuse to cohabit with uncircumcised men. [16]

It is one thing, however, to determine the origin of circumcision as a purely utilitarian measure; quite another, as a social or religious institution, and insofar as the Jewish rite is concerned, it is the development of the former into the latter that is the really significant thing. How did the purely "functional" practice become the symbol of the Covenant?

Anthropology and comparative religion furnish the answer.

Among primitive peoples, circumcision is almost always performed not individually but *en masse*, as part of the ritual of the major annual or seasonal festivals. It provides a means of periodically replenishing the life and energy of a community by formally integrating into it a body of new members physically "conditioned" (at least in theory) to ensure its continuance. It therefore consti-

· · · · ·

* Cp. Arabic ḥatana. The bride's father is called ḥoten, lit. "one who circumcises," and this would suggest that it was he that originally performed the operation. (The fem. ḥoteneth, denoting the bride's mother, would be but a secondary formation).

tutes a rite of initiation: the child or youth who *sub*mits
to circumcision is automatically *ad*mitted to the bond of
kinship—*that is, to the communal covenant.*

Now, in ancient Semitic society, the community consisted not only of its human members but also of its local
genius or god—the personification of its corporate being.[17] Entry into the bond of social kinship therefore im-
plied also entry into the covenant with the god. *Mutatis
mutandis,* it established the same relationship as is created
today between the newly naturalized American and "Un-
cle Sam."

The idea is brought out in dramatic fashion in a curious
legend embodied in the Book of Exodus (4:24-26). When
Moses was returning from Midian to Egypt, so we read,

... it happened upon the journey that Jehovah* encountered him
at an inn and sought to kill him. So Zipporah [the wife of Moses]
took a flint and cut off the foreskin of her son and cast it at his
[Jehovah's] feet; and she said: Verily, thou art a kinsman unto me
by the blood of circumcision.† Thereupon he let him alone.

In the course of the ages, Judaism found an even more
striking method of expressing this relationship: circumcision was described as "the seal of God" imprinted on
the flesh.‡ [18]

. . . . .
* Some of the ancient versions, followed by modern scholars, read here
"an angel of Jehovah." But this is simply an attempt to palliate the
implications of a very archaic tale. In the original source of the legend,
Jehovah was probably no more than the local god of Midian.

† The Hebrew expression is *"ḥatan* of blood," and since *ḥatan* normally
means "bridegroom," it is usually rendered "a bridegroom of blood." From
this all sorts of speculative deductions have been drawn. The fact is,
however, that the story was derived from an extremely ancient source,
in which the word *ḥatan* still bore its primary meaning of "one who is
circumcised" (cp. Arabic *ḥatana*) or "who is related by ties of circumcision." A later glossator tried, indeed, to make the point clear by adding
the note (v. 26): "She was then applying the expression *'ḥatan* of blood'
to circumcision." Unfortunately, however, his note has been misunderstood
and hence mistranslated!

‡ Sometimes, too, it is called "the seal of Abraham."

The expression represents a characteristically Jewish adaptation of a common pagan institution.

It was customary among many ancient peoples to brand or "seal" slaves in order to prevent their running away or to punish them for trying to do so. By a natural extension of this practice, votaries of gods and goddesses developed the habit of marking their flesh in order to signify that they were the deities' servants and chattels. Among the Babylonians, for example, persons dedicated as acolytes in the service of a temple were wont to bear a distinguishing sign on their persons,[19] and in Egypt, the priests of Isis had a cross-shaped mark on their foreheads.[20] Lucian of Samosata tells us, in the second century C.E., that a similar custom obtained among the worshipers of the Great Goddess at Hierapolis in Syria;[21] the church father Tertullian says of the god Mithra that "he signs his soldiers on the brow,"[22] and the ecstatic devotees of the Phrygian Attis were branded with "the seal" in token of their initiation into his "mysteries."[23] Similarly, on Greek vase-paintings, the Maenads, or female followers of Dionysus, are often depicted with tattoo marks,[24] and in agreement with this is the statement in the Third Book of the Maccabees (2:29) that Ptolemy VI compelled the Jews in his realm to be branded with the sign of that god.

The custom passed even into Christianity. In early centuries, baptism was known as "sealing,"[25] and this was also the ancient name for the rite of Confirmation, which originally followed immediately. Nor did the custom survive only in a figurative sense. To this day, the Catholics of Central Bosnia tattoo themselves with religious symbols;[26] while in the neighborhood of Loreto (Italy) it is common to do likewise in honor of the celebrated local Madonna.[27] Similarly, too, Syrian Christians who have been to Jerusalem mark their brows with the sign of the Cross,[28] and it is recorded of the German mystic, Heinrich Seuse, that he impressed the name of Jesus over his heart.

The brand was commonly regarded as a mark of divine protection, since the devotion and dedication of the worshiper imposed a reciprocal obligation on the god. Herodotus informs us, for instance, that in ancient Egypt, if a fugitive slave reached the temple of "Heracles" at the Canobic mouth of the Nile, and there submitted to branding with the mark of the god, he could not be reclaimed by his master.[29] Similarly, in the Babylonian Epic of Gilgamesh, that hero's friend, Enkidu has to be protected by the sign of the goddess Ninsun before embarking on his series of adventures; [30] while the real purpose of the so-called "brand of Cain" was, as the Bible states expressly (Gen. 4:15), to indicate that once he had been punished by God, he was under His protection against further reprisals at the hands of men. In the same way, too, the prophet Ezekiel bids those who are faithful to Jehovah to set a mark upon their brows in order to spare themselves from a general massacre destined for apostates (Ez. 9:4).

In calling circumcision "the seal of God" the Jews were thus manifesting once again their remarkable genius for articulating a distinctive message in traditional, time-honored terms, "understanded of the people."

Today, circumcision has long since outgrown its primitive significance. When the Jews ceased to be a nation, those of their traditional institutions that had originally been bound up with their national status, or that had stemmed in the first place from their whilom social structure and economy, tended more and more to assume a wider, universal significance and to be interpreted in terms of religious and spiritual symbolism. Circumcision thus developed from a rite of admission to the social group into a symbol of that basic Covenantal commitment which is the *raison d'être* of the Jewish faith and of which all distinctively Jewish experience is a living expression. The Covenantal commitment imposes upon the Jew the obligation of exemplifying and transmitting the Law of God.* He therefore carries in his flesh a constant reminder of the fact that his own self-perpetuation is also the perpetuation of Israel's mission, and that the off-spring which he begets are not merely his own heirs but also the prospective agents and witnesses of an eternal God.

To be sure, the relevance and importance of circumcision have been challenged more than once in modern times. The early Jewish Reformers, for example—motivated, as they too often were, by an excess of nineteenth century rationalism and by an obstinate inability to recognize symbol behind form—were inclined to regard it as a somewhat barbarous institution long since outmoded,[30a] and at the present day some of their followers no longer require it of adult proselytes. By and large, however, the deeper significance of the rite has indeed come to be apprehended, and the vast majority of present-day Jews would probably subscribe to the classic words in which, over a century ago, Leopold Zunz, the master of the modern scientific study of Judaism, protested its proposed abrogation:

Circumcision [he wrote] is, like the Sabbath, an institution, not a mere ceremony. It is not the operation itself (which might indeed be described as a ceremony), but the state of being circumcised

. . . . .

* See my *Festivals of the Jewish Year* (New York, 1953), pp. 3-5.

from one's eighth day onward, that is the core and essence of the commandment. All other rites and ceremonies recur periodically through life, and any single act of omission is in no way final and decisive. They permit of varying degrees of observance, so that remissness on any one occasion can be made up by increased zeal on the next. Not so circumcision; once neglected, the neglect remains permanent and irreparable. Circumcision is a symbol at once of the unity and of the eternity of Israel; an act which exemplifies in concrete form the inheritance of God's Law from the past and the transmission of it to the future. Neglect of this rite is more than a personal matter; it compromises the succeeding generation. For it is unlikely that one who has been denied circumcision on principle will on principle retain his Jewish affiliations. To abrogate circumcision . . . therefore amounts to repudiating the past on the one hand and renouncing the future on the other. It is to sever the thread of Jewish continuity. It is suicide not reform.[31]

Scripture prescribes (Gen. 17:12; Lev. 12:3) that circumcision must be performed on the eighth day after birth, and this rule is rigidly observed, no matter whether the day in question happens to be a sabbath or festival or even the solemn Day of Atonement itself. Postponement is permissible only on grounds of health. A male child who has died between the third and eighth day after birth must be circumcised before burial,[31a] and an adult proselyte is required to submit to the operation before he can be formally received into the fold.

According to the traditional law, circumcision may be performed by any competent male Jew, and in cases of emergency even by women. In practice, however, it is usually entrusted to a specially trained person (often a physician) known as a *mohel* (Hebrew for "circumciser").

The operation consists in three acts: (*a*) the initial cutting of the foreskin (*mîlah*); (*b*) the subsequent removal of it from the glans (*perî'ah*); and (*c*) the stanching of the blood by oral suction (*meẓîẓah*) or by the application of salves.

In Biblical times, the cutting was performed with a flint knife (cf. Exod. 4:25; Jos. 5:2-3), and in certain Jewish communities this usage persisted until as late as the eighteenth century.* Nowadays, however, the general practice is to use an iron or steel blade. The latter must be double-edged, because otherwise the child might be injured if the blunt side were to be applied to it by mistake. Moreover, it is customary for the *mohel* to provide himself with *two* such knives, in case one should prove defective or in case he should find it necessary to make a second incision without delay.

Circumcision must be performed in daylight, and since it is essentially an initiation into the House of Israel, preferably in the presence of ten adult males, the minimal quorum of a Jewish congregation. No women—not even the mother—may be present.

In Western countries, the ceremony usually takes place in the home or in the hospital where the child has been delivered. In the Middle Ages, however, the custom grew

· · · · ·

* Such ceremonial retention of ancient forms is, of course, commonplace in all religions; witness the ram's horn (*shofar*) instead of the trumpet and the manuscript Scroll of the Law instead of the printed book, in Judaism, and the vestments of priests and ecclesiastics in Christianity. Similarly, in Scottish popular custom, a stone hammer has to be used in making the *clavie,* or Yuletide fire-wheel; and both in ancient Rome (Livy, xxi, §45, 8) and in modern Mexico sacrificial knives were made of stone. What is here of special interest, however, is that, according to Herodotus (iii, 8), the Arabs likewise used stone knives for circumcision, and this usage obtains also among the Hottentots and among several North American Indian tribes. It is attested also in parts of Abyssinia and in Australia. Roman writers (e.g. Catullus lxiii 5; Ovid, *Fasti* iv, 237) inform us that the votaries of Attis used stone knives in the rite of castration, and in Egypt, they were employed in making the incision for mummification.

up of holding it in the synagogue, and this is today the more common practice among Oriental Jews.[32]

The child is usually carried to the ceremony by a female relative or friend of its mother, escorted by other women. The ladies retire, however, as soon as they reach the door of the room where the menfolk are assembled. There, a member of the company known as the *sandek* receives it. As he brings it in, all rise and welcome it with the traditional Hebrew greeting, "Blessed be he that cometh!" The *sandek* then hands the child to the *mohel*, who proceeds with it to a gaily decorated chair placed in a prominent position. "This," he declares, "is the Chair of Elijah," and lays the child upon it. Meanwhile, the *sandek* takes his seat on an adjoining chair, likewise gaily beribboned. After a few moments, the *mohel* picks up the child and deposits it on the knees of the *sandek*, where it is held throughout the operation.

The service is introduced by the following verses from Scripture:

I wait for Thy salvation, O Lord (Gen. 49:18).
I hope for Thy salvation, O Lord, and perform Thy commandments (Ps. 119:166).
I rejoice at Thy word, as one that findeth great spoil (Ps. 119:162).
Great peace have they that love Thy Law, and they have no occasion for stumbling (Ps. 119:165).
Happy is he whom Thou choosest and causest to come near, that He may dwell in Thy courts (Ps. 65:4).
Let us, then, be sated with the goodness of Thy House, even of Thy holy temple (ibid.).

Between the second and the third of these quotations it is customary in many communities to insert the following curious sentence: "O Elijah, thou Messenger of the Covenant, that which is for thee stands before thee."

In the present form of the ritual, these verses are put

into the mouth of the *mohel,* but this obscures their whole point and purport. Originally they were recited severally by the various participants in the ceremony and served as a prelude to the actual operation.

First, the *mohel* stepped forward to receive the child, and as he did so, expressed his reliance on Divine aid to prevent his doing aught amiss. "I wait for Thy salvation (*i.e.* power of deliverance)," he declared, in reference to the making of the incision (*mîlah*), and "I hope for Thy salvation," in reference to the tearing of the foreskin (*perî'ah*).

Next, the father gave voice to his joy at initiating his son into the Covenant. "I rejoice at Thy word," he exclaimed, "as one that findeth great spoil."

Nevertheless he could not altogether conceal his nervousness, and the bystanders thereupon reassured him that those who cherish the Law "have no occasion for stumbling."

Lastly, as the child was readied for the operation, those same bystanders cried out, "Happy is he whom Thou choosest. Let us be sated with the goodness of Thy house," etc.

As for the curious sentence that is sometimes addressed to Elijah, this was originally spoken by the *sandek.* Before taking his own seat, he pointed deferentially to the Chair of Elijah and bade the Prophet occupy it: "that which is for thee stands before thee."

The service proper begins with the pronouncement by the *mohel* of the words: *Blessed art Thou, O Lord our God, King of the Universe, Who hast hallowed us by Thy commandments and commanded us concerning circumcision.* Thereupon he performs the operation.

As soon as it is completed, the father exclaims: *Blessed art Thou, O Lord . . . Who hast hallowed us by Thy*

*commandments and commanded us to initiate (our sons)
into the covenant of Abraham, our father.* And to this he
adds the customary blessing on a joyous occasion: *Blessed
art Thou, O Lord . . . Who hast kept us alive and sus-
tained us and enabled us to reach this moment.*

The company responds: *Even as he has now been led
to the Covenant, so may this child be led in due time to
the Law, to the marriage bower, and to good fortune!*

The *mohel* then recites the blessing over wine and proceeds: *Blessed art Thou, O Lord our God, King of the
Universe, Who didst hallow Abraham, dear from the
womb, and didst set the mark of Thine ordinance in his
flesh and seal his offspring with the sign of Thy holy covenant. By virtue thereof, O Living God, our Portion, our
Rock—yea, for the sake of the covenant which Thou hast
set in our bodies—vouchsafe to deliver from corruption
them of our flesh that are dear unto us. Blessed art Thou,
O Lord, Who didst make a covenant (with us).*

After this, he announces the child's Hebrew name and
invokes blessings upon it and its parents. Then he drinks
of the wine and applies a few drops of it to the child's
lips, sending the goblet also to the mother.

This brings the proceedings to a close, except that
among Sephardic Jews it is customary before leaving
to chant in unison the One Hundred and Twenty-eighth
Psalm:

O happy every man that feareth the Lord,
    that walketh in His ways!
The fruit of thy labors shall thou eat;
    O happy, and how goodly thy lot!
Thy wife shall be as a fruitful vine
    at the sides of thy house;
Thy children around thy board
    as olive shoots!

THE COVENANT OF ABRAHAM

It should be added that throughout the ceremony all present remain standing, in accordance with the Scriptural phrase: (II Kings 23:3) : "All the people *stood* to the covenant."

Jews living in Christian countries have often tended to regard circumcision as the Jewish equivalent of baptism, and this attitude has left its impress not only on the formal religious ceremony but also on the accompanying popular customs.

Insofar as the ceremony is concerned, the clearest instance of indebtedness to Christian usage is, perhaps, the use of the name *sandek* for the man who holds the child on his knees. The office performed by this person is, of course, readily explained by the fact that in the East the knees usually serve the purpose of a table. The name, however, has been "lifted" directly from the vocabulary of the Greek Church, where *synteknos* (literally, "he who accompanies the child") is the technical term for the baptismal "sponsor" or "godfather."

Now, in the Christian rite, the godfather has a definite doctrinal function. Baptism is a sacrament, and a sacrament implies the conferment or transmission of Divine grace ("the Holy Spirit") in return for what may best be described as a spiritual or religious "loyalty oath" (Latin, *sacramentum*). The rôle of the godfather or sponsor (i.e. "pledger") is to pledge that oath on behalf of the inarticulate infant or, by extension, of the adult neophyte (lit. "newly born"), who is regarded as such an infant until he has been "signed" and "redeemed." He stands guarantor that the child or neophyte will indeed adhere to the Christian faith, and it is he who answers the priest's preliminary questions on this score. In Judaism, however, there are no sacraments, and the rite of circumcision, while it admits to the fold, involves neither the conferment of grace nor the pledging of an oath. Consequently there is no need for a "sponsor" or "godfather," and the use of that term for a man who in fact performs quite a different office can therefore be regarded only as a mechanical and meaningless borrowing from Christian usage.

The name *sandek*, it may be added, seems first to have been introduced in the tenth century—at least, it is not mentioned in any earlier source[33]—and this is particularly interesting in view of the fact that it was only some hundred years earlier—namely, in 813—that the institution of godfathers was first decreed by the Church at the Council of Mainz.

In all probability, it was due also to the seeming analogy of baptism that it became customary to name male children on the occasion of their circumcision. In the Old Testament—as, for instance, in the case of the Patriarchs or of the sons of Jacob—children appear to have been named *at birth*. In Christianity, however, a person does not possess a Christian identity, and hence cannot bear a "Christian name," until he or she has been baptized and thereby received into the Church. Once again, the Jews took over the standard practice of their neighbors without regard to its doctrinal implications.

Scarcely less arresting is the manifest similarity between popular customs connected with baptism and those associated with circumcision. In some cases, to be sure, we may be dealing with genuine parallels, but in others, as we shall see, the indebtedness of the latter to the former is patent and obvious.

Until a child has been formally received into the Church and stamped, so to speak, with the sign of redemption, it is considered to be still exposed to the assaults of the

Devil—so much so, in fact, that in the Catholic ritual of baptism the solemn exorcism of the Evil One, by the officiating priest, forms a cardinal element of the ceremony. In popular usage, this exposure to demonic influences often calls for stringent countermeasures. On the way to the font, an unusual and circuitous route must be followed in order to throw off the malicious spirits.* [34] The child must be brought into church through a special door.[35] Trumpets must be blown to scare away the princes of darkness.[36] Amulets or demon-averting sachets of salt must be tucked into the infant's clothing,† or it must be bound with red threads.‡ [37] During the ceremony, the northern door of the church must be kept open to give egress to the Evil One,§ [38] and as soon as it is over, the child must be rushed home at full speed in case, by chance, its demonic adversaries have not yet taken their departure but are still lying in wait for it.[39] Once indoors, it must be further protected by the lighting of twelve small candles and one large one, symbolizing the beneficent presence of the Twelve Apostles and of Jesus himself.[40] Finally, magical and medicinal virtues are commonly attached to the baptismal water; what remains in the font after the child has been dipped or signed is religiously conserved in bottles and distributed among those who have attended the ceremony.[41]

Several of these practices have found their way into Jewish popular usage.

. . . . .

* The same thing is done also at funerals. See below, p. 144.

† In the Catholic ritual, the priest actually places salt on the child's mouth. This has been reinterpreted as a symbol of the "salt of wisdom." In popular custom, salt is also placed on the bodies of the dead to keep away demons.

‡ See above, pp. 12 ff.

§ Demons are popularly believed to live in the north. Hence, they go home in that direction.

The night before a circumcision, for example, is likewise deemed especially critical for both mother and child inasmuch as it is Lilith's last chance to work her mischief upon them. It is therefore customary among many Jews to observe a vigil on this occasion, and in the Judaeo-German (Yiddish) vernacular, this night is known as *Wachnacht,* that is, Night of Watching. At dusk, children enter the bedchamber, accompanied by their religious instructor, and after reciting the statutory Prayer upon Retirement (*Keriath Shema'*), chant in chorus the words with which Jacob is said to have blessed his grandchildren, Ephraim and Manasseh (Gen. 48:16): "May the angel who hath redeemed me from all evil [harm] bless the lads." Moreover, it is deemed propitious if the *mohel's* knife lie throughout the night under the mother's pillow—a clear adaptation of the custom of protecting women in confinement by placing swords or iron weapons beside them.*

The practice of performing circumcisions in the synagogue led to further imitation of Christian customs connected with baptism in church. A document of the seventeenth century relates, for instance, that in the German city of Worms, the child used to be brought into the building through a special entrance known as "the Circumcision Door," *[42] and in this it is not difficult to recognize an imitation of the special door often used at the Christian ceremony. Like his Gentile counterpart, the child was rushed home immediately after the ceremony,

. . . . .

* See above, pp. 9 ff.
* The German expression was *Jüdisches Tor,* i.e. "Jewish Door." But since all the doors of a synagogue are necessarily Jewish doors, it is obvious that the word *jüdisches* was here employed in the sense of the Judaeo-German *yiddishen,* "to circumcise"—itself a clear imitation of "christen" for "baptize."

and there, too, it was a common practice to illuminate the
room with twelve small candles and one large one. Among
the Jews, however, these were taken to symbolize the
twelve tribes of Israel and the Patriarch himself!

Lastly, even the custom of attributing special properties
to the waters of baptism found an echo in Jewish circles.
Incongruously enough, it was believed in some parts that
if a barren woman drank of water placed under the "Chair
of Elijah" during the performance of the ceremony she
would be cured of her condition.[43]

Nor is it only to Christian prototypes that the popular
customs connected with circumcision are indebted. Pagan
usages also were freely adopted and adapted.

The "Chair of Elijah," for instance, really goes back
to the ancient Roman practice of spreading a meal for
the household gods—and especially for the deities Pilum-
nus and Picumnus—on the occasion of a birth. Such a
meal was called a *lectus* ("couch"), and the seats on which
the divine guests were expected to recline were known as
"thrones." [44] The Jews simply took over this custom and
"naturalized" it, choosing Elijah as the patron of the
ceremony by virtue of the fact that in the First Book of
Kings (19:10) he is said expressly to have been "very
zealous for Jehovah" when the children of Israel "for-
sook the Covenant"; while in the prophecy of Malachi,
he appears to be described as "the messenger of the Covenant" (3:1; cf. 4:5). This latter idea is caught up and
developed in a passage especially inserted into the Grace
after Meals following a circumcision:

O Thou Whose mercies ne'er have ceased,
Send to us the righteous priest*
. . . . .

* Actually, Elijah was not a priest. In popular legend, however, he was
identified with Melchizedek, the priest-king of Salem, who blessed and

Who, when Thy Covenant was spurned,
Wrapped him in his cloak and turned
And vei'd his face;† who stands withdrawn
Until at last that day shall dawn
When, in a sudden blaze of light,
Upon a throne translucent bright,
Thou shalt rule us as a king
And in our ears Thy message ring:
'My Covenant shall never cease;
Behold, I give you life and peace.'

There is, indeed, an even clearer survival of the pagan usage, for in some parts of the world it is customary on the eve of a circumcision to set out a table of rich fare which no member of the household and no guest may touch, or to spread a couch on which none may lie.[45] This, of course, is nothing but a relic of the table and couch (*mensa* and *lectus*) which the Romans spread for Juno, the goddess of childbirth, and, in the case of male births, also for Hercules.[46] In Jewish tradition, this is known as "the table (or couch) of Gad," [47] an allusion to the words of Isaiah 65:11 in which this practice is denounced. Gad was really the Canaanite god of Fortune (cf. Gen. 30:11), and what the prophet actually had in mind was the custom of the more assimilated and apostatic Jews of his day of offering sacrifices and libations to heathen deities. In later ages, however, the rabbis took the words in a somewhat different sense. To them, the word *gad* was associated with the Arabic *jadd*, "ancestor," and they therefore saw in the prophet's words an allusion to the custom, familiar in their own day, of set-

---

befriended Abraham (Gen.14:18-20) and who was believed to live forever (cf. Ps. 110:4; Heb. 7:1-3). This legendary association with the patriarch would, of course, have lent special point to the introduction of Elijah into the ceremony of "the Covenant of Abraham."
† Cf. I Kings 19:13.

ting tables and spreading couches for ancestral spirits. Indeed, the very fact that they usually speak of the "couch" rather than the "table" of Gad is a sure indication that they are thinking of Roman practice, for this reproduces to a nicety the technical Roman term, viz. *lectus*. Moreover, we are told explicitly that "the couch of Gad" often stood in the household as a regular element of the furniture, without reference to any particular ceremony, and this conforms also to general Roman practice.

Circumcision, the most sacred and the most ancient of all Jewish institutions, thus provides at the same time a striking illustration of the way in which the Hebraic heritage has been expressed by Jews throughout the ages in terms of their own immediate environments.

2

COMING OF AGE

The Ceremony of Bar Mitzvah

At the age of thirteen, in accordance with the precept of the Mishnah, every male Jew is regarded as *bar mitzvah*. The term means literally "son of the commandment" and denotes a legally responsible member of the Jewish community. That status is not automatically acquired by mere physical transition from boyhood to manhood, nor—like Christian grace and salvation—by the performance of a ritual act. It is, in essence, an academic degree, and a Jew can only become bar mitzvah if he satisfies the proper rabbinical authorities concerning his mental and intellectual competence and his intention to accept in deed, and not merely in word, the full responsibilities of the Jewish faith. Like citizenship, the status of bar mitzvah is not a matter of a single moment; it is a continuing condition.

The graybeard of eighty is just as much a bar mitzvah as the youth of thirteen, and when we use the term, we should think not of a young boy on a Saturday morning, but of any conscious, "committed" Jew through the whole of his adult life.

The occasion is marked, in modern usage, by a formal ceremony. After due training and preparation, the lad stands up in the synagogue, on the morning of the Sabbath nearest to his thirteenth birthday, and reads from the Scroll either the whole or a portion of the weekly lesson from the Law, sometimes adding also a reading from the Prophets. By this ceremony, he is automatically recognized as an adult Jew, with all the privileges and obligations thereunto appertaining. In further celebration of the event, it is customary for his parents to hold a banquet or reception and for relatives and friends to bestow presents upon him. In some parts of the world, it is the practice also to cut the boy's hair on or about the thirteenth birthday—a Jewish counterpart of the widespread custom of shearing the locks at puberty.*

The synagogal ceremony is not prescribed in Jewish law and was not even known before the Middle Ages. It is in no sense a sacramental rite. It confers nothing, imparts nothing, creates nothing; it merely celebrates. When the fledgling bar mitzvah stands up in the synagogue and reads his "portion," he is, in fact, in much the same position as the citizen who goes to the polls for the first time. That citizen is not thereby acquiring citizenship; all he is doing—albeit with an extra flourish—is to exercise for the first time one of its particular privileges to which he has now become entitled.

Viewed in proper perspective, the institution of Bar

• • • • •

* See below, p. 106.

Mitzvah stands in the same relationship to Jewry as citizenship to a nation. It is predicated, however, upon a unique conception. That conception is that the Jewish people is not a mere fortuitous aggregation of individuals, but a sacred society—a self-dedicated "kingdom of priests"—dedicated to the practical expression of the Torah (as interpreted progressively throughout the generations) and to the attestation of God's presence in the world of men: Ye are My witnesses. Jews are not considered automatically—either by divine fiat or by race—participants in this mission, but for the mission to be fulfilled, it is necessary that every individual Jew shall be a trained and active combatant in the ranks. This and this alone is what is meant by being bar mitzvah. Anyone who evades this obligation, or denies the premise upon which it is based, is simply not a Jew in any proper sense of the term; he has no portion of Jacob, nor inheritance in Israel—no stake in the emergent future, no "share in the world to come."

Once its true basis is grasped, the actual procedure by which the status of bar mitzvah is acquired becomes readily intelligible.

First, as to the age. A Jew becomes bar mitzvah at thirteen because, in Eastern countries, that was (and often is) the customary age of marriage. Accordingly, at the age of thirteen a youth actually became the founder of a household, and it was therefore both logical and appropriate that he should then be admitted as an adult member of the community. In other words, the choice of age was neither arbitrary nor artificial; it was determined by the consideration that at thirteen the young man did, in fact, qualify for the status which the institution envisaged.

Second, as to the antecedent training. This was not

a mere perfunctory preparation for a specific event. It was a solid initiation into Jewish life, based on the premise that all human conduct should be channeled and controlled by sound factual knowledge and the ability to form judgments by it. For that reason, it was deemed necessary that the bar mitzvah candidate should demonstrate to the authorities not only his command of actual data but also his *ability to think;* he had to show that he could follow a rabbinic disputation and that the involutions and subtleties of pilpulistic argument were not beyond his comprehension. He was expected, in fact, to produce something very like a dissertation in the form of an oral discourse (*derashah*) publicly delivered. Pedagogues may criticize the matter and frown on the manner of this ancient curriculum, but its underlying principle can scarcely be contested—the principle that no one who is not generally literate, specifically versed in its traditional lore, and actively conscious of its mission should be admitted to full membership in the House of Israel or have a voice in its affairs.

In setting up this principle, Judaism offered a positive and valuable contribution to the concept of social responsibility. The principle was entirely democratic: every Jew was eligible to become bar mitzvah; the knowledge by which he qualified for that status was knowledge in the public domain and not, as in the puberty rites of so many cultures, special and secret lore, and the society into which he was admitted was the community as a whole and not, as elsewhere, some particular, esoteric group within it. At the same time, the principle protested the facile assumption that social privilege is an inherent and inalienable right, and it demanded that it be earned by qualification. What applies to the professions of law and medicine today was thus applied also to social status: license had to be earned by requisite knowledge. To the principle "No taxation without representation" Judaism replies, "No representation without taxation," but the taxation which it envisages is that of the mind and heart. No representation without education.

Third, as to the actual ceremony of Bar Mitzvah. From the strictly historical point of view, this would appear to be a relatively late innovation, not definitely attested before the fourteenth century. Traditionally, the duty of the Jewish father is simply to see that his son, by the time he reaches the age of thirteen, is equipped with sufficient religious education to enable him to discharge the responsibilities of that adult state upon which he enters. It is, however, a sound instinct which now requires that the new bar mitzvah present himself in the synagogue and there attest his status by means of a public ceremony. For this requirement is founded on the truth that the House of Israel, to which he is admitted, is not an ideal abstraction but a concrete reality and consists actually in the aggregate of Jewish congregations. It is a society, not a concept, and a man cannot be a member of it except through the medium of communal affiliation. At the same time, the congregation is itself but an aggregate of households, not an independent, transcendental entity. Accordingly, the bar mitzvah does not become a full member of the congregation without also becoming a responsible member of a particular household. The "initiation" is thus twofold, and for this reason the ceremony takes place both in the synagogue and in the home. Then, too, it must be borne in mind that, while the bar mitzvah *enters* the community, the community *receives* him, so that the synagogal ceremony in fact possesses the double character of an introduction on the one hand and a reception on the other.

To the average Jewish father, his son's Bar Mitzvah is scarcely less important than his daughter's wedding. However far he may himself have strayed from the ancestral fold, he usually insists that at the prescribed age his male offspring shall be duly and properly inducted, with all attendant traditional ceremony, into full membership in the House of Israel. What attitude the boy may later adopt toward this commitment is, he concedes, his own concern, but at least he must be given the chance, on entering manhood, to take his place in the community of his fathers. To deny him that chance is to deny him his birthright and gratuitously to repudiate both the past and the future. Above the din and clamor of the world, the muffled cry of the exiled Divine Presence still makes itself heard.

This feeling about Bar Mitzvah has been strengthened, no doubt, by the force of recent events—by a deepening sense of Jewish solidarity, a clearer apprehension of the truth that survival entails obligation and that every Jew has a duty today to stand up and be counted. Quite apart, however, from this understandable reaction to persecution, genuine religious sentiment on the one hand and mere atavistic nostalgia on the other have themselves proved sufficient, over several generations, to make of the ceremony and celebration one of the major institutions of Jewish life. Indeed, it is doubtful whether any other institution (short of circumcision and burial) can claim so widespread and devoted an adherence.

Nevertheless, it must be confessed that in the changed conditions of modern life, especially in Western countries, the traditional institution has tended to lose much of its original significance and to become more and more a mere formality.

In the first place, in Western society today a boy of

thirteen is not, in fact, an adult; he is still a minor. He does not marry, does not become a responsible member of a household, and cannot enter into legal obligations. Moreover, within the sphere of the Jewish community itself, he is not—as a rule—eligible for full membership in the congregation and certainly not for any active voice or executive position in communal affairs. (Indeed, even if—theoretically—he were to be appointed to such office, the law of the land would automatically withhold from him the necessary powers to discharge it.) Even in the State of Israel, the status of bar mitzvah does not of itself admit to the rights of an adult citizen. To be sure, the bar mitzvah boy is reckoned thenceforth as one of the ten males required to form a *minyan,* but the *minyan* itself—which is really the minimal community—has degenerated to the level of a mere formal quorum for public devotions. Moreover, on the American scene, the boy actually is often relegated, in point of fact, to membership in a "junior congregation"—a device which deprives him of his "civil rights" and which amounts to handing him the latchkey and then telling him to find other accommodation! In short, the status to which he is admitted by the ceremony of Bar Mitzvah is today entirely nominal; what is granted *de jure* is denied *de facto.*

Then there is the question of preliminary training. In most cases, this is purely perfunctory; it is totally insufficient to equip the bar mitzvah for the status which the institution properly envisages. As often as not, it is a mere preparation for the ceremony itself, and its frame of reference is solely the ritual of synagogue and home. It is presented as something *in*jected into, rather than *pro*jected out of, the life of the Jew—a kind of creedal indoctrination. The Hebrew which is taught is described, with disarming candor, as frankly "functional," the function being to enable the bar mitzvah candidate to "find the place" in the prayer book and to "follow the service."

Lastly, it should be observed that when the ceremony of Bar Mitzvah is today performed in the synagogue, the implications are appreciably different from what they were in the past. In former days, the synagogue was the center of all collective Jewish life, not merely a house of worship. To be introduced into the synagogue was therefore to be inducted into the community. Today, however, almost all communal activities that are not strictly religious are distributed over extra-synagogal organizations. In point of fact, therefore, the new bar mizvah is introduced only into a congregation of worshipers (and even that is not usually present in full force), not into a community.

To be sure, several more enlightened rabbis and educators have sought, in recent years, to remedy this parlous state of affairs by insisting that the ceremony of bar mitzvah be performed only after so many years of continuous attendance at the religious school. Yet even this can scarcely suffice without radical revision of the traditional curriculum. For more is needed at the present time to equip a responsible Jew in a predominantly Gentile world than was required in the days when life was concentrated in a more exclusively Jewish environment and less liable to be buffeted, at almost every turn, by the impact of different and conflicting ideologies. An educational program today has to do more than merely impart traditional lore; it has also to provide the student with at least an elementary understanding of the factors which determine the status of the Jews in the contemporary world. Moreover, much of the traditional lore itself now stands in a different light from heretofore. (Archaeology, for example, has placed a new complexion on the Exodus and the conquest of Canaan—events which occupy a cardinal and quasi-dogmatic position in Jewish religious thought.) It no longer suffices, therefore, to spend the hours of instruction in mere repetitions of Bible tales, formal descriptions of Jewish observances, inspirational talks about Jewish ideals. Accordingly, to prescribe a length of time during which a child must be subjected to the present curriculum is no solution of the problem. What is important is not the length but the quality of the training.

Reduced to bare essentials, the problem of Bar Mitzvah at the present day has a twofold character. First, in terms of the institution *per se,* the question arises: how, if the present form is inadequate, can its broad purpose and objective—that of guaranteeing that every member of the House of Israel shall be fully conversant with its traditions and actively participate in its mission—now be secured? Second, there is the question: how, if at all, can the traditional ceremony be salvaged and given meaning?

During the past hundred years, under the initial impetus of the Reform movement, the favorite solution has been to substitute for the individual Bar Mitzvah ceremony a collective "confirmation" of juveniles at the festival of the Feast of Weeks (Pentecost), this date being chosen because it is the traditional anniversary of the Conclusion of the Covenant and the Giving of the Law and therefore peculiarly appropriate as the time when new Israelites shall be formally inducted into the fold. The advantage of this system, it is claimed, is that the festival of Pentecost happens to coincide, more or less, with the end of the school year, and the ceremony can thus become one of graduation—the logical climax to years of study. Moreover, on this basis, it can be open to girls as well as boys and thus take cognizance of the fact that the social and communal status of women has indeed changed appreciably since the days when the traditional Bar Mitzvah was established.

This solution, however, is tenable only on the express assumption that confirmation is not a mere amended form of Bar Mitzvah but something entirely different—a ceremony of graduation and affirmation of faith. For if it is intended to serve the original purpose of Bar Mitzvah— namely, to admit the adolescent Jew as a full member of the community—then clearly, it no more effects its pretensions than does the time-honored usage. The confirmand is *de facto* just as much debarred as is the bar mitzvah, and his preparation is as incomplete. From this point of view, the problem remains exactly where it was, and the ceremony, though more spectacular, is no whit less artificial.*

A more constructive approach to the problem might be, perhaps to recognize the present ceremony as a kind of initial matriculation, and add another, at a more mature age, which would have the value of full graduation, and which would really take over the function of the Bar Mitzvah institution.

At the present moment, what happens is that the two stages are confused. The lad of thirteen is, so to speak, being handed a cap and gown but denied any graduate standing, or a certificate of citizenship without enjoying civil rights. And the fact of the matter is that he is indeed

. . . . .

* It should be observed, in this connection, that the name "confirmation" is, in any case, misleading. The term has been adopted, albeit unconsciously, from Christian practice, where confirmation is a *sacrament*. What it confirms is not, as is often thought, the adherence of the individual to the Christian faith, but rather the baptismal bestowal of grace. Originally, in fact, baptism and confirmation (called "sealing") took place at the same time or within a very short interval. To avoid misunderstanding, therefore, it would be well if the use of this name were given up; "religious graduation" would be more to the point.

not yet qualified, by age, knowledge, or experience, to receive such standing or enjoy such rights. On the other
hand, when he really attains majority and is actually qualified to be bar mitzvah—that is, to be a full member of
the community with all its privileges and obligations—
there is no ceremony whatsoever, no test of his qualification or of his intention actively to play his part.

By the approach here suggested, the first ceremony—
the present Bar Mitzvah at thirteen—would have the
force of confirmation. It would mark the close of initial
religious education—a graduation from high school. But
it would not admit to adult status in the House of Israel,
nor to membership in the adult congregation. The confirmand could become, however, a member of the junior
congregation, which would thus acquire an organic place
in Jewish life. Then, after a further period of preparation,
when he is indeed legally an adult, he would be admitted
to the senior congregation. But such admission would
again be dependent on a test of qualification and an accompanying ceremony of induction. In this way, a guarantee would be furnished that every congregation of Jews
really consists of trained, conscious, responsible, and active members of the House of Israel. It would be a
method of turning the profession of Judaism into an active campaign, instead of a mute acquiescence; it would
eliminate malingering in the ranks of God.

From the practical point of view, such a system would
also facilitate the drawing up of adequate curriculums of
Jewish education. At the present moment, one of the major problems is that a great deal of adult knowledge has
to be crammed into the head of the thirteen-year-old because there is small chance of his remaining in school after
Bar Mitzvah, and he has consequently to be prepared for
Judaism in his childhood or not at all. By the proposed

system, however, the progress of Jewish education could be properly organized and graded, and there could be a proper and methodical distinction—which there is not to-day—between high school and undergraduate instruction. There is nothing in Jewish traditional law which would militate against such a change. On the contrary, the spirit of the rabbinical precept is that the assumption of the status of bar mitzvah is merely one stage in a progressive course of education. In ancient times, it happens to have been the graduate stage, but that—as we have explained —is because the antecedent training was more intensive. Today, it may well represent a lesser stage, and the in-tellectual requirement be correspondingly lowered.

Jewish tradition wisely leaves the solution of these problems to the discernment of the prophet Elijah at the time when he comes to herald the Messiah. In the present instance, however, the long interval may well prove disas-trous, for it may in fact deprive the Messenger of any fully responsible Jews to whom he may convey his tidings.

III

Betrothal

TROTH AND RING

To us, Betrothal consists essentially in "popping the question" and receiving an affirmative answer. In ancient times, however, it was not so much a private understanding between a young man and woman as a business arrangement concluded by their families.

Originally, wives were purchased. The primary consideration was to compensate a family for losing one of its female members. The father of the bridegroom therefore paid a sum of money to that of the bride. The ceremony took place in the latter's home. A formal contract was drawn up and witnessed; the bridegroom presented gifts to his betrothed; and there was often also an exchange of "pledges." Although actual delivery of the bride might be deferred for some time, the couple was regarded from that moment as legally bound or "espoused." [1]

A graphic description of these early betrothal ceremonies is contained in a Canaanite poem of the fourteenth
century B.C.E. discovered in recent years at Ras Shamra,
site of the ancient city of Ugarit, on the north coast of
Syria:

The bride's guardian sets up the scales,
her mother adjusts the trays,
her brothers compute the cash,
her sisters attend to the weights.[2]

Later, the emphasis shifted and the main factor became
that of making provision for the prospective wife in case
she should subsequently be abandoned by her husband or
divorced through no fault of her own. In place of the
original "brideprice" paid to her father, the bridegroom
was now required to put down a security of at least two
hundred "Tyrian *zuzim*" and to hand that sum directly
to the bride. This, however, often imposed an intolerable
hardship on him just at the time when he needed every
penny to establish the new home and to set himself up
in a remunerative trade or profession. Accordingly, in
the first century B.C.E., an important modification was introduced by Simeon ben Shetah, president of the Sanhedrin, or supreme rabbinical assembly, during the reigns
of Alexander Jannaeus and his successor, Queen Salime.
Henceforth it was ordained the prospective husband
could legally "borrow back" the cash deposit, by insert-
ing in the marriage contract a clause imposing a lien on
all his present and future property in favor of his wife.[3]

This ancient form of the betrothal contract survives
substantially at the present day. A significant addition has
been made, however, to the accompanying ceremony for,
since about the fifth century, it has become customary to
seal the engagement by having the "bridegroom" present
the "bride" with a ring.[4]

The wedding ring (more properly, the betrothal ring) is usually interpreted nowadays as a symbol of the "link" or bond forged by matrimony, or, in view of the fact that, being circular, it has neither beginning nor end, of "the eternity, constancy and integrity of love." [5] In Jewish tradition, however, it possesses quite a different significance. It is simply a deliberate substitute for the small coin (Hebrew, *perūṭah*) which the "bridegroom" was originally required to put down in token of his ability to meet the financial obligations of the contract. So long as it has at least the value of that coin, the ring need not be made of gold nor even of silver, but if any baser metal is employed, the "bride" must be duly apprised of the fact, for otherwise, it is held, she will have been "short-changed." [6] Nor need the ring be necessarily a *finger* ring. Indeed, such specimens of Jewish engagement rings as have survived from ancient times are almost invariably too large and uncomfortable for that purpose, and it has been plausibly suggested that they were designed rather as holders for the bridal bouquet! [7]

The custom of using a ring instead of the original token coin was, in all probability, a clever adaptation of current pagan practice, for we know that Roman bridegrooms often included a ring among the "pledges" presented at the ceremony of espousal.[8] Moreover, it was common usage in the Middle Ages for people to present rings or bracelets to parting friends or lovers as a sign of the enduring alliance between them,* and this would have been particularly appropriate in the case of a betrothed couple in view of the very prevalent convention which prohibited

．．．．．

* In the Saga of Fridthjof the Bold, for instance, the hero gives a ring to his beloved Ingeborg on bidding her farewell; while in the Nibelungenlied, Gotelind, the wife of Rudeger, gives a bracelet to the warrior-minstrel, Folker.

them from seeing each other until the actual marriage ceremony.

Nor, as a matter of fact, was the substitution peculiarly Jewish. In the Christian marriage service, the ring is likewise characterized as "a token and pledge" of the "vow and covenant" made between the bridal couple, and the word "covenant" is there to be understood in reference to the older legal contract. Moreover, traces of the more ancient practice do indeed survive sporadically even in the ritual of the Church. In Cumberland (England), for instance, it was customary, as late as the nineteenth century, that when the bridegroom recited the words, "With this ring I thee wed . . . and with all my worldly goods I thee endow," he not only placed the ring on the bride's finger but also poured gold and crown pieces into a handkerchief held by the bridesmaid. This was called *"dow-purse."* [9]

In common Jewish parlance, the betrothal ceremony is known as "Sanctification" (Hebrew, *Kiddūshin*). This, however, has no reference to "holy matrimony," nor even to the sanctity of the marriage vows. It is simply an imitation of the Roman term *sacramentum,* which meant originally "the rite of making a pledge" and was thence applied specifically to the plighting of troth.

The ceremony originally took place a considerable time —sometimes as much as a year—before the actual wedding or handing over of the bride. The holding of two celebrations, however, often imposed a severe strain upon families of moderate income. In the Middle Ages, therefore, the custom grew up of performing the two ceremonies together—a custom which was likewise adopted by the Church. The modern Jewish wedding thus consists in reality in *two* ceremonies, formally separated by the reading of the contract. All that precedes the reading is *betrothal* (Hebrew, *kiddushin*); all that follows is *marriage* (Hebrew, *nissuin*); and for each ceremony a separate cup of wine must be used and blessed. This, it may be added, applies also to the Christian service. Indeed, the older Christian prayer books prescribe specifically that the first part of the wedding ceremony must be performed at the church door, and only after the couple has exchanged the formal pledges of matrimony may they enter the church for the second part.

EXCHANGE OF GIFTS

It is a common custom in many parts of the world that a betrothed couple exchange gifts of apparel shortly before their wedding. In the rural districts of Germany and Austria, for instance, the bride sends the groom an embroidered shirt, while he reciprocates with a present of slippers, handkerchiefs, and scarves.[1] Similarly, Mongolian brides receive a shawl on the eve of their marriage;[2] while the Roman historian Tacitus informs us that in ancient times, the prospective wife of a Teuton gave him, among other things, "divers articles of armor."[3] In all cases, these gifts were originally part of the token "pledges" by which a betrothal was sealed.

The Jews, too, adopted this custom, but they gave it a new and distinctive significance, for the particular articles of apparel which they exchanged symbolized in very pointed fashion the demands which each of the partners to the marriage made upon the other. They became, so to speak, *instruments of matrimony*.

The usual present from the bridegroom is a *sash* or *girdle,* often gaily ornamented. Now, the unloosing of the girdle—today a mere figurative expression—was in ancient times the almost universal symbol of wedlock; so much so, indeed, that among the Greeks and Romans the word "girdle" was itself a recognized synonym for "marriage." Among the Arabs of Palestine, the bride makes a point of leaving off her waistband or girdle, or of using it as a veil, until the day after the wedding ceremony, thereby symbolizing the surrender of her virginity,[4] and in Morocco, she resumes it only after several days have passed, in order to mark the transition from the status of bride to that of matron.[5]

The bride, for her part, sends the bridegroom a *tallith,* or fringed prayer-shawl, usually made by her own hands. This he wears at the wedding ceremony.

Now, in ancient times, the *tallith* was not simply a prayer-shawl, but an outer wrap or mantle, and the spreading of such a garment over another person signified the taking of that person under one's protection[6]— an idea which underlies the very word "protect" (i.e. cover over) and which survives also in the common expression, "to cast the mantle of charity" over someone. It is related in the Bible, for instance, that when Ruth sought the protection of her kinsman Boaz, she bade him *spread thy garment over thy handmaid* (Ru. 3:9); and the prophet Ezekiel represents Jehovah as assuring Israel that *I will spread My garment over thee and cover thy nakedness, and plight troth with thee, and enter into covenant with thee . . . and thou shalt be Mine* (Ezek. 16:8). Mohammed, we are told, took to wife the Jewess Safiya, whom he had acquired after the battle near Khaibar, by summarily casting his mantle over her,[7] and at the present day, this is the regular gesture of marriage

among the bedouins of the Sinai Peninsula.* [8] Similarly,
in the wedding service of the Russian Orthodox Church,
the bridegroom used formerly to throw the lap of his
gown over the bride in token of his protection.[9] When,
therefore, the Jewish bride sent a *tallith* to her future
husband, she was symbolically committing herself to his
care. The rabbis, however, invented a fanciful explanation of the custom. In the Law of Moses, they pointed
out, the commandment enjoining the wearing of the
fringed garment is followed immediately by the words,
If a man take a wife . . . (Deut. 22:12-13). This, they
said, implies clearly that the *tallith* is pre-eminently the
garment of a married man and might therefore be most
appropriately presented to him by his bride! Furthermore, they observed, the statutory fringes of that garment are made up of thirty-two skeins, and thirty-two is
the numerical value of the Hebrew letters which spell the
word for "heart" (viz. *LeB*). By this gesture, therefore,
the bride in effect "gives her heart" to her prospective
husband!

The girdle is usually brought to the bride by a male
friend of the bridegroom specially delegated for the purpose. In Austria, for instance, he is called the *Wortmann,*
and carries it to her, along with other gifts, on the wedding morn.[10] This has recently inspired a particularly interesting conjecture. In most of the Semitic languages,
the word for "best man" (e.g. Hebrew, *shoshbîn;* Aramaic, *shushbînâ;* Assyro-Bablyonian, *shushapinu*) bears
a strange resemblance to another (viz. Aramaic, *shosîfâ;*
Assyro-Babylonian *shusuppu*) meaning "a dyed or embroidered cloth." It has therefore been suggested that

. . . . .

* In pre-Mohammedan times, sons took over the care of their deceased
fathers' wives by casting their mantles over them.

the original function of the "best man" was to serve as the conveyor of the bridal sash or veil.[11] In support of this conjecture, the further point may be adduced that in Amharic—a Semitic language spoken in Abyssinia—the related term *shafashift* denotes specifically "a white piece of cloth which has not touched water and *which the 'best man' ties around the head of the bride*." [12]

SPINNHOLZ

Among the Romans, the ceremony of betrothal was known as *sponsalia,* because the bride was then solicited from her father or guardian by the formula *spondesne* (Do you pledge [her]?), to which in turn he replied, *spondeo* (I do). The commitment was sealed by an exchange of presents—called "pledges"—between the couple involved, the bride sometimes receiving an engagement ring (*annulus pronubus*), and the occasion was marked by a family banquet and celebration.[1]

Although the ceremony itself subsequently underwent changes, the old name persisted down to the Middle Ages as the regular term for espousals. Thence, in an intriguing disguise, it percolated into Jewish usage.

In the afternoon of the sabbath which precedes her marriage, it is customary among Ashkenazic Jews to hold a reception in the home of the bride's parents, and at this reception she formally receives her trousseau. The "shower" is known as *Spinnholz*—a designation which can be traced back to medieval times. Since that name would seem, on the face of it, to be identical with the German word for "distaff," it is usually explained by reference to the fact that distaff and spindle are everywhere the standard symbols of feminine domesticity—so much so, indeed, that in several parts of Europe (as was likewise the custom in ancient Rome) they are actually carried before the bride in the wedding procession.[2] The fact is, however, that *Spinnholz is* here simply a popular corruption of the Latin *sponsalia,* the ceremony itself being nothing but a lingering survival of the old Roman usage! In the course of its adoption, however, it received a characteristically Jewish complexion by being transferred to the sabbath preceding the wedding. The reason for this was that in Jewish custom the entire week in which a wedding took place was regarded—in accordance with Oriental practice—as a family festival, the inauguration of which was celebrated appropriately on the sabbath.

Nor, indeed, is the bridegroom overlooked on that day, for it is customary to include him among the seven persons called to read the Lesson from the Law in the morning service of the synagogue.* At the same time, relatives and friends who attend that service pledge † offerings to charity in order to induce the Divine blessing upon the marriage.

. . . . .

* The weekly Lesson from the Law, i.e. Pentateuch, (Hebrew, *parashah* or *sidrah*) is divided into seven sections, and seven members of the congregation (the first, a Cohen or descendant of Aaron; the second, a Levite) are called successively to the rostrum to read them aloud from the sacred Scroll. So unredeemed are our times, however, that this office, once performed literally, now consists in merely reciting the appropriate blessings and standing passively beside the professional cantor, while the latter does the actual reading.

† Actual payment of cash is prohibited on the sabbath.

IV

Marriage

WEDLOCK

A contract of eternal bond of love,
Confirm'd by mutual joinder of your hands,
Attested by the holy close of lips,
Strengthen'd by interchangement of your rings.
SHAKESPEARE, *Twelfth Night.*

Marriage is regarded in Jewish tradition as the fulfillment of the Biblical command to "be fruitful and multiply"— the first charge laid by God upon man (Gen. 1:28). It therefore ranks not only as a Divine institution but also as a paramount human duty. To neglect that duty, say the sages, is as serious a crime as to commit murder, and in support of this contention they point out acutely that in the text of Scripture (Gen. 9:6-7) the law prohibiting homicide is in fact followed immediately by that enjoining the propagation of the species!

Marriage is regarded also as inherently holy, not because it is a sacrament or because marriage vows are sacred bonds, but because it issues in the reproduction upon earth of that Divine "image and likeness" in which Man was originally created.

Nevertheless, whatever high and holy doctrines may have been entertained about it, it has also been the common belief (if not, indeed, the common experience) of humanity from time immemorial that marriage is attended with hazard and that those who embark upon it stand in very special need of protection from malicious spirits all too eager to assail them and from an Evil Eye which seems to be cast all too steadily in their direction. Accordingly, it has been the custom throughout the ages to accompany the formal rites of marriage with all sorts of popular practices and procedures designed specifically to that end.

The Jews have been no more immune to this attitude than anyone else, and in consequence of their dispersion among the peoples of the earth they have come also to absorb many of the "pagan" usages which follow from it. If, therefore, we wish to understand the true character of Jewish wedding ceremonies—to understand, that is, why the bride wears white and carries a bouquet; why the bridal couple stands under a canopy (Hebrew, *huppah*); why they are attended by bridesmaids, groomsmen and a "best man"; why they are pelted with rice, nuts or confetti; and why the bridegroom smashes a glass at the close of the proceedings—it is necessary, in most cases, to search for prototypes and counterparts in pagan and gentile usage, and to go back to that earlier stage of civilization in which the mating of man and woman was an occasion not so much of joy as of vital and imminent peril.

At the same time, it must be borne in mind that here, as elsewhere, the Jews did not copy mechanically. Wherever possible, they transmuted what they borrowed into the terms of their distinctive religious heritage, giving to the originally "heathen" customs new meanings based, as often as not, on deft and ingenious applications of Holy Writ! Hence, even though they may be pagan in origin and outward form, Jewish marriage customs are, by and large, thoroughly Hebraic in contemporary significance, an excellent example of "the beauties of Japheth in the tents of Shem."

A TIME TO EMBRACE

All over the world, and in all ages, it has been considered of special importance that weddings take place on auspicious dates.

Since in ancient times, they were usually solemnized at nightfall—as they still are in the Orient—particular attention was, and is, paid to *the phase of the moon.* The Parsis of India, for example, will not perform a marriage in "the dark o' the moon";[1] neither will the Moroccans.[2] To do so, it is held, is simply to court disaster, for at such times the demons have a special opportunity to work their mischief without being detected. Similarly, according to Tacitus, the ancient Germans were loth to embark on any new enterprise when the moon was invisible[3]—a practice which survives among many of their modern descendants[4] and which allegedly led Hitler to call off his projected invasion of Britain at the last moment! This idea is well attested in Jewish superstition, and several of the most prominent of the medieval and later rabbinic authorities

were constrained, in view of its prevalence, to condemn it
expressly as a "heathen" superstition.

Equally important is it to choose a propitious day of
the week. The particular choice, however, has varied from
age to age, and from country to country. In Talmudic
times, the favorite day—especially for the marriage of
virgins—was Wednesday.[5] This finds a curious parallel
in early Teutonic practice, where Wednesday was deemed
peculiarly auspicious because it was sacred to the high god
Wotan.[6] Similarly, too, a traditional English rhyme prescribes:

Monday for health,
Tuesday for wealth,
Wednesday the best day of all;
Thursday for crosses,
Friday for losses,
Saturday no luck at all.*

During the Middle Ages, however, preference was
given to Friday. The primary reason for this was economic: poor families were thus enabled to combine the
wedding feast with the regular festive meal in honor of
the Sabbath, thereby avoiding double expense. But there
were also other considerations. According to the Bible,
the creation of man took place on a Friday, and it was
then that he was enjoined to "be fruitful and multiply"
(Gen. 1:26-31). Moreover, in Mohammedan countries,
the change was doubtless influenced also by the fact that
Friday is the Moslem Sabbath; it is known, in fact, as "the

. . . . .

* On the other hand, Wednesday is considered by many peoples as
peculiarly unlucky. In Alsace, for instance, marriages are avoided on that
day, and among some of the native tribes of Madagascar, every Wednesday throughout the year is an occasion of public sorrow and, in former
times, children born on a Wednesday were put to death. The belief still
obtains in some parts of Germany that Wednesday is "no day at all,"
because, alone of all the days of the week, it is called by a name (viz.
Mittwoch, "midweek") which does not contain the element—*tag* ("day") !

day *par excellence"* (Arabic, *el-fadileh*),* and weddings
are very commonly celebrated on Friday night.† Conversely, in Christian lands, the choice of Friday stood in
pointed contrast to general usage and thus provided a
means whereby the Jews might preserve and assert their
distinctiveness instead of adopting "the ways of the
Amorite." To the Christians, Friday was especially unlucky because it was the day when Jesus was crucified. As
late as the nineteenth century, for instance, Christian
mariners in Germany would not leave port, if they could
help it, on a Friday,[7] while in 1840, the omnibus in Paris
charged extra fares for carrying passengers on that day,
since it was deemed ominous for travel.‡ [8]

In modern times, Tuesday too has come into favor
among Jews as a day for weddings. The reason in this
case is that in the Book of Genesis (1:10, 12), the words,
God saw that it was good occur *twice* in reference to things
created on Tuesday, but only once in reference to those
created on the other days!

Weddings have also their open and closed seasons.
Among the ancient Romans, for example, marriages in
May were considered unlucky. The poet Ovid declares
flatly that such marriages will not last;[9] while a similar
ban sometimes applied also to the month of March.[10]
Moreover, such beliefs survive to the present day in many

• • • • •

* Friday is likewise regarded by the Hindus as the most auspicious day
of the week.

† It was partly under this influence that the Jewish mystics of Safed,
in the sixteenth century, adopted the custom of composing sacred hymeneals in honor of "Bride Sabbath" and of chanting them on Friday night.
The famous *Lechah Dodi* by Solomon Alkabetz is a specimen of this
genre. See fully my *Festivals of the Jewish Year*, p. 283.

‡ The aversion to Friday is likewise attested in the pagan world. Among
the ancient Finns and Estonians, no bethrothals or marriages were celebrated on that day. If the king of the Bambarra has a son born to him on
a Friday, he straightway condemns him to death.

European countries. A North Country rhyme current in Britain asserts tersely, "Marry in May—rue for aye." Similarly, in several parts of Germany, marriages in May are discountenanced,[11] and a work on Kentucky superstitions, published as late as 1920, bears evidence that the notion has percolated also to the New World.[12]

The original reason for the restrictions was that, in different agricultural and pastoral calendars, the periods in question preceded the real beginning of the year or annual cycle, and therefore marked the time when the life of the community was believed to be in eclipse, prior to its regeneration. That period was signalized by public austerities and other forms of "mortification." Thus, in Cambodia, the first three days of the year (which begins in mid-March) are a period of solemn and rigorous abstinence, when sexual relations are forbidden, and in many other parts of the world, the reaping of the harvest is preceded by a lenten period.[13]

The Jews took over from their neighbors this system of "closed" seasons. At three times of the year the celebration of marriages is forbidden not merely by custom but actually by law; * viz. (*a*) during the first thirty-two days of the "Omer-period" between Passover and the Feast of Weeks; † (*b*) during the three weeks from the Fast of Tammuz until that of Ab, inclusive; ‡ and (*c*) during the Ten Days of Penitence, from New Year until Yom Kippur.*

Jewish tradition has attempted, however, to justify

. . . . .

* Marriages may not be solemnized, of course, on the Sabbath, on a festival or holy day, and during a period of mourning.
† See *Festivals of the Jewish Year*, pp. 32 f.
‡ *ibid.*, pp. 192 f.
* See *Festivals of the Jewish Year*, pp. 123 ff.

these restrictions on seemingly historical grounds. The ban on marriages during the earlier portion of the Omer-period is said to commemorate the fact that, during the second century C.E., a severe plague decimated the disciples of the illustrious Rabbi Akiba at that season; while the prohibition during the three weeks from the seventeenth day of Tammuz until the ninth of Ab is explained as due to the fact that this is a period of mourning, the walls of Jerusalem having first been breached by the forces of Nebuchadnezzar on the former date, and the Temple having been sacked and burned on the latter.

The Jews, however, were not alone in reinterpreting the time-honored usage. The Christians likewise attempted to bring it into line with their own faith. In England, for instance, the ban on marriages in May takes the form, "If you marry in Lent—you will live to repent"; while in Italy, weddings in that month are regarded as inauspicious because it is dedicated to the Virgin! [14]

BRIDE AND GROOM

Nowhere, perhaps, are primitive ideas concerning marriage better exemplified in Jewish usage than in the Hebrew terms for bride and bridegroom.

The bride is called *kallah,* a word which means primarily "one who is shut in, secluded." [1]

Now, it is common belief among primitive peoples that on the eve of her marriage a girl is exposed especially to the attacks of evil and malicious spirits.* *Au fond,* such spirits are merely personifications of the phobias, neuroses and apprehensions which so often beset the prospective bride. The primitive, however, is less capable of distinguishing between personification and reality—the figurative and the real—than is his more civilized brother or descendant. The evil spirits are therefore conceived to be very real beings, lying in wait to wreak their mischief in the form of sudden death, sickness, or—especially—impotence or incompatibility. Far from being regarded as mere projections of the bride's mood and temper, they are regarded rather as the powers that inject them into her. Consequently, she must be protected from them, and the best method of ensuring such protection is obviously to seclude her and keep her out of reach at the crucial time. Accordingly, she is kept secluded for a few days prior to the nuptial ceremony. Among many bedouin tribes, for example, she has to withdraw to the hills, and the bridegroom has to go in search for her; [2] while among various primitive peoples of South Africa, she remains in hiding either in her own or in the groom's hut for several days before connubial relations may take place.[3] Similarly, among the Sulka of New Pomerania, during the days immediately preceding her wedding, she must take care not to be seen by any man when she goes out of doors, and to this end must wrap herself from top to toe in a long cloak; [4] while in Swabia (Germany), she is forbidden to leave the house after curfew from the moment of her betrothal until that of her marriage.[5]

· · · · ·

* This belief is further encouraged by the fact that in primitive societies girls are often married at puberty, which is likewise regarded as an especially critical and "dangerous" period during which they must be similarly secluded.

Nor, indeed, does the period of seclusion end with the actual consummation of the marriage. The demons are in no hurry to depart, and it is only when the couple have got used to each other—when, as the psychiatrists would say, they have really shed their phobias and achieved sexual adjustment and harmony—that interference on the part of these malevolent beings need no longer be feared. Accordingly, the bride is usually required to go into temporary retirement not only by herself *before* the marriage but also together with her husband *after* it—a custom which survives, of course, in the modern honeymoon. Thus, among the bedouins of Palestine, the couple usually repair to the hills and remain in seclusion for eight days; [6] while among those of the Sinai Peninsula, they sometimes withdraw from the community for as long as two months. [7] In Tangier, the bride was formerly obliged to remain indoors for a whole year after her marriage; * [8] and in the Kingsmill Islands, the home of newlyweds is screened with mats for ten days, and the bride is not allowed to go out. [9]

The Hebrew term *kallah* evidently refers also to such postnuptial seclusion.

Primitive ideas survive likewise in the Hebrew word for bridegroom. He is called *hatan,* which means primarily "one who is circumcised." The reference, as we have explained in a previous chapter,† is to the ancient and primitive custom of performing circumcision before marriage as a means of preventing or correcting any untoward condition—either physical or magical—of the sexual organs that might be thought to threaten the propagation of the

.....

* Nowadays the period is curtailed to two or three months.
† See above, p. 49.

species. Moreover, the fact that the bridegroom's father-in-law is called *hoten,* or "circumciser," would seem to suggest that it was he who originally performed the operation.

BRIDE'S ADORNING

Bride and bridegroom come to the wedding specially dressed and coiffured to symbolize the significance of the occasion and to protect them against its perils.

They wear new clothes. The primary reason for this is that, in primitive thought, "clothes makyth man," so that whenever a person enters a new phase of life and thereby undergoes a change of outward character and status, he has to assume also a new outward vesture; as we say today, he *invests* himself with a new personality. Kings, for example, don new raiment (and assume new names) at their installations, and so do neophytes when they are initiated into the mysteries of a cult or communion and thereby shed their previous individualities.[1]

Other ideas, however, also enter into the picture. *The bride's garments are usually white.* In Jewish tradition, this is explained as a symbol not only of innocence but also (as on Yom Kippur) of penitence, since it is deemed appropriate that she should repent her former sins and misdeeds before embarking upon her "new life."[2] Actually, however, the custom of wearing white was determined in the first place by the fact that white represents the unstained and unsullied state of all new things. It was, indeed, on that account that it was so frequently prescribed in antiquity as the statutory color of festal attire (e.g. at the Feast of Cerealia in Rome).[3] Says Cicero (borrowing from Plato): "White is the color most acceptable to the gods. Dark hues should be avoided [for sacral purposes] except on military ensigns."[4]

The bride also wears a veil. This practice is explained traditionally by reference to the fact that Rebekah "took a veil and covered herself with it" when she first met Isaac (Gen. 24:65). This, of course, is simply an attempt to accommodate to Jewish tradition what is in fact a fairly universal custom.

The true significance is disputed. According to one view, the original purpose of the veil was to "shut out" the previous personality of the bride, now that she in effect acquired a new character and "became one flesh" with her husband. In support of this interpretation it is pointed out that among primitive peoples veils are in fact worn not only at marriage but also on all occasions on which a person is believed to assume a new rôle. Initiants, for example, commonly wear veils when they are received into a religious community, and the dead are veiled, to signify—according to this theory—that they are "defunct."[5]

An alternative view maintains, however, that the veil served originally to screen the bride from the "evil eye," and for this view, too, impressive evidence can be cited. The Zulus of North East Africa, for instance, make a point of keeping the bride closely muffled;[6] while in Melanesia, she is usually wrapped in a mat.[7] The Koreans have her cover her face with the wide sleeves of her gown,[8] and in Arab weddings she is led to the ceremony under a draped canopy borne by her bridesmen.[9] For the same reason also, Moroccan brides are required to close their eyes throughout the proceedings.[10]

The unveiling of the bride, it may be added, was a cardinal element of ancient wedding ceremonies, and it has even been suggested that the familiar Biblical use of the word "know" to denote sexual relations * referred originally to the bridegroom's coming to know the features of his bride by lifting her veil before the consummation of the marriage.[11] The Arab bridegroom, we are told, often sees his bride's face for the first time on that occasion,[12] and in Turkey, the present which he then gives her is known explicitly as "the gift of the seeing-of-the face." [13]

Sometimes, the wedding costume serves expressly as a means of rendering the bride and bridegroom unrecognizable by malicious spirits. In the fifteenth century, for example, it was customary for the Jewish bridegroom in the Rhineland to wear mourning garb and to strew ashes on his head.[14] This was interpreted as a reminder of the destruction of the Temple—a somber thought which, it was held, ought properly to temper all moments of joy. In point of fact, however, it was simply a means of foiling demons by disguise. In the same way, among the Moslems of the northwest provinces of India, bride and groom wear dirty clothes for a few days before their marriage.[15]

· · · · ·

* A similar usage obtains in the other Semitic languages and in Greek.

TRESSES AND WIGS

The Talmud tells us that in ancient times *the bride came to her wedding with her hair dishevelled or at least unbraided;* [1] while even at the present day it is customary among "orthodox" Jews to cut it off before she "goes under the *huppah*" and to pile it up on her head in the form of a wig (Judaeo-German, *sheitel*). Jewish tradition explains the former custom as a mere preliminary to the latter, and validates it by the legend that Eve, the first bride, had her unkempt locks carefully trimmed by God before she was presented to Adam! Actually, however, the two things are quite independent of each other, and here again we are confronted with general rather than specifically Jewish usages. Shakespeare, for instance, speaks of the Devil's coming "in likeness of a new *untrimmèd* bride"; [2] his predecessor, John Heywood says of the "blushing bride" that she proceeds to her wedding "with hair dishevell'd 'bout her shoulders"; and this was likewise common practice in medieval Germany [3] and in Lapland. [4] Behind it lay the notion that, since magic consists essentially in binding spells, it can be averted by the reverse process of leaving all things loose and untied. For the same reason, it may be observed, all knots are untied in the garments of a woman in labor, and her hair may not be braided, and by a similar line of thought, the clothes of the dead must be free of knots and loops.*

· · · · ·

* See below, p. 164.

As for the custom of shearing the bridal locks, this again has worldwide parallels. In ancient Greece, the bride's tresses were cut before marriage and dedicated to the goddess;[5] while among the Romans they were parted with the so-called "bachelor's spear" before the nuptial ceremony.[6] In the steppes of Southeast Russia, on the shores of the Caspian and Black Seas, the bride has her hair cut off when she returns home after visiting relatives and friends on the eve of her wedding. Thenceforth she is required to wear the *platoke* (turban), a woolen or linen shawl wound tightly around the head, this distinctive article of apparel being presented to her by her husband.[7] In Prussia, the bride's hair used formerly to be sheared at her wedding by a specially designated girl friend,[8] and in the province of Trapani in Sicily, it was ceremonially parted by her mother-in-law.[9] The basic custom is attested also in Japan [10] and among the Kaffirs of Natal.[11]

The custom is to be explained as the sacrifice of a part for the protection of the whole. The hair is regarded in many cultures as a "life-index" or as a seat of the vital spirit; witness the story of Samson. It is, indeed, a common superstition that it may not be cut during the first year of life lest future health and vigor be impaired, and it is likewise a widespread belief that warriors must let their hair grow long lest they loose their strength and invite defeat.* The surrender of the hair is therefore a

· · · · ·

* In the *Iliad,* for example, the Achaeans are frequently described as "long-haired," which may perhaps be understood in this sense. Some scholars would also find a reference to the custom in the Bible; for the opening words of Deborah's war-song (Judges 5:2), which are usually translated, "For that the leaders took the lead in Israel (or, For the avenging of Israel), for that the people offered themselves willingly, bless ye the Lord," could also be rendered (by deriving their crucial verb from a different root), *"For that men let grow their hair* in Israel, for

surrender of one's essential "life-spirit," and it is deemed
an appropriate gesture whenever a person in fact assumes
a new character. For this reason it was a common practice in antiquity to shear one's locks and dedicate them to
the deity at the moment one reached puberty and "put
away childish things." [12]

SWORDS
AND DAGGERS

Besides special provision concerning costume and coiffure,
there are also other methods by which the demons are for-
fended at the wedding ceremony.

In the East, the bride and bridegroom are often
escorted by armed men. The custom is mentioned already
in the Biblical Song of Songs (3:7-8), where it is said of
the bridegroom—facetiously identified with King Solomon—that he comes borne on a palanquin surrounded by
threescore mighty men,

all of them grasping the sword,
expert in war;
every man with his sword on his thigh,
against terror by night.*

Similarly, among the Palestinian Arabs of the present
day, when the bride is led to the scene of the festivities,

---

that the people volunteered," etc. The present writer believes, however,
that the correct meaning of that passage is: "For that men threw off
all restraint in Israel, for that (consequently) a whole army volunteered," etc.

* "Terror by night" is not just a general expression, but alludes specifically
to a nocturnal demon or hobgoblin; cp. Ps. 91:5.

her camel is preceded by a man carrying a sword;[1] while among the Mordvins of Eastern Russia, the best man circles the bridegroom three times, drawing his sword and calling down curses upon ill-wishers.[2] In parts of China, a Taoist priest rides ahead of the bridal procession, brandishing a knife,[3] and in India, the bridegroom sometimes shoots arrows, crying, "I pierce the eyes of the spirits who surround the bride!"[4]

In the Usambara country of East Africa, the chief bridesmaid walks ahead of the bridal procession, bearing a sword and gun;[5] while among the Abkhassians of the Caucasus, two men guard the couple's new home by standing in the doorway with crossed swords.*[6] Similarly, in the rural districts of Prussia, the bride used to be accompanied to church by male friends sporting daggers.[7]

Sometimes, however, the weapons are carried by the bride and bridegroom themselves. Again the Bible provides early evidence of this usage, for in the Forty-fifth Psalm—specifically entitled "a song of loves"—the bridegroom is bidden (v. 4), *Gird thy sword upon thy thigh as a warrior,* and to this day, the Palestinian Arab goes out to welcome the arrival of his bride, carrying a sword which he presses thrice against her face and with the tip of which he subsequently lifts her veil.[8] So, too, among the Maronites of Syria, he greets her by holding a sword over her head, and when she enters her new home, he stands on the flat roof and waves the weapon over her, to keep away the demons.[9] Conversely, in pagan Norway (as at the marriage of Rolf with the daughter of Erik), it was the bride who came armed with sword, ax, and shield,[10] and, according to Maimonides, a similar custom

· · · · ·

* Of similar purpose, of course, is the archway of crossed swords at military weddings.

obtained among the Jews of Egypt in the eleventh century.[11] Nor, indeed, was this an exclusively Oriental usage. A stage direction in the 1597 quarto of Shakespeare's *Romeo and Juliet* prescribes that the heroine is to wear a *knife* during the scene in the friar's cell; while in Dekker's *Match Me in London,* a bride exclaims to her jealous husband:

See, at my girdle hang my *wedding knives!*
With those dispatch me!

TORCHES

Demons can also be frightened off by fire and light, and it was primarily for that reason—and not merely because they took place after dark—that wedding processions were usually escorted, in ancient times, by persons carrying torches or candles. The custom is familiar especially from the parable in the New Testament concerning the ten virgins who "took their lamps and went forth to meet the bridegroom" (Mat. 25:1-12). In modern Arab usage, the bridegroom is usually preceded by one or more men holding flaming cressets (*mesh'als*)[1] and that the custom is indeed of high antiquity is attested by the fact that it is mentioned already in a Canaanite text of the fourteenth century B.C.E.![2] Torches were likewise a standard feature of Greek and Roman weddings, and in Latin, the word for "torch" (viz. *taeda*) is not infrequently employed as a poetic synonym for "marriage."[3]

Among the Jews, the most common practice is for the

bride and bridegroom each to be accompanied to the
wedding canopy (*huppah*) by attendants carrying *two*
candles. This is popularly explained by the fact that the
letters of the Hebrew word *NeR* meaning "candle," when
taken in their numerical value and doubled, add up to the
same total (viz. 500) as those which spell out the commandment, *Be fruitful and multiply* (Gen. 1:28)![4]
There were, however, a number of variations. At Pesaro
and Modena (Italy), for instance, the bridegroom used to
be greeted with a short ditty sung by a man carrying "a
torch to which were attached six other lights, three on
each side." This was called *menorah* in allusion to the
seven-branched candelabrum in the Tabernacle and
Temple.[5]

2

THE WEDDING
CEREMONY

Huppah: The Bridal Canopy

The most striking feature of a Jewish wedding is the *huppah,* or canopy, under which the bridal couple stand throughout the ceremony. In its modern form, the *huppah* usually consists of an awning of white silk or satin, supported on four poles and embroidered with some such Biblical motto as the words, *The voice of mirth and the voice of joy, the voice of the bridegroom and the voice of the bride* (Jer. 16:9; 25:10). It is customary to adorn it also with flowers and green leaves.

The *huppah* is a survival of the bridal bower in which the newlyweds were anciently confined at the conclusion of the ceremony. It is in this sense that the word is used in the Hebrew Bible. In the Nineteenth Psalm, for example, the rising sun is likened (v. 5) to *a bridegroom*

that cometh forth from his huppah; while the prophet
Joel describes (2:16) how, in a time of alarm, *the bridegroom cometh forth out of his chamber, and the bride out
of her* huppah. Similarly, in the apocryphal Third Book
of the Maccabees (4:6), it is related that when Ptolemy
VI decreed the annihilation of the Jews of Alexandria,
*maidens who had but recently entered the bridal chamber,
to partake of the joys of wedlock, exchanged bliss for
anguish; and, with dust scattered upon their myrrh-
anointed heads, were hurried along unveiled, the while,
to the accompaniment of coarse insults, they set up dirges
in place of hymeneals.*

The *huppah* was erected by the bridegroom's father in
the courtyard of his house, and in Talmudic times, the
covering was a purple cloth studded with crescent-shaped
spangles.[1] In the Middle Ages, it often took the form of
a portable baldachin rather than a fixed structure, and it
was held over the couple by the groomsmen.[2]

Once again, the institution was by no means exclusively
Jewish. The Greeks, we are told, used likewise to set up
a bridal bower (*thalamos*) for every wedding and to em-
bellish it with gay figures and flowers, and sometimes also
with images of the Erotes, or gods of love—that is, with
Cupids or *amoretti*.[3] So, too, at Brahmin weddings, the
bride and groom are placed under a canopy supported by
twelve poles. This is really the regular "arbor" or "sun-
porch" which stands at the entrance of every house. On
such occasions, however, the structure is gaily adorned
to give it an especially festive appearance.[4] The custom
was likewise prevalent in former times among the country
folk of Spain;[5] while in the mining districts of Fife, Scotland, it used to be the practice, in the nineteenth century,
to "bower" newlyweds beneath an arch of green boughs
on their way home from the church.[6]

In the course of the ages, however, although the original name was retained, the *huppah* came more and more to be regarded as a mere stylized substitute for quite another feature of the traditional wedding ceremony— namely, the custom of spreading a cloth or other covering over or around the bridal couple in order to screen them from assaults of demons and from the "evil eye." This is an extremely widespread usage. In Sweden, for example, the bridesmaids often hold a canopy of shawls over the bride throughout the ceremony.[6a] In Serbia, two of the bridegroom's brothers hold an umbrella over her when they escort her to the church.[7] And in Tahiti, bride and groom are actually rolled up in a mat.[8]

Among Western Jews, yet a further development took place. The *huppah* came to be regarded as a conventional substitute not only for the protective screen, but also for the *tallith* which it had now become customary to spread not, as originally, over the bride alone but over the bridal couple together. This use of the *tallith,* it may be added, finds its direct counterpart in the Anglo-Saxon care-cloth, a square piece of material held over the bridal couple by four tall men, each grasping a corner of it. Both the Sarum and York Missals prescribe that before the celebration of the nuptial mass, bride and bridegroom are to kneel at the foot of the altar, while clerics hold a *pallium* over them.[9]

KETUBAH: THE MARRIAGE CONTRACT

The marriage service begins with the reading of the contract (Hebrew, *Ketubah,* lit. "writ"). Theoretically, this may be composed in any language; in practice, it is redacted in Aramaic, the vernacular of the exiled Jews after the destruction of the Temple. The deed is drawn up in accordance with rigid specifications. It must begin with a record of the date, given unambiguously in terms of the day of the week, the month, the year, and the era. Among Western Jews, the latter is the era of Creation (i.e. 5712 = 1954); among Oriental Jews, it is the Seleucid Era which opened in 312 B.C.E., while elsewhere the Byzantine and other local systems are adopted. After the date, comes the place. This must be defined in unambiguous terms. In ancient times, villages and hamlets were precisely identified by reference to neighboring large cities, and cities by the rivers on which they lay. Today, however, when Jewish marriages are registered in any case with the civil registrar, such precision is considered unnecessary, and the city alone is usually mentioned.

There follow immediately the names of the bride and groom. Here again, greater precision was required in antiquity than is necessary today for, until comparatively recent times, Jews had no surnames, so that a particular "Mordecai" or "Ruth" could be identified only by mention of his or her parents or grandparents or by the inclusion of such other particulars as place of residence, occupation, etc. In the East, the names are often introduced, with typical Oriental exuberance, by a string of high-sounding complimentary epithets, but these flourishes are generally discarded in the Western world.

The body of the document is introduced by a statement that the bridegroom actually sued for the hand of the bride and that she accepted him. This is expressed in the standard traditional formula. Thereafter come a series of clauses specifying the amount of dowry received making provision for succession, and possible divorce, guarantying to the bride maintenance, cohabitation, ransom if imprisoned, and burial.[1]

The marriage contract is not mentioned in the Bible, but its antiquity among Jews is shown by the fact that writs of this type have been found among the Aramaic papyri emanating from the Jewish garrison colony settled at Assuan (Elephantine) in Egypt during the fifth century B.C.E.;[2] while in the apocryphal Book of Tobit, it is stated explicitly that the latter's father-in-law Raguel "called his daughter Sarah and took her by the hand and gave her to wife unto Tobit and said, Behold, take her unto thyself after the law of Moses, and lead her away to thy father. And he blessed them and called Edna his wife and he took a book and wrote an instrument and sealed it" (7:12-15).*

The *ketūbah* is often embellished with artistic designs and miniatures, sometimes of symbolic purpose. In a specimen from Ancona (dated 1776), for example, the text is flanked by exquisitely executed representations of the signs of the Zodiac and at the top and bottom there are pictures of the bridal crown and the Temple respectively —the latter captioned by the sobering reminder: "If I forget thee, O Jerusalem, let my right hand forget her cunning" (Ps. 137:5). Similarly, if the bride's name happened to be Esther, it was deemed appropriate to decorate the *ketubah* with scenes from the Bible book; and a *ketubah* from Rome (dated 1816) honors a bridegroom named Elijah with an illustration depicting his great namesake being borne aloft on the fiery chariot (cf. II Kings, 2:11).[3]

• • • • •

* It has been doubted by some scholars whether the document written by Tobit was a marriage contract or a mere marriage certificate, and it is certainly true that in early rabbinic sources mention is made both of a "writ of betrothal" and of a "writ of marriage." Louis M. Epstein has shown, however, in the *Jewish Marriage Contract,* that they were probably the same thing.

The reading of the contract is followed by a short blessing over the cup of betrothal and by another in which reference is made to the fact that "only those are permitted to us who have been taken to wife under the bridal canopy and with the due rites of betrothal (*kiddushin*)." The bridegroom then places a ring upon the forefinger of the bride's right hand, meanwhile repeating, word by word, after the officiant the traditional formula: "Behold, thou art wedded (*mekuddesheth*) unto me by this ring, according to the religion of Moses and Israel." (The ring, as we have already explained, is a mere token pledge and possesses in itself no mystic significance.)

Thereupon the service passes over into the ceremony of marriage, as distinct from betrothal. This part of the proceedings consists in the recital of Seven Blessings. The first is the regular blessing over wine, now pronounced over the cup of marriage as it was previously over that of betrothal. The remaining six read as follows:

2. Blessed art Thou, O Lord, our God, Who hath created all things to Thy glory.

3. Blessed art Thou . . . Creator of Man.

4. Blessed art Thou . . . Who didst fashion man in Thine image, in the image and pattern of Thy similitude, and didst furnish unto him out of himself a perpetual fabric. Blessed art Thou, O Lord, Creator of Man.

5. May Zion that now is barren rejoice exceedingly and be glad when her children are gathered once more unto her, speedily

and in joy. Blessed art Thou, O Lord,
Who causest Zion to rejoice through her
children.

6. Cause thou this loving couple to rejoice
   exceedingly, even as of old Thou didst make
   Thy creature (Adam) to rejoice in the
   Garden of Eden. Blessed art Thou, O Lord,
   who causest bridegroom and bride to rejoice.

7. Blessed art Thou . . . who hast created
   joy and gladness, bridegroom and bride,
   love and brotherhood, pleasure and delight,
   peace and concord. Speedily may there be
   heard in the cities of Judah and in the
   streets of Jerusalem the sound of joy and
   the sound of gladness, the sound of the
   bridegroom and the sound of the bride,
   the sound of wedding revels, of bridegrooms
   at their feasts and youths at their carousals.
   Blessed art Thou, O Lord, Who rejoicest the
   bridegroom along with the bride.

These blessings possess several striking points of similarity to passages in the Anglican marriage service. With
the second, third and fourth of them, for example, may
be compared the words:

O God, Who by Thy mighty power hast
made all things of nothing; Who also
. . . didst appoint that out of man
(created after Thine own image and
similitude) woman should take
her beginning. . . .*

while the sixth, with its reference to the state of Adam in
Paradise, finds a close parallel in the invocation:

     . . . . .

* The similarity is even closer if, as some authorities believe, the words
"didst furnish unto him out of himself a perpetual fabric" refer not to
the power of procreation but to the creation of Eve from Adam's rib.

Almighty God, Who at the beginning
didst create our first parents, Adam
and Eve, and didst sanctify† and
join them together in marriage: Pour
upon you the riches of His peace,
sanctify and bless you. . . .

THE CUP OF BETROTHAL

After the recital of the blessings, the celebrant hands
the cup of betrothal first to the bridegroom and then to
the bride, and each drinks from it.

Today this has become a mere logical sequel to the
blessing of the wine. Originally, however, the essence
of the rite lay not in the drinking of the wine *per se* but
rather in the drinking from the same goblet. For the sharing of food and drink—that is, the absorption of a common substance—is everywhere a standard method of sig-
nifying and cementing an alliance, as witness the very
word "companion," which means properly "one who
shares bread with another." A few examples must suffice.
Abraham, we are told, concluded a treaty with Melchizedek, king of Salem, by proffering food and drink (Gen.
14:18-24), and Abimelech did the same when he made
an alliance with Isaac (*ibid.*, 26:30). So, too, it is a recognized principle among the Arabs that if anyone eats even
the smallest portion of your food, he is forthwith under
your protection; while in Madagascar, drinking out of the
same bowl establishes brotherhood. Our own custom of
"having a drink on it" is, of course, a relic of the same
usage.

The custom is a prominent element of marriage cere-

· · · · ·

† A clear reminiscence of the Hebrew terms *ḳaddesh, ḳidduschin;* see
above, p. 84.

monies in many parts of the world, and goes back to remote antiquity. A recognized form of wedlock among
Roman patricians, for example, was that of *confarreatio*
which consisted originally in having the bridal couple eat
sacred bread (*panis farreus*) together in the presence of
priestly authorities.[1] In Germany, the bridal couple eat off
the same plate;[2] in Scandinavia[3] and in Russia,[4] they drink
from the same cup. In the island of Romany, such drinking
constitutes of itself a rite of marriage,[5] and the same holds
good also among the Hos and Lepehas of Bengal[6] and in
several parts of Japan.[7] Indeed, even in modern American
life, when a boy and girl "share a coke" by sipping, with
two straws, from a common glass, the gesture—as everyone knows—often has amorous undertones and, psy-
chologically, is simply an attenuated version of the ancient
time-honored method of sealing a union!

SMASHING THE GLASS

At the conclusion of the wedding ceremony, the bridegroom takes the cup of betrothal and, facing toward the
north, smashes it against the wall or crushes it beneath his
foot, whereupon the bystanders at once cry out *Mazal
tov,* i.e. Good luck!

The custom is by no means exclusively Jewish nor, indeed, is it mentioned in the earlier Jewish sources. Once
again, it is something that the Jews picked up from their
neighbors. It is, for instance, a regular feature of Gypsy
weddings, and it is attested also among many other
peoples.[1] In Transylvania, the bride breaks a jar or dish
in the presence of the local magistrate (*gako*) to signify
acceptance of the bridegroom at the ceremony of betrothal.[2] In several parts of Germany, she smashes a
glass from which the guests have previously drunk.[3] In

Bohemia, she throws over her shoulder a glass or cup of wine proffered by her mother-in-law at the entrance to her new home, although there the interesting detail is added that if the glass breaks in the process, this betokens ill luck rather than happiness.[4] In Hanover, Prussia, Thuringia and other areas of Germany, village children fling old crockery against the door of the bride's house; the higher the heap of broken fragments, it is said, the greater will be the prosperity of the newlyweds.[5] It is recorded, in fact, that when, in 1791, Lord Malmesbury married a Prussian princess as proxy for the Duke of York, he found a veritable mountain of broken dishes outside her royal highness' door the next morning.[6]

The original purpose of this rite was symbolically to smash the powers of the demons and, indeed, of all ill-wishers. This was a very common magical gesture in the ancient Near East. The Egyptians, for example, used for this purpose to inscribe the names of their enemies on clay pots and then break them to pieces, and the same imagery occurs, of course, in such Old Testament expressions as "thou shalt dash them in pieces like a potter's vessel" (Ps. 2:9).

Of especial interest is the fact that the gesture has to be performed facing *northwards*. The reason for this is that demons were believed to live in the north and hence to come from that direction. This was a common idea among the Iranians, the Mandaeans, the Manichaeans and the Greeks, and it survives to this day in Mexico and elsewhere. Plutarch there locates the demonic monster Typhon, and Milton has the rebel angels assemble in the north. Similarly, in Shakespeare's first part of *King Henry the Sixth*, La Pucelle invokes the aid of spirits "under the lordly monarch of the north." [7]

The Jews gave to the traditional custom a new and distinctive meaning: to them it symbolized the destruction of the Temple and served as a reminder that even the most joyful occasion must be tempered by the somber recollection of that unhappy event—the source of Israel's agelong woes. A modern modification of the custom is perhaps worthy of record: during the Second World War, used photographic flash bulbs took the place of the traditional wineglass at Jewish military weddings solemnized at Fort Benning, Georgia. The bulbs, declared the local chaplain, "were far the most easily available and least extravagant substitutes"![8]

RICE, NUTS, AND CONFETTI

Not all marriage customs, however, were designed originally to *ex*pel evil; some, on the contrary, were designed rather to *im*pel bliss—that is, more specifically, to promote fertility, and ensure offspring—and these, too, are well represented in the Jewish wedding ceremony.

Prominent among them is the practice of showering the bridal couple with rice or grains of wheat. This, too, was taken by the Jews from their pagan and Gentile neighbors. It was, for instance, a standard feature of Greek and Roman weddings,[1] and down to the present day it is current usage in most parts of Europe and in many Oriental countries (*e.g.* among the Arabs of Syria and Palestine).[2] Originally, of course, it was simply a piece of "sympathetic magic"; the seeds, it was thought, would convey their own fertility to the couple upon whom they were pelted. In characteristic fashion, however, when the Jews took over this time-honored usage, they found for it a particular authority in Scripture and a particular validation in their own distinctive terms. The grains of wheat, they said, bore specific allusion to the statement in the Psalms (Ps. 147:14) that (*God*) *filleth thee with the finest of the wheat;* while the scattering of seeds in general alluded to the Divine assurance through the prophet Isaiah (53:10) that *My servant . . . shall see seed, shall prolong his days.* Similarly, the pagan custom of throwing nuts at newlyweds—a custom which really originated in the fact that the nut is everywhere a symbol of fertility[3]—was validated in Jewish popular lore on the grounds that the letters which compose the Hebrew word for "nut" (viz. *egoz*), when taken in their numerical value, add up to the same total as those which spell the word for "bliss" (viz. *tôb*) !

INSULT
AND RIBALDRY

One of the most singular, yet persistent methods of averting the evil eye from a person is to hurl abuse at him! This is intended to beguile ill-wishers and demons into thinking that he is not worth troubling about.

Derogatory songs and jests at the expense of the bridegroom were therefore a common feature of ancient weddings. He was roundly lampooned and accused—especially

by the bride and her relatives—of all sorts of objection-
able traits and repulsive habits, a device which served at
the same time to flatter her own vanity and her family's
pride by creating the illusion that she was really better
than he.

The custom is still widely practiced by primitive
peoples. Among the Kaffirs of Natal, for instance, the
bride is required to hurl insults at the bridegroom (though
this is rationalized nowadays as a sign that she will not
easily submit to him!).[1] Similarly, in the Punjab, her relatives hurl all kinds of abusive epithets at him.[2] Naturally
enough, this sort of invective was well seasoned with bil-
lingsgate, and in course of time it became a popular convention to chant bawdy songs at weddings without particular reference to the bridegroom. Among the Romans, for
instance, such songs—known as Fescennine verses—
were a regular feature of the nuptial ceremonies.[3] Says
the famous hymeneal of Catullus:

Raise the torches, lads; I spy
The groom resplendent coming nigh.
Swell the chorus, raise the cry:
    Hymen hymeneal, ho!
    Ho, Hymen hymeneal!
Chant aloud, and none too soon,
The ribald fescennine lampoon![4]

The songs came then to be interpreted as charms to promote fertility, for among primitive peoples it is widely
believed that fecundity and increase can be induced not
only by imitative actions but also by suggestive words.
Such songs, for instance, are very commonly sung at seasonal festivals in order to stimulate the growth of crops.[5]

Chants of this character never became a formal part of
the Jewish wedding, as they did of its Roman counterpart.
In the Talmud, however, we hear of rabbis who made a

particular point of denouncing ribaldry in marriage songs,[6] and it is by no means impossible that this was intended as a protest not only against obscenity in general but also, more specifically, against a growing tendency on the part of the Jews to adopt the common fashion of chanting "Fescennine verses" at nuptial celebrations.

Such tendency might also explain the rabbinical ban on singing snatches from the Song of Songs on those occasions. Although, to be sure, that Biblical book seems to be composed in large part of songs originally designed for such ceremonies, the ancient rabbis were inclined, on the whole, to interpret it in a symbolic or allegorical sense— as rehearsing the love of God for Israel. The use of it as a purely secular poem—more especially, the consequent application to human beings of epithets and intimate descriptions believed to refer properly to the Holy-One-Blessed-be-He or to His Torah—was therefore regarded in any case as impious; it was doubly so when the sacred strains were chanted in such circumstances as might make them appear to all the world as a mere Jewish equivalent of the salacious pagan ditties!

ROUND AND ROUND

When the bride is conducted to the *huppah,* the groomsmen often make a point of leading her around the bridegroom *three times.*

This curious performance is a relic of the ancient and primitive custom of asserting title to a piece of property by walking round it and "prescribing its boundaries."[1] A standard feature of African coronation ceremonies, for example, is that the newly installed king has to march ceremonially around his domain,[2] and when the new sultan of Malaya was enthroned at Perak in 1944, he had likewise to circumambulate his royal territory seven times.[3] It has been suggested that the ancient Roman rite whereby men clad in skins raced round the walls of the city at the festival of Lupercalia was really a survival of such an annual "taking of possession" by the primeval kings;[4] while in England and Germany, the practice still obtains of going in procession round a church or parish on certain days of the year and "beating the bounds" at selected spots *en route*.[5]

But the procedure is common also in more domestic settings and, more especially, in wedding ceremonies. In Croatia, for instance, the bride is led around the hearth *three times* on entering her new home;[6] while in Serbia, she is not permitted to set foot within it until she has ridden three times around her mother-in-law.[7]

Once again, the Jews found significance and authority for a borrowed custom by a deft application of the words of Scripture. The practice was interpreted by a reference to a passage in the Book of Hosea (2:19-20) where God declares to Israel, with threefold iteration: *I will betroth thee unto Me for ever; I will betroth thee unto Me in righteousness and justice and in loving kindness and mercy; I will betroth thee unto me in faithfulness*, words which may very probably reproduce an ancient formula of marriage. Alternatively, it was asserted, it is a method of bringing to literal fulfillment the prophecy of Jeremiah (31:22) that the female shall encircle the male! *

. . . . .

* So the Hebrew literally rendered. The English Bible translates: *A woman shall encompass a man*.

3

THE TWO COVENANTS

Thy beloved, Lord, are we;
Thou our Lover e'er shalt be.
High Holiday hymn.

Traditional teaching holds that the life of the Jew should be permeated at every moment with a consciousness of his commitment to actualize and exemplify the Divine Law (Torah) and thereby advance the establishment of the Kingdom of God on earth. In line with this teaching, the ancient rabbis read into the marriage service an effective reminder of the Jew's basic obligation, tracing in its main features a remarkable parallel with those that Scripture associates with the conclusion of the Covenant between God and Israel at Mount Sinai.

First, they averred, in both cases a marriage relationship was involved. For had not the prophet Hosea likened God to a bridegroom and Israel to His bride? And what, after all, was the Biblical Song of Songs if not the idyll of their mystic wedding?

Second, in the marriage service, the bridegroom proceeds first to the *huppah* and there awaits the bride. Was not this, asked the sages, precisely what God did when, as the Scripture says (Deut. 33:2), *Jehovah came from Sinai, and rose from Seir, unto them; He beamed forth from Mount Paran and proceeded . . . unto them?*

Third, the marriage contract, specifying the conditions and obligations of the union, is read to the bride before she is required finally to commit herself. Is not this, again, a perfect reproduction of what God did when He said to Israel from Sinai: *Now, therefore, if ye will indeed obey My voice and keep My covenant, ye shall be Mine own especial possession* (Exod. 19:5)? And does not the Scripture go on to say explicitly: *Then Moses came down and summoned the elders of Israel and set before them all the things which Jehovah had commanded him; and all the people answered and said, All that Jehovah hath spoken we will do* (*ibid.*, 7-8)? Fourth, the marriage ceremony is (or, at least, was originally) performed by the light of torches.* Once again, observed the sages, does not this run parallel with the fact that the Revelation at Sinai was accompanied by what the Scripture expressly describes as voices *and torches* (Exod. 20:18)? †

Lastly, is not the marriage service known in Hebrew parlance as "sanctification" (*kiddushin*)? And is it not written that when they had signified their acceptance of the Covenant, *Jehovah said unto Moses, Go unto the people* and sanctify *them* (Exod. 19:10)?

. . . . .

* See above, p. 109.

† The English Bible renders *thunderings and lightnings*, which is, of course, what is actually meant. But the Hebrew term used for *lightnings* literally signifies *torches*.

Thus, in Jewish tradition, the marriage of man, created in the image of God, becomes a replica in miniature of that which binds God Himself to the people which has entered into covenant with Him. And as a natural corollary to this idea comes the further affirmation that every Jewish home is in fact a temple—a place where that bridegroom takes up earthly abode.

AN ANCIENT HEBREW WEDDING

One of the oldest and most illuminating descriptions of a Jewish wedding is to be found, if one looks closely, in the Forty-fifth Psalm, which is actually entitled "a song of loves."

Unfortunately, the true sense of this poem has been but imperfectly perceived and is therefore not brought out clearly in the standard English translations. Because it is said to have been indited "for a king" (v.2),* and because it refers to his anointment (v.3) and enthronement (v.7), and makes specific mention of a princess (v.13), it has been commonly assumed that it was composed for the marriage of a particular monarch, and scholars have broken their heads to determine who he may have been. Once we recall, however, the common convention both in the Near East and elsewhere of treating a bridal couple as royalty,[1] it becomes apparent that "His Majesty" is simply an ordinary bridegroom and that the allusion to his regal status and dignity are no more than *jeux d'esprit*. The entire psalm is then seen to be a singularly vivid and detailed description of a typical Oriental wedding.

Such weddings invariably involve the presence of a professional

• • • • •

* Verses are cited according to the *Hebrew* numeration.

poet or minstrel (Arabic *sha'ir*) who improvises songs in honor of
the bridal couple and leads the guests in chanting them.[2] Accordingly, our poem begins with that songster's reply to the summons
for his services. He playfully expresses his excitement at being
ordered to perform for a "king":

My heart is a-flutter—Oh, joy!
'Tis for a king himself
I am now to indite my works!
My tongue shall be like the pen of a fluent scribe!

(v.2)

The scene then turns to the bridegroom's house. He is being
dressed and perfumed for the ceremony, and each stage of the procedure is accompanied by appropriate verses. As the oils and un-
guents are poured over him, the poet exclaims:

Fairer thou wast than human kind,
with a magic shed o'er thy lips!
Some godhead must have endowed thee
*   with an immortal grace!*

(v.3)

In these lines the poet plays on the custom of sprinkling oil or
honey on the lips of a child shortly after birth.* No ordinary oil
or honey was it that was shed on *your* lips, he says in a graceful
compliment to the bridegroom, but rather divine magic. You were
born superhumanly fair and handsome; some god must have conferred upon you the quality of immortal *berakah* or "grace."

And as he buckles on the sword usually worn by Oriental bridegrooms as a protection against demons,† the action evokes a snatch
of song in which such martial attire is said to be the outward
token of his royal prowess and splendor:

Champion that thou art,
as thy regal array and adornment
gird (this) sword on thy thigh!

. . . . .

* See above, p. 14.
† See above, p. 108.

Next, as he mounts his steed in order to ride forth and meet the bride, and as he distributes largesse (Hebrew, *zedakah*) to the poor at the entrance to his house, the poet again cries out:

Ride forth, fare on, in behalf of truth,
    and befriend the poor! ‡

And as the groomsmen ride beside him fully armed against the demons, the words ring out:

and may thy right hand guide thee
    to awe-inspiring deeds—
to the sinking of thy darts
    (darts well-sharpened to boot!)
in the hearts of thy Majesty's foes,
to the falling of (whole) peoples at thy feet!

Then, as he rides forth through the courtyard to meet the bridal procession, relatives and friends gaze with admiration on his sumptuous attire and, under the leadership of the professional poet, heap compliments upon him, comparing him with a king newly invested and enthroned:

Thy throne hath some god [set firm] *
    to endure for all time!
A sceptre of equity is the sceptre of thy kingship!

Because thou hast loved the right,
    and hated the wrong,
some god with (this) festive oil
    hath now anointed thee (king)!

Thine undergarments *are scented*
    like myrrh and aloes;
like cassia all thine outer robes!

· · · · ·

‡ In a few passages, the traditional Hebrew text appears to be corrupt. I have, however, eschewed radical emendation, and have been able to make sense by very slight changes, often involving only a different vocalization of the consonantal letters. Such changes are indicated by the use of roman type.
* A word has apparently dropped out of the traditional Hebrew text.

Moreover, with typical Oriental exuberance and in order to enhance his worth, they pay tribute to his former triumph in the lists of love:

Among thy lady loves
who have brought delight unto thee
have been very princesses themselves
hailing from ivory halls!
At thy right hand hath stood
(full many) a harem-queen
decked in the gold of Ophir!

Meanwhile, corresponding ceremonies take place in the home of the bride, and the next verses of our poem represent the snatches of song sung by *her* relatives and friends as she is being prepared for the ceremony. As they dress her and address her, they seek to allay her apprehensions and to overcome that bashfulness which convention demands of her:

Hearken, maiden, and see,
and bend thine ear:
Forget thy kin and thy father's house;
His Majesty craves thy beauty;
He is thy lord—make obeisance to him!

Then, as a counterpart to what the bridegroom's friends have been chanting about *him,* they make a point of extolling the girl's powers of captivation:

Thyself a Tyrian heiress,
the richest men of the people
used to *court thee with gifts.*

Finally, they turn her this way and that in order to show off her finery. As they take in the various details of her costume, they break out into enthusiastic cries:

Very princess that she is,
her finery is of pearls
set amid braids of gold!
She is clothed in broidered robes!

When all is in readiness, the procession moves off to conduct her to the scene of the ceremony. As it wends its way, those who take part in it strike up gay music and shout in chorus:

Let her be led to the king!
Let virgins, walking *behind her,*
escort her *with gladness and glee,*
bring her *into his Majesty's halls!*

After the ceremony, the company turns once more to shower congratulations on the bridegroom:

In place of thy fathers be thy sons!
Mayest thou make them to be lords throughout the earth!
May they *keep thy name in remembrance*
     for age upon age!
May peoples heap upon thee
     everlasting praise! [3]

"CHILDREN UNDER THE MANTLE"

It was a common usage of the medieval Church that children born to a couple before marriage could be legitimized at the wedding ceremony by having them stand under the ample crape of the bride's veil or under the cloth (*pallium*) of the altar during the pronouncement of the nuptial benediction.[1] This constituted formal adoption, and in Germany, such children were actually known as "mantle-children" (*Mantelkinder*).[2]

There is no trace of this custom in the Jewish marriage ceremony itself, but a survival or borrowing of it may perhaps be recognized in another familiar Jewish usage. On the Feast of the Rejoicing in the Law (Simhath Torah), it is customary to call collectively to the reading of the Scroll all children under the age of thirteen who, having not yet attained religious majority, are not normally entitled to that privilege. They are escorted to the rostrum by an adult member of the congregation (usually one distinguished for piety and learning) who recites the statutory blessings on their behalf. While the sacred text is being read, a large *tallith,* or praying-shawl, is spread over their heads like a canopy. At the end of the reading, the rabbi or precentor turns to the children and pronounces a blessing over them, repeating especially the words uttered by Jacob when he blessed his grandchildren, Ephraim and Manasseh, viz. *The angel who hath redeemed me from all evil, bless the lads* (Gen. 48:16).

Now, the service on this occasion is, as is well known, a symbolic parody of the wedding ceremony.* The men who are chosen to read the opening and closing sections of the Law are called "bridegrooms"; the Scrolls are decked in bridal white; they are carried in procession around the synagogue; the procession is usually headed by children carrying candles or other lights; and in many communities nuts and "confetti" are thrown. Moreover, the festival itself seems to have originated in Western Europe in the eleventh century.

Is it not possible, then, that this ceremony with the *tallith*-covered children was simply a further "take-off" of a wedding custom with which the Jews had become familiar from their Gentile neighbors? The children, each of whom was not yet a *bar mitzvah* —that is, literally, a son of the commandment—were "legitimized" ad hoc at the symbolic wedding!

What lends added support to this suggestion is the fact that the blessing pronounced over them might itself be understood in this context as a kind of formula of adoption. The angel who is invoked to protect the children is described in the Hebrew text as a *goel* (E.V. "that hath redeemed"), and this is also the technical term for the next-of-kin who had the duty of protesting and defending relatives left in helpless circumstances (cf. Lev. 25:25 f.). Moreover, we learn expressly from the Book of Ruth (3:9) that one of the ways in which he expressed acceptance of that responsibility was by spreading his garment over his charges! The time-honored words of the benediction may thus have acquired added meaning in this instance by means of a neat and subtle *double-entendre.*

. . . . .

* See my *Festivals of the Jewish Year,* pp. 99 f.

V

Death

1

LAST RITES

Man goeth to his long home, and
the mourners go about the streets.
Ecclesiastes 12:5.

A Jew is expected to die, as to live, with the name of God on his lips. At the approach of death, he prays for divine forgiveness of his sins, acknowledges the sovereignty of God and the truth, or validity, of His Law (Torah), and, with his last breath, repeats the declaration, "Hear, O Israel, the Lord is our God, the Lord is One" (Deut. 6:4).

It is a strict rule of the Jewish religion that one must not touch the bed of a dying person nor disturb him in any way lest one thereby hasten his death. If, however, he happen to be lying on a pillow made out of chicken feathers, this may be (and often is) gently removed from under his head.

As soon as life is extinct, the window is opened for a brief moment, and then immediately slammed shut.

The eyes and mouth of the deceased are closed by his eldest son or by a near relative. The face is covered, and the body is left undisturbed for one hour. At the end of that time, it is transferred to the ground (often strewn with straw), feet turned toward the door. This is taken to symbolize that "the dust returneth to the earth as it was" (Eccl. 12:7).

Until the body is prepared for burial, it must be watched continuously, without intermission. An indigent coreligionist of the appropriate sex is usually engaged for this purpose, and spends the time reciting psalms or reading devotional books.

The preparation itself (Hebrew, *taharah*, "cleansing") is entrusted, in the case of males, to the members of a voluntary local society known as "the Holy Brotherhood" (*Ḥebrâ Ḳadîshâ*), and in that of females, to women especially appointed by the local congregation or community.* The rites are performed in strict silence.

The body is washed in warm water, scented with spices, and in ancient times it was often sprinkled also with myrtle leaves. Sometimes, too, a beaten egg is used as an additional cleansing agent.

Originally, the garments of the dead could be either black or white. Nowadays, however, the latter color is the general rule. In the case of males, the garments are patterned after those worn in ancient times by the high priest when he entered the holy of holies on the Day of Atonement: "He shall put on the holy linen coat, and he shall have the linen breeches upon his flesh, and he shall be girded with the linen girdle, and with the linen headdress

. . . . .

* The modern practice of employing professional morticians, though perhaps inevitable in large cities, turns into a commercial transaction what Jewish tradition has always regarded as the supreme voluntary service (*mizvah*) which one Jew can render another.

[cap] shall he be attired" (Lev. 16:4). The "linen coat" takes the form of a long cloak which the traditionally minded Jew wears also at his wedding, at the services of the High Holidays and at the celebration of the Seder, or paschal supper. It is known most commonly today by the Judaeo-German name of *kittel*, but the older term—still retained among Oriental and Sephardic Jews—was *sargenes*, a word connected with the English "serge," in the archaic sense of twilled silk or wool.

The burial clothes must be free of knots or bows. These, it is said, prevent both the egress of the soul and the natural dissolution of the body. They constitute an impediment to the Divine Will.

The body of a male is wrapped also in the prayer-shawl (*tallith*). One of the corner fringes, however, is previously removed or mutilated, in order to indicate that the deceased is now—as the Scripture has it—"free among the dead" (Ps. 88:5) and that the garment is being worn solely as a "robe of honor" and no longer in obedience to the commandment (Deut. 22:12) to "make unto thee fringes on the four corners of thy garment wherewith thou coverest thyself." The wearing of the prayer-shawl by the dead is regarded in Jewish traditional lore as a preparation for the robes of glory which the righteous are destined to put on in the next world. In the case of rabbis, it is customary to use the same *tallith* as they wore when they received their diplomas.

Jewish tradition insists on the utmost simplicity in the cerements of the dead. Originally, we are told, grave-clothes were often elaborate and ornate, but this convention tended to strain the resources of the bereaved and to introduce invidious distinctions between rich and poor. In the first century, therefore, the great Gamaliel the Elder set an example by enjoining on his disciples that they bury him only in plain white linen garments, and ever since, traditionally minded Jews have followed this precedent.

There is a curious rule—more honored today in the breach than the observance—about the graveclothes of a person who has been the victim of murder. If, at the time when his body was discovered, his garments were bespattered with his blood, he must be buried in them, the normal cerements being placed above them, for, so it is said, the blood of the slain cries to God for vengeance and must not be concealed when the deceased appears before him.

In ancient times, Jews were frequently buried without coffins, it being considered more meritorious to be brought into direct contact with the earth, and even today it is the custom in some parts of the world (especially at the interment of distinguished rabbis) to remove the body from the casket at the last moment and to lay the latter beside it in the grave.* In most Western countries, however, the civil law requires burial in coffins. A compromise is therefore often effected: a nether plank is removed, or small holes are drilled in the underside.†

A sachet of Palestinian earth is enclosed with the body. This is regarded as a substitute for actual burial in the Holy Land, the soil of which is believed to have the property of expiating sins.‡ Among the Sephardim of London, a "custodian of the holy soil" is a statutory officer of the

. . . . .

* Until as late as the nineteenth century, this was the regular practice of the Spanish and Portuguese Jews of London at the burial of their *haham,* or rabbi. It was formally discarded only in 1939.

† Children less than three days old are buried without coffins. They must be carried in the bosom to the grave.

‡ The belief is based on a fanciful interpretation of Deut. 32:43 ("God will make expiation for His land, for His people") which was construed to mean, "God's land will make atonement for His people."

congregation, and a collection for the purchase of it is taken up annually during the morning service of the Feast of Purim.

Sometimes, too, the deceased is provided with a trowel so that he may dig his way to Zion, where—according to Jewish belief—the resurrection of the dead and the "ingathering of the exiles" will take place; their books and writing instruments (formerly also a Scroll of the Law) are commonly placed beside them or laid on the coffin during the funeral.

2

LAST JOURNEY

Burial * takes place as soon as possible; in the Orient, usually before sundown. This practice was justified by the ancient sages as an extension of the Biblical law (Deut. 21:23) that the body of a criminal who has been hanged "shall not remain all night upon the tree." [1] In the Middle Ages, however, the belief was widespread (not only among Jews) that death could not be definitely ascertained until after three days, and that what appeared to be such might really be a cataleptic trance. The custom therefore arose—though it was indeed discountenanced by the rabbis—of deferring burial until that period had elapsed. [2] In all cases of such postponement, the grave which has

. . . . .

* Cremation, though today not uncommon among Western Jews, is forbidden by traditional religious law.

been dug may not lie open overnight, but must be covered with boards; otherwise, it is held, another death will occur in the community within a few days.[3]

The dead is borne from his house feet foremost. Because the Hebrew word for "coffin" is the same as that which is used in the Bible for the Ark of the Covenant, it was customary in former times, in conveying it to the cemetery, to carry it on the shoulders, in the manner of that sacred receptacle, rather than to mount it on a hearse. Nowadays, however, the size of large cities and the distances thus involved have made the perpetuation of this usage impracticable.

The pallbearers must go unshod or wear felt slippers, lest they trip over loose shoestrings.[4] They are exempted, on the day of the funeral, from the duty of wearing phylacteries at their morning devotions.

At the moment when the cortege leaves, all standing water is poured out in the house and, in some parts of the world, also in the two adjoining houses, if they are occupied by Jews.[5] Mirrors are covered, blinds are drawn, and sometimes too chairs are overturned, pots broken, and clocks stopped.

In ancient times, the funeral procession was invariably accompanied by at least one professional wailing woman and by at least two flute players;[6] but this custom has long since been discarded. At the obsequies of a distinguished rabbi, however, it is the practice in some Jewish communities to sound the shofar, or ram's horn—not as a mere equivalent of the "Last Post" but rather as a method of announcing the death and assembling the mourners or, more symbolically, as a foreshadowing of the Last Trump which will herald the resurrection. Occasionally, in such cases, blasts are sounded also on the way from the mortuary chapel to the grave, and each time the Scriptural verse is chanted: "The Lord shall fight for you, and ye shall hold your peace" (Exod. 14:14).

A circuitous route is followed, in order to give as many persons as possible an opportunity to join the procession.[7] A precedent for this is found in the Biblical statement that when Joseph brought up the bones of his father Jacob from Egypt to Canaan, he did not travel by a direct route but made a point of going first to "the threshing floor of Atad, which is beyond Jordan" (Gen. 50:10). It is considered the duty of every Jew who meets a funeral procession to accompany it, at least symbolically, by taking a few steps in the direction in which it is moving. This, in fact, is the traditional Jewish equivalent of removing one's hat at the passing of a hearse.

In days when the cortege proceeded on foot, it was usual to make three or four short stops on the way. This custom (which has many parallels in Gentile usage) was explained in Jewish tradition as designed to give the various mourners the privilege of each shouldering the coffin on the last journey.

At the burial of a male, it is customary among Sephardic Jews to make seven circuits around the bier in the mortuary chapel. The circuits are accompanied by the chanting of the so-called "Song against Plagues"—that is, the Ninety-first Psalm combined with other appropriate Scriptural verses—or of a mystical poem describing, in highly fanciful terms, the journey of the soul after death:

I

O God, Who art a living God,
    O Thou Eternal King,
from Whom, as from a fountainhead,
    the stream of life doth spring,*

. . . . .

* Ps. 36:10

Now in the realm of larger life
in grace let him abide;†
and in the tether of all souls
may his soul too be tied.‡

2

Lord, look upon his goodly deeds
—his sins removèd far—
and in Thy presence let him rest,
where all Thy faithful are.

Now in the realm, etc.

3

O let the record of his days
commend him unto Thee,
that Thou, his Maker, let him share
Thine immortality;
and, as Thy prophet said, his light
shine for all time to be! §

Now in the realm, etc.

4

O may he reach the heav'nly gates
and find them open'd wide,
and see the Citadel of Peace,
where cares are laid aside.
And for to usher him therein
may joyous angels come,
and Aaron and the high priests all,
to bid him welcome home.

Fare on until thou reach the goal,
and rest, and rise again, O soul! ||

5

First to Machpelah may he come,
and thence to where they wait—

. . . . .

† Ps. 116:9   ‡ I Sam. 25:12   § Dan. 12:3 || Dan. 12:13

the holy cherub sentinels
    before the Eden gate.¶
And may they give him permit there
    that onward he may wend
to where the giant pillar stands
    whereby all souls ascend!

Fare on, etc.

6

May Michael lead him on to God,
    opening the portals wide,
and may his guardian angel walk,
    an escort at his side,
from height to height to lead him on,
    that he at last may dwell
in that most fair of heavens all,
    where dwelleth Israel.

Fare on, etc.

7

Where God in one great tether ties
    the greatest and the least—
the men who teach, the men who lead,
    the people and the priest—
there, in that great bond of souls,
    O may his soul be bound;
and may he sleep in Eden's close
    until the trumpets sound.

Fare on, etc.[8]

Improvised dirges and laments written by local poet-
asters are also frequently recited. The following, in use
among the Jews of Corfu, will serve to illustrate this type
of composition:

. . . . .

¶ Gen. 3:24.

Alas, the living lay it not to heart:
Tomorn the wind blows o'er them; they depart.

Be done with worldly gain and worldly greed!
For in the end the fire on these shall feed.

Remember: at the last we slumber all;
Remember: even reddest roses pall.

Ah, how the fool exulteth in his prime!
Ere raven locks be silver'd o'er by Time,

How few the days; the rapture, O how brief!
The glory fadeth from the driven leaf.

All lustre dulls, all radiance turns to gloom;
Mute are all voices; silent is the tomb.[9]

At the funerals of rabbis or communal dignitaries, it is customary furthermore to deliver eulogies beside the bier.

The dead are buried with their feet toward the east, ready—so it is said—to rise again in the customary direction assumed at prayer. As the coffin is lowered into the grave, the bystanders murmur softly, "May he (she) come to his (her) place in peace." Each of them then strews three handfuls, or shovels three spadefuls of earth upon it. In the latter case, the spade must not be handed from one to another but must be replaced each time in the soil and picked up afresh.

The chief mourners then recite a special form of the *Kaddish*—that is, the great liturgical formula of Sanctification—in which they acknowledge the greatness and holiness of God "Who will yet renew creation and quicken the dead and raise them to life everlasting."

Before re-entering the chapel for the conclusion of the service, everyone washes his hands in clean water and repeats the words, "Our hands have not shed this blood, neither have our eyes seen it" (Deut. 21:7), the formula anciently recited by the elders of a city after they had given burial to the victim of homicide by an unknown hand. Then they place their hands over their eyes, accompanying the gesture with the verse from Isaiah (25:8), "He will destroy Death for ever; yea, the Lord God will wipe away the tear from off every face."

On leaving the graveyard, it is customary to cast a handful of dust over one's shoulder, saying quietly, "He remembereth that we are dust" (Ps. 103:14); or to pluck a few blades of grass and murmur, "Out of the city may men flourish like grass of the earth" (Ps. 72:16).

The return from the funeral should be made, according to tradition, by a different route, and be punctuated by seven stops.[10] This latter custom is explained by the sages in two ways. According to the one view, the seven stops serve to recall the sevenfold repetition of the phrase, "this too is vanity" in the Book of Ecclesiastes (viz. 2:23, 26; 4:4, 16; 6:2, 9; 8:10). According to the other, they symbolize the seven things that are perennial and upon which the order of the world is based, viz. (1.) sowing; (2.) reaping; (3.) heat; (4.) cold; (5.) summer; (6.) winter; and (7.) the succession of day and night.[11]

On arriving home, the bereaved are regaled by friends and neighbors with a special meal of bread, hard-boiled eggs, and lentils. No one is permitted to join them in this meal except the sexton. If, however, there is only one male mourner, two other males share the repast with him in order to make up the minimum quorum of three which is required by Jewish tradition before the complete form of Grace can be recited. From this moment the formal period of mourning begins.

3

A TIME TO MOURN

For thirty days the bereaved may not cut their hair,* pare
their nails, wear new clothes, listen to music, celebrate
weddings, go to parties, appear at public gatherings, or
visit places of entertainment. In many communities it is
the custom also that when they attend divine services in
the synagogue they do not occupy their usual seats.

The austerity is even more severe during the first seven
days, known as *Shiv'ah* (Hebrew for "seven"). Throughout this period the bereaved must remain at home, abstain
from all work or preoccupation with business, wash only
their hands and faces, wear no clean linen, and sit on low

. . . . .

* Shaving is forbidden in any case by traditional Jewish law, but even
those Jews who normally ignore the prohibition are often punctilious about
observing it during a period of mourning.

stools, unshod or—at best—in felt slippers. They may read nothing except the more mournful portions of the Bible, such as the book of Job and Lamentations, or devotional works calculated to arouse in them a sense of the evanescence of human life. Even the study of the Torah is forbidden, for such study, it is held, is really a pleasure and a delight. (Teaching, however, is permitted.) Moreover, throughout the seven days a lamp is kept burning in memory of the deceased.

There is a special protocol about the giving and returning of greetings during the period of mourning. For the first three days, a mourner may neither give them nor acknowledge them. From the third to the seventh day, he may not give them, but he may return them if offered by persons who do not know that he is in mourning. From the seventh to the thirtieth day, he may extend them, but not acknowledge them.

In the case of the death of parents, the period of mourning is extended from thirty days to a full year.

The ancient sages attempted to find authority in Scripture for these traditional customs. For the "thirty days" this was easy enough: is it not written explicitly (Deut. 34:8), that "the children of Israel wept for Moses . . . thirty days"? The "seven days," on the other hand, presented something of a difficulty, for the verse in the Book of Genesis (50:10) which relates that Joseph "made a mourning for his father seven days" refers, in point of fact, to exercises performed *before,* not *after* burial. The ingenuity of the rabbis, however, was equal to the problem. It is said in that same Book of Genesis (7:4, 10) that the Flood did not commence until seven days after God had warned Noah of its imminent approach. The delay, they asserted, was to allow for a seven day mourning for the pious Methuselah! Then, too, they pointed out, had not the prophet Amos declared expressly (Am. 8:10) that God would "turn all your feasts into mourning," and, since there are in fact seven festivals (or holidays) mentioned in the Bible,* did not this foreshadow the institution of seven-day periods of mourning?

Morning and evening devotions held in the house during the "seven days" are characterized especially by the chanting of appropriate psalms. In the evening, the service is introduced by the Forty-ninth Psalm, the theme of which is the vanity of earthly possessions and the inevitability of the grave:

> Hearken to this, all ye peoples;
> give ear, all ye that dwell
> in what seems so stable a world;
> high and low alike,
> rich and poor together!
> My mouth will utter wise saws,
> and the thought of my heart be sound sense;
> I will turn my mind † to a parable,
> and e'en as I twang my harp,
> I will a riddle resolve:
> (*Question:*) Why should I be dismayed
> if, by casual mischance,
> my tracks from Fortune stray,
> and lead me on roundabout paths? *
> (*Answer:*) Men that rely on their wealth
> and boast of their riches so great
> can none of them ransom his fellow
> nor bail him out from God.
> Too costly even for them
> is the ransom-price of a soul,

. . . . .

* *viz.* Passover, the Feast of Weeks, the Feast of Booth, the Day of Solemn Assembly, the Day of Memorial (New Year), the Day of Atonement, and the Feast of Purim.

† *Literally,* ear, i.e. attention.

* *Literally,* Why should I fear, in days of evil, the deviation of my tracks that carry me around in circles?

that a man ⌐might live for ever⌐*
and never see decay.
Nay, what it is that he sees
is that all men die and perish—
the wise, the fool and the brute,
and leave to others their wealth.

"Ever-enduring houses,
dwellings that last for all time"—
what have they of such but ⌐graves⌐?†
All they can claim as their own
are—so many mounds of earth!

> *Man in his glory bright*
> *lasts not through the night;*
> *like as dumb beasts men fare,*
> *that know not when nor where.*

This is the fate of those
—those fools in their sleek complacence
and of them that in their wake
go mouthing whatever they please:
Like as sheep they are
herded and ⌐driven⌐ by Death,
bound for the netherworld,
⌐their flesh doomed to rot,⌐ §
their ⌐skin⌐¶ to waste away;
no more mansions for them,
but only the netherworld.

· · · · ·

---

* The traditional text is disfigured by several scribal errors which distort the sense. My rendering incorporates the emendations (marked ⌐ ⌐) generally adopted by modern scholars.

† The traditional text reads, *Their inward thought is that their houses shall continue for ever (and) their dwelling-places for all generations,* but for *qrbm,* "their inward thought," we must read, with several of the ancient versions, the very similar qbrm, "graves."

§ For the traditional text's obscure *wa-yorᵉdū bām yᵉshārîm la-bôger,* commonly rendered, 'And the upright shall have dominion over them in the morning,' we should read the very similar, *wᵉ-yirdeh bām; bᵉ ṣārām li-rᵉqôb.*

¶ For the traditional text's *ṣîrām,* an unparalleled form usually taken to mean "their form, frame," I read the very similar *ᶜôrām,* 'their skin'; cf. Lamentations 3.4.

But as for this soul of mine,
when the netherworld would take me,
God, yea, God Himself
will ransom me from its grasp.
'Pay, then, no regard'
when a man grows rich,
when the pomp of his household increases,
for nought shall he take when he dies;
his pomp shall not follow him down!
What though, during his life
he count his soul as blessed,
(telling it,) "Men acclaim thee
because thou art faring so well,"
in the end it needs must go
to join his sires of old*
who shall never see daylight again!
    Man, though with glory bedight,
    if lacking all inner light,
    doth to dumb beasts compare
    that know not when nor where.

Among Sephardic Jews it is customary also to preface the service by spelling out the name of the deceased in verses selected from the One Hundred and Nineteenth Psalm, which is composed in the form of an alphabetical acrostic. The Requiem (Hebrew, *Hashkabah*) and the Acknowledgment of Divine Justice (Hebrew, *Zidduk Ha-Din*)—prayers also recited at the burial—are likewise intoned, and on the seventh evening, the former is concluded with the comforting assurance of Isaiah (60:20) that "thy sun shall no more go down, neither shall thy moon wane; for the Lord shall be unto thee an everlasting light, and the days of thy mourning shall be ended."

Throughout the week, appropriate additions are also made to the customary Grace after Meals. God is besought to comfort "them that mourn for Zion and them

. . . . .

* Literally, *To the generation of his forefathers.*

that mourn for Jerusalem, and likewise them that share in this mourning," * and the usual formula which proclaims Him to be "our Father, our King, our Stalwart, our Redeemer" is amplified into an acknowledgment of Him as "the God of truth, Who judgeth aright, Who taketh men's souls and ruleth the world in accordance with His will—the God whose people and servants we are."

There are no special rules about the costume of mourners, other than that one must rend one's garments at the death of a parent, spouse, brother, sister, son or daughter. The "rending" takes the symbolic form of a gash to the extent of a hand's breadth. For a parent, it is made on the left side, and in all the garments; for others, on the right side and only in the upper garment. The performance of this rite is accompanied by the words: "Blessed art Thou, O Lord our God, King of the Universe, Who judgest aright"—a formula which every Jew is expected to recite on hearing of a death.

For the rest, mourning costume varies from country to country, in accordance with local usage. The Bible speaks, to be sure, of mourners' wearing sackcloth or dark raiment,† a common usage among the ancient Semites, but this custom has not persisted among all Jews everywhere. Sometimes, for instance, white is preferred to black, and among the Jews of Cochin, mourners wear upon their heads a small square of white cloth which is ceremoniously removed by the rabbi on the seventh day.[1] In Algiers, on the other hand, the distinctive dress of Jewish mourners is a pair of black gloves[2]—a custom which,

. . . . .

* The customary formula for consoling mourners is: "May the Lord comfort you along with all that mourn for Zion.
† e.g. Gen. 37:34; Isa. 15:3; Job 5:11 (Heb.).

incidentally, finds a curious parallel in some parts of England.[3]

4

THE FOLKLORE OF DEATH

Most of the customs observed by Jews in connection with death and mourning are by no means original or exclusive, but have been picked up from their Gentile neighbors. They therefore vary considerably from land to land and, in some cases, even from city to city. By and large, their original significance has long since been forgotten and they have been cleverly—though often somewhat tortuously—reinterpreted in the light of distinctive Hebraic ideas and "justified" by assumed Biblical precedents or by reference to a seemingly appropriate quotation from Scripture. This, however has not always proved possible, and not a few usages therefore persist simply as meaningless survivals.

Take, for instance, the custom of *snatching feather pillows from under the heads of the dying*. Though widespread among European Jews and though sanctioned even by rabbinic authority, this lacks any satisfactory explanation from Jewish sources. For at least five hundred years, however, it has been a common superstition in several parts of the continent that pillows stuffed with pigeon or partridge feathers prevent the approach of death and thereby prolong the final agony. Shakespeare's Timon of Athens, for instance, specifically derides the pusillanimity of those who, in an effort to reduce the normal pangs of death, "pluck stout men's pillows from below their heads," [1] and even in more recent times it has been widely believed in the rural areas of England that a person must on no account be allowed to die on a feather bed.[2] Indeed, only seventy years ago, it was reported from the City of Wakefield that an old family nurse had insisted, at the deathbed of a young man, on substituting a flock pillow for one made of game feathers, so that he might die calmly.[3] The belief obtains likewise in Germany,[4] Norway,[5] Russia,[6] and Portugal;[7] and in 1698 a learned scholar at Jena was able to compile a fairly lengthy dissertation citing instances of it from many parts of the world.[8]

Various reasons have been given. According to one view, the spirits of the birds from which the feathers have been plucked cry out to the Angel of Death to avenge their untimely ends, whereupon he delays bestowing the *coup de grâce* on the expiring human being. Another explanation, common alike in Britain and (at least, formerly) among the peasants of Russia, is that the use of dove's down or pigeon's feathers is sacrilegious, because the dove is the emblem of the Holy Spirit (cf. Mat. 3:16; Mk. 1:10; Lu. 3:22; John 1:32). God therefore requites such sacrilege by withholding the mercy of an easy demise. This purely Christian interpretation is, however, in all probability, a mere afterthought, for the fact is that a clearly comparable practice is likewise known to "the heathen Chinee": the matting on which a dying person lies is often pulled from under him at the last moment in order, so it is said, to prevent his being visited with lingering sickness in his next incarnation! [9]

Equally inexplicable from purely Jewish sources is the custom of *opening the window for a few moments immediately after the last breath has been drawn.* The original purpose of this act was to provide a means of exit for the departing soul, and here, too, we have a mere survival of a worldwide usage which the Jews took over mechanically from their Gentile neighbors. Students of English literature will recall at once the familiar lines in Shakespeare's *King John:*

Ay, marry, now my soul hath elbow-room;
It would not out at windows nor at doors.[10]

Analogously, among the Hottentots,[11] the Samoyeds,[12] the Siamese,[13] the Fijians,[14] and the Redskins,[15] it is customary to make a hole in the hut to allow passage of the spirit; and in China, an opening is provided in the roof.[16]

Special care is usually taken, however, to shut the window in short order lest the spirit return through it and harass or frighten the survivors. That the ghosts of the departed do indeed hover for a time about their whilom habitations is an exceedingly widespread superstition. In Silesia, it is believed that they actually knock on the panes or shutters during the night after burial,[17] and among the Huzuls[18] and Ruthenians,[19] children who have died unbaptized are thought to appear at the windows at midnight clamoring for that sacrament. Alternatively, it is held that unless the window be shut immediately, Death himself may be tempted to pay a second visit, or the family may be disturbed by the unwelcome attentions of some other noxious demon. That Death and demons enter through the window was a common notion among the ancient Semites. The prophet Jeremiah declares expressly (9:21) that "Death is come up through our windows, hath entered our palaces"; while a magical incantation from Asshur, the ancient capital of Assyria, explicitly exorcizes demons against forcing their way into a house through the side windows or the skylight.[20]

For the same reason, it is customary to draw all blinds in a house until after a funeral, and in many European countries, neighbors do so while the cortège is passing. This is conventionally explained as a "mark of respect," but—as in so many other instances—what has now degenerated into a somewhat meaningless courtesy was originally a more deliberate method of forfending evil and contagion. For it is very commonly supposed that demons can work mischief by merely glancing through the windows. In Lower Germany, for example, Heidmann, the dread "Man on the Heath," is thought to peer through windows at night, and anyone on whom he fixes his gaze is destined to die within a year and a day.[21] Similarly, it is a popular notion that Berchta, the hideous beldam who brings plague and carries off children, creeps around under cover of darkness, peeping through lattices in order to select her victims.

It has been suggested—perhaps too rationally and prosaically—that such beliefs originated in the fear of fatal pneumonia caused by draughts and by the damp night air.

The closing of the eyes is yet another practice which has survived obstinately from primitive usage but the original significance of which has long since been forgotten. The usual explanation nowadays is that it is designed simply to remove the terrifying stare which often remains on the face of the dead. This, however, is mere latter-day rationalization. Originally, the practice was inspired by the belief that the soul of a man rests in his eyes. Babrius, the Greek fabulist, speaks, for instance, of "the souls in the eyes of the dying";[22] the Elder Pliny says that the eye is the habitation of the spirit;[23] and it was a common ancient superstition, surviving today in Scotland and elsewhere, that when the mannikin was no longer visible in the eye, a man was about to "give up the ghost." Accordingly when the soul had actually departed, the door, as it were, was shut behind it.[24]

The custom is already attested in the Bible: when God reveals himself to Jacob at Beersheba, He expressly assures him that "I will go down with thee into Egypt, and I will also bring thee up again; and Joseph shall put his hand upon thine eyes" (Gen. 46:4). But it was by no means confined to the Hebrews. In the *Iliad,* the ghost of Agamemnon complains that by being murdered he was denied this last mercy,[25] and in the *Odyssey,* Laertes wonders whether his son Odysseus may not be lying dead on foreign soil, with neither father nor mother to close his eyes.[26]

Analogous is the practice of *closing the mouth;* for it was a very prevalent belief in antiquity—as it still is among primitive peoples—that the soul departs *via* the lips, along with the last breath. The Greeks, for instance, spoke of a man *in extremis* as "having his soul on his lips," and in one of the mimes of Herondas (third cent.

B.C.E.), an angry mistress bids a schoolmaster beat her disobedient slave "till his soul hangs from his lips." [27]

A curious offshoot of this belief was the custom of kissing the mouth of the dying in order to catch his "spirit" so that it might be transmitted to future generations. Joseph, for example, is said so to have kissed his father Jacob (Gen. 50:1); and in the pseudoepigraphical Book of Jubilees it is said (23:10 f.) that Jacob himself printed no less than seven kisses on the mouth of his grandfather, Abraham. Similarly, in Vergil's *Aeneid*, when Dido, queen of Carthage, commits suicide upon the departure of Aeneas, her sister Anna rushes forward to the pyre, exclaiming:

If the last breath yet linger on thy lips,
Suffer me with my mouth to gather it; [28]

while Cicero speaks of mothers who were cruelly "withheld from the last embrace of their sons—mothers who prayed for nothing more than to be allowed to catch with their mouths the last breath of their offspring." [29] The idea is echoed also in English literature: Alexander Pope has Heloise cry out to Abelard,

Suck my last breath and catch my flying soul;

while Shelley invokes Adonais:

O let thy breath flow from thy dying soul
Even to my mouth and heart, that I may suck!

Moreover, there are some curious variations on this time-honored theme. Thus, among the Seminoles of Florida, it used to be the custom, when a woman died in childbirth, to hold the infant over her face so that it might receive her parting spirit. [30] And only a century ago, the superstition prevailed in Lancashire (England) that a witch could not die unless an associate caught her last breath, and with it her familiar spirit, into her own mouth.[31]

At the present day, the closing of the mouth usually takes the form of binding up the jaws. Sometimes, extra precautions are taken. Among the Jews of Bukovina,[32] and likewise in parts of India,[33] sherds are placed on the mouth to prevent its falling open, and among the pagan peoples of antiquity, it was often sealed with a golden plaque or "muzzle." Such plaques have been found, for instance, in interments of the fourteenth-thirteenth centuries B.C.E. at Mycenae and Enkomi, and the custom was subsequently imported into Palestine and Syria, for it is evidenced in graves excavated at Beth Shean and Tell Halaf.[34] Moreover, some seven hundred years later, an inscription on the sarcophagus of a royal lady at Byblus, Syria, declares that she is "lying with a veil and a headpiece upon me, and with a golden muzzle over my mouth." [35]

Somewhat more difficult to explain is the custom of *rending the garments* as a sign of mourning. This was common not only among the ancient Hebrews—as the Bible abundantly attests (e.g. Gen. 37:29; II Sam. 1:2, 11; Isa, 37:1; Job 1:20)—but also among the Canaanites and among the Romans.[36] Two theories have been advanced to account for it. According to the one, it is a natural, emotional expression of anguish, analogous to tearing one's hair or biting one's nails, and is simply a later form of the more primitive practice of gashing the flesh. According to the other, however, it is a conscious and deliberate method of disguising oneself so that hovering demons may be foiled if they have previously marked one out as their next victim.

It was likewise as a method of forfending demons and

expelling contagion that *the graveclothes were left free of knots and bows.* The original idea was to provide ready egress not so much for the spirit of the deceased as for the dread power of Death which had invaded his body. That power had to be expelled not for the benefit of the deceased, on whom it had already done its evil work, but rather for that of his survivors who might otherwise be contaminated by it.

As for the custom of *laying the body on the floor* shortly after death, this is a somewhat meaningless modification of the older Gentile practice of so placing a person during his last moments, the modification being necessitated by the fact that Jews are forbidden by their religious law to touch or disturb the dying.

The custom can be traced back to ancient India,[37] and Servius, the famous fourth-century commentator on Vergil, tells us that it was likewise the practice of the Romans, when men lay dangerously ill, to place them on the ground outside the doors of their houses, "so that they might return their last breath to the earth" whence they sprang.[38] The Jews, however, probably adopted the usage at a far later date from their Gentile neighbors. Says Aelfric, the celebrated medieval English churchman:

It was the custom to spread a sheet of sackcloth on the floor and on this to sprinkle ashes in the shape of a cross. Just as the dying person was in the last agony, he was taken out of bed and stretched on the sackcloth and ashes; it being deemed more becoming that sinful man should yield up his soul thus than on a soft bed, when his divine Redeemer died on the hard wood of the cross.[39]

Moreover, it is related both of Bishop Benno of Osnabruck, in the eleventh century,[40] and of St. Francis of Assisi, in the thirteenth, that they ordered their disciples to deposit them on the ground during their last moments.[41] Nor, indeed, was the custom altogether extinct, in more recent times; it was common as late as the nineteenth century in several parts of England and Ireland,[42] and it still obtains sporadically in such regions of Germany as Vogtland, Silesia, and East Prussia.[43]

Here again, opinions differ about the true significance of the procedure. One theory is that it was designed in the first place to permit the soul to enter more readily into the nether regions;[43a] another, that it was intended to symbolize a new birth from the earth and thereby to procure new life for the dying.[43b] A third view contends that it was simply a ceremonial survival from that early stage of civilization when men had no beds,[43c] and a fourth, that it was inspired by the purely economic consideration that the bed on which a person had actually died was believed to be charged with perpetual contagion, so that it could not be used in the future.[43d]

The washing and perfuming of the corpse was not, in the first place, merely a sanitary act. In primitive thought, cleanliness is next to godliness in more than a symbolic sense, for the removal of impurity or contagion from the body amounts to the removal of demons which are believed to be infesting it. Washing is a peculiarly effective means to this end because demons, like witches and warlocks, have a pronounced aversion to water.

Even better than washing, however, is the use of perfumes and spices. A document from Asshur, their ancient capital, informs us that the Assyrians used to burn "goodly reeds" and "fine ointments" at funerals;[43e] while the Biblical Book of Chronicles records (II Chr., 16:14) that Asa, king of Judah, was laid on a bier "filled with sweet perfumes and divers kinds of spices prepared by the apothecaries' art." This custom, which was likewise prevalent among the Greeks and Romans, subsequently became standard Jewish practice. The Gospel of John states expressly (19:40) that "they took the body of Jesus and swathed it in linen cloths, *with the spices, as the custom is of the Jews to bury"*; and it is related that the proselyte Onkelos piously burned no less than thirty *manehs* of balsam at the obsequies of his teacher, Gamaliel the Elder.[43t]

The original purpose of the scenting was to drive away the demons, and the effectiveness of the measure was enhanced if the spices were *burned,* for in that case the evil beings were at the same time "smoked out." This use of fumigation is common to virtually all religions, and it is this idea that really underlies the employment of incense. Says an early Christian writer: "No one will be surprised at the widespread use of fumigation, if he but bear in mind that . . . demons who flit unseen through the air can at once be lured into the open by the vapors thus exuded. It is said, for instance, that they flock around immediately whenever coriander, parsley or henbane is burned." [44]

An engaging variation upon the same theme is the common notion of ancient mythology that divine beings themselves exude a special aroma which both announces their presence and protects them from the assaults of demons.[45] 'Anat, the Canaanite Diana, is said, for example, to have been perfumed with coriander and with "the camphor of maidens sevenfold," [46] and Demeter to have shed a wondrous scent from her robes;[47] while of Venus, Vergil declares that

from her head divinest odors breathed
In her ambrosial hair.[48]

The custom of *dressing the dead in white* was common also in ancient Greece, though variations did indeed occur.[49] Similarly, the avoidance of knots in graveclothes was likewise an established practice in Germany until relatively modern times.[50] The usual explanation was that knots and bows would serve only to restrain the demon of death from departing and would thus entail the speedy demise of some other member of the household. In Zurich, however, the alternative interpretation is offered that knots and bows impede the egress of the soul to eternity.[51]

The kindling of lights beside an unburied body and the use of torches at funerals are well-nigh universal usages and can be traced back to ancient Greece and Rome. Indeed, the very word "funeral" derives from the Latin *funus*, "torch." In general folklore, these lamps are usually interpreted as a means of guiding the soul of the deceased to its eternal abode, and in the burial service of the Samaritans, a fine "twist" is given to this idea, when it is said:

> Long is the way.
> Ere on it thou essay,
> Let the lamp of purity
> Make bright the gloom as day! [52]

Often, however, the light is regarded—as among the Jews —as a symbol of the soul, and it then becomes customary to keep it burning perpetually in the tomb. Such an "eternal light" glows, for instance, over the alleged tomb of Jesus in the Church of the Holy Sepulchre at Jerusalem, and it is reported that in the reign of Pope Paul III (1534-49), the grave of a girl was discovered on the Via Appia near Rome, in which a light had been burning steadily for some fifteen hundred years! [53]

Nevertheless, modern scholars believe that the original purpose of funerary lights was the same as that of lights lit at childbirth and marriage—namely, to keep away demons and evil spirits, who can operate only under cover of darkness.[53a]

Interment without coffins is yet another usage which the Jews shared with their Gentile neighbors, though in general European practice this was not reserved for dignitaries. In Flanders, the dead were often wrapped only in straw;[54] while in Upper Bavaria, even at the present day, the shrouded body is often removed from the casket at the last moment and slid into the earth on a board.[55] Similarly, in the German province of Baden, a common coffin used formerly to be used for all funerals, the corpse being lifted from it at the graveside.[56] Coffinless burial was likewise prevalent in Italy as late as the nineteenth century.[57]

Nor, indeed, is the Jewish custom of removing the nether plank from the casket or of boring holes in it altogether without analogies elsewhere. For it is recorded that, less than eighty years ago, it was not unusual among Irish country folk to remove the nails from a coffin in order to facilitate the emergence of the deceased at the Resurrection![58]

To the practice of *enclosing in the coffin a sachet of Palestinian earth* as a substitute for actual burial in the redemptive soil of the Holy Land there is an interesting parallel in former English usage. As is well known, Christianity likewise holds the belief that burial in consecrated soil helps to ensure resurrection. Until the middle of the nineteenth century, however, Catholic priests were not permitted by English law to officiate in churchyards. The funeral service of Catholics was therefore often read in the home, and the priest blessed a small satchet of earth, sprinkled it with holy water, and placed it in the coffin, so that in this token fashion the dead might still be said to lie in holy earth.[59]

Although Jews were accustomed, even in Talmudic times, to *place keys, pens and the like in the coffins* of graves of scholars and dignitaries, there is no reliable evidence that they ever adopted the practice of providing the dead with coins in order to pay his fare to the next world. This custom, familiar especially from Greek antiquity ("the obol for Charon"), is still prevalent in many countries as, for instance, in modern Greece, in Estonia and in parts of Germany, as well as among the gypsies of Alsace—if, indeed, there be any of them left.[60] Its absence from Jewish folkways is therefore somewhat remarkable. There is, however, a possible reminiscence of it in the custom observed occasionally by Oriental Jews of placing seven silver coins on the corpse while the seven circuits are made around it at the cemetery. As each circuit is completed, a member of the company takes one of the coins and flings it away, at the same time reciting the Biblical verse (Gen. 25:6): *And unto the sons of the concubines which Abraham had, Abraham gave gifts, and he sent them away from Isaac his son, while he yet lived, eastward, unto the east country.* It is pretty obvious this Scriptural passage has simply been dragged in as an afterthought to justify a traditional custom the original significance of which was no longer remembered or no longer acceptable. Not impossibly, therefore, the whole curious procedure is but an elaborate transmogrification of the "heathen" practice of supplying the dead with money for his "fare," and in this connection it is interesting to observe that the Japanese somewhat similarly present him

with a bag (*dzudabukuro*) containing six pieces of money
designed for that purpose.* [61]

There is likewise no clear evidence among Jews of the
widespread practice of *providing the dead with a "passport"* to the afterworld—a practice which can be traced
back to the ancient Egyptians[62] and which survives especially in the popular usages of the Greek Church.† [63] The
underlying idea, however, finds expression in that verse
of the Sephardic funeral dirge (p. 146) in which the
mourners pray that the deceased, after passing the Cave
of Machpelah, may come upon the guardian cherubim
and receive from them a "ticket" or "passport" (Hebrew, *pinkas*) to the Garden of Eden.

On the other hand, the custom of supplying the dead
with a *trowel* wherewith he may dig his way to the Holy
Land possesses a direct counterpart in the practice reported, in the past century, from various counties of
England and Wales of providing him with a *hammer* to
knock on the celestial doors! [64]

The rule that *burial must take place as soon as possible*—in Palestine, on the very day of death—may have
its practical foundation in the climatic conditions of
Near Eastern countries. Nevertheless, other considerations would seem also to enter into the picture, for it is
significant that in the *Iliad* of Homer (xxiii, 71), the

· · · · ·

* The precise amount often varies, and sometimes paper drawings are
substituted for actual coins.
† When the body is brought into church, the priest places on its breast a
"passport to heaven" consisting in a piece of paper inscribed with the
Christian name of the deceased, the dates of his birth and death, and a
statement that he has received final absolution. The custom, however, is
not formally prescribed in the liturgy.

speedy burial of Patroclus is regarded as a pious duty, and Xenophon tells us that the Greeks in general held it inconsiderate toward the dead to delay their interment.[65] English superstition asserts, in the same spirit, that to keep a body unburied over Sunday invites another death in the family within three weeks.[66] The basic idea is, of course, to forestall the malevolent attentions of a disgruntled and errant ghost.

The tradition that *the pallbearers must walk barefoot* conforms to a common ancient gesture of mourning. Not only is it mentioned in sundry passages of Scripture (e.g. II Sam. 15:30; Ezek. 24:17), but it is also well attested in Greek and Roman antiquity. The women who accompanied Demeter in her mourning for the abducted Persephone are said expressly to have walked unshod,[67] and it was in the same condition that Aphrodite (Venus) bewailed Adonis.[68] An even more direct parallel to the Jewish usage is afforded, however, by the statement of Suetonius, the biographer of the Roman emperors, that the nobles who removed the ashes of Augustus from the funeral pyre went barefoot.[69] Moreover, it is not without significance that in times of grievous drought the Romans used to perform a supplicatory mourning rite known as *nudipedalia*—that is, "the barefoot ceremony." [70]

The custom of *pouring out all standing water* in the house of the dead is not mentioned in Jewish sources before the thirteenth century and appears to have been borrowed from Gentile usage. It is extremely common in modern Greece[71] and among adherents of the Russian Orthodox Church,[72] and it is attested also as a popular practice in various rural areas of Germany.[73] The Greeks say that it is designed to provide refreshment for the soul during its journey to the future world, but another and more plausible explanation connects it with the widespread belief that *the dead suffer excessive thirst.* Among the Babylonians, for instance, the netherworld was sometimes known as "the field of thirst," [74] while in ancient Egyptian funerary texts, the dead is often represented as begging for water.[75] Similarly, the prophet Isaiah speaks (5:13) of man's pomp and glory's being eventually "dried out by thirst," and in modern Palestinian superstition, the soul of the departed is said to revisit his tomb every Friday night in quest of water.[76] Jews in the island of Djerba periodically pour water for the dead into little hollows especially carved upon their flat tombstones.

There is, however, even a third interpretation. All over the world, it is observed, the belief obtains that demons and warlocks cannot cross water. The purpose of pouring it out in front of the house at a funeral may therefore have been to prevent a speedy return of the "Angel of Death."

Somewhat different in intention is the practice of *overturning chairs and breaking pots.* This was designed originally to prevent the spirit of the deceased from being tempted to remain in the house and enjoy its amenities. The overturning of chairs is paralleled in Germany and in several European countries,[76a] and gives rise to the practice whereby mourners—sharing, as it were, the experience of death—sit on the ground.

For God's sake, let us sit upon the ground
And tell sad stories of the death of kings,

cries Richard the Second in Shakespeare's play of that name, and to this day, when Jews mourn the destruction of the Temple on the alleged anniversary of that event, they abandon their usual seats in the synagogue and sit on the floor.

The breaking of pots at the moment the cortege leaves the house finds an exact parallel in the funeral usages still current in the isles of Greece,[77] and it may be compared also with the more drastic practice of the Gypsies whereby the caravan is smashed to pieces and burned upon the death of its owner.

In *halting the cortege* several times on the way to the graveyard, the Jews were once again adopting and adapting a time-honored custom of their non-Jewish neighbors. Similarly, in Germany[78] and in Portugal,[79] for example, it used to be the practice to make regular stops on the funeral route in order to shake off evil spirits that might still be hovering around the deceased; while among the remote Tigrē of Abyssinia, the march to the church is made in seven short stages.[80]

There are several intriguing variations upon this custom. Thus, in the Upper Inn region of Bavaria, the funeral procession is often halted thrice, and each time the coffin is tipped up so that the dead may see his home once again and take a final farewell of it;[81] while in other parts of Germany, the casket is deposited thrice at the threshold before the cortege moves off. This is said to prevent the soul of the departed from re-entering the house.[82] Similarly, the report of a Scottish funeral in 1871 states that the coffin was "bumped" three times on the way to the cemetery, and that on each such occasion a traditional dirge (composed in the reign of Henry VIII) was duly intoned;[83] while the halting of the cortege is mentioned expressly in an account of popular usages in North Wales.[83a]

Even more widespread is the custom of *making circuits around the body* of the deceased. An ancient Assyrian document, now in the British Museum, records how a bereaved bride encircled the bier of her husband three times, and how similar circuits were made around the mortuary chapel.[84] In Mohammedan tradition, it is related that the corpse of Antar's father was circuited by wailing women seven times,[85] and among the Indians, it was customary to walk ceremonially around a funeral pyre.[86] In the *Iliad,* Achilles is said to have driven his chariot around the pyre of Patroclus,[87] and in the Anglo-Saxon poem of Beowulf, twelve noblemen are said to have done likewise around the ashes of that hero.[88] In the Russian Orthodox ritual, officiating priests, carrying candles (as in the Sephardic Jewish practice in the case of dignitaries) used formerly to walk around the bier when it was placed in the church before a burial.[89] A similar rite performed (usually thrice) by relatives is recorded also in several parts of Germany[90] and even in such relatively faraway places as Jamaica[91] and Sierra Leone.[92] Sometimes, to be sure, the circuits are made in the house before the funeral, and sometimes also around the grave. But the purpose is always and everywhere the same—namely, to prevent the approach of demons. They are thus of the same order as those made around a woman in labor or around a bride.

The *strewing of earth upon the coffin* after it has been lowered into the grave is, once again, by no means an exclusively Jewish custom. Sometimes it is regarded as the pious duty of all who attend the funeral; sometimes—as among the Annamese,[93] or among certain tribes in Southern India,[94] or even in the German province of Baden[95]—its an office reserved to the relatives of the deceased. In the Greek Church, the earth is scattered by the officiating priest,[95a] and this was also the form prescribed in the English Prayer Book of Edward VI. In 1559, however, the rubric was changed, and the Anglican ritual now enjoins that the priest is merely to recite the appropriate words *while the earth shall be cast upon the body by some standing by.*

Both Judaism and Christianity have given their own distinctive interpretations to this ancient practice. The former sees in it a symbolic reminder of that wider mourning for Zion which the Jew must never allow to be obscured by his own private sorrows. The earth symbolizes the soil of the Holy Land, of which the Psalmist said: *They that are servants of Thee hold dear its very rubble and cherish its very dust* (Ps. 102:14).* The latter, on the other hand, construes the gesture as an outward token of the fact that the body of the deceased is committed to the ground, *earth to earth, ashes to ashes, dust to dust, in sure and certain hope of the Resurrection to eternal life, through our Lord Jesus Christ, who shall change our vile body, that it may be like unto his glorious body.* It is probable, however, that in origin the custom represented nothing more than a token burial of the dead in accordance with the principle that, out of sheer charity, a few handfuls of dust should always be scattered by the passerby on an exposed, unburied body. Of the same order, indeed, is the widespread rule that a wayfarer should never pass a roadside cairn without adding a stone to it.

That those who have attended a funeral should be required immediately to *wash their hands* is easily explained

. . . . .

* The King James' Version renders: *Thy servants take pleasure in her stones, and favour the dust thereof,* which does not quite reproduce the nuance of the original.

from the fact that death is always regarded in primitive thought as a contagion. Jewish tradition is, in fact, very conscious of this notion, for it is prescribed by several rabbinic authorities that the hands must not be subsequently wiped on a towel, lest the impurity cling to it.

Here again we have but the Jewish form of a virtually universal practice. At modern Greek funerals, mourners are met on their return to the house by a servant who stands at the door and pours lustral water into a basin. All must rinse their hands in it before re-entering.[96] A similar custom, we are told, obtained in ancient India,[97] and in many parts of Europe, water and a towel are provided ceremonially for mourners when they arrive home after an interment.[98] Manganja mourners bathe on that occasion and rub themselves with "medicine water";[99] while among certain of the tribes of Luzon everyone is obliged to dip forthwith in the river.[100]

Certainly one of the most picturesque of all Jewish funeral rites is that of *throwing a few blades of grass or a handful of dust over one's shoulder* upon leaving the cemetery. The Biblical verses by which this rite is traditionally explained (viz. *He remembereth that we are dust,* or *Out of the city may men flourish like grass of the earth:* Pss. 103:14; 72:16) are, of course, inspired afterthoughts. The custom itself does not appear to be attested in Jewish sources before the twelfth century, and it was simply an adaptation of the common European practice of throwing things behind one in order to drive away pursuing demons—a motif which recurs time beyond number in folktales.[101] The use of grass for this purpose, and specifically in connection with funerals, is mentioned, however, in medieval German documents.[102]

Observance of this custom, it may be added, was not

always successful in keeping the demons at bay. During the Middle Ages, the accusation was leveled against the Jews that what they were really trying to do was symbolically to cast evil upon their Gentile neighbors! The rabbis, however, were equal to the charge and promptly sought to disencumber the practice of its original pagan significance. The dust, they pointed out, was sprinkled *upwards over the head,* and this was simply an ancient gesture of mourning, for is it not written of Job's comforters that *they rent every one his robe and sprinkled dust above** *their heads toward heaven* (Job 2:12)? [103]

The meal of eggs and beans served to mourners on their return from a funeral—the *funeral meats*—bears a striking resemblance to that which was offered to the dead themselves in the religious practices of the Greeks and Romans.

Eggs—either real or model—were often placed in Greek and Roman tombs as a symbol of eternal life, and scenes depicted on Athenian vases show that they were also bought in baskets to the graves of the departed.[104] Moreover, the custom survives in European usage. At Beihingen (Ludwigsberg), in Germany, it was still the practice, only forty years ago, to present eggs to the dead,[105] and in the Ukraine, they used to be deposited on graves on Saint Thomas' Day.[106] Similarly, in certain parts of Bavaria, a basket of eggs is given to the village sexton on the Feast of All Souls.[107] The Maori place an egg in the hand of the dead before interment.[108]

Beans, too, have definite mortuary associations. The Romans used to throw them to the spirits of the departed at the Feast of Ghosts (*Lemuria*) in May,[109] and they

. . . . .

* The Hebrew word usually translated "upon" can also mean "above."

were likewise offered to the dead in more direct fashion.[110] Pliny tells us that they were a standard dish at Roman commemorative banquets,[111] and to this day, bean soup is regularly served on the Feast of All Souls in parts of the Tyrol.[112] During the Middle Ages, they were a frequent article of funerary fare among the Germans, and it was customary to make a point of eating them during Holy Week.[113]

It would seem, therefore, that the "mourners' breakfast" goes back to an earlier custom whereby the bereaved shared with the dead his first meal in the afterworld—a kind of sentimental communion with him by the time-honored method of commensality, or "breaking bread" together.

In characteristic fashion, the Jewish sages found a precedent for this popular usage in Scripture itself. The prophet Ezekiel, they pointed out, was instructed specifically not to mourn over the just doom appointed for the wicked city of Jerusalem, and therefore not to go barefoot nor "eat the bread of men" (Ezek. 24:17).* This, they inferred, implies that even in his day, some special type of meal was a feature of mourning ceremonies. Even more fancifully, they traced the custom of eating *lentils* during mourning to the fact that Jacob "gave Esau bread and a pottage of lentils," when the latter sold his birthright (Gen. 25:34). The patriarch, they said, had been cooking lentils because it happened to be the anniversary of his grandfather Abraham's death! *

· · · · ·

* Some of the ancient versions actually read "mourners" instead of the rather vague "men."
* Actually, a dish called *mujedderah,* composed of lentils stewed with onions, rice and oil, is to this day common fare among the poor in the Near East.

5

THE HOUSE OF LIFE

In addition to those concerned with actual burial and mourning there are a number of traditional rules and customs relating to the cemetery.

The cemetery must lie at least fifty cubits from the city, and the graves must be laid out in rows. Rabbis must be buried in a separate row; so too, must children. No flowers may be plucked from a cemetery, and no waterpipes or conduits may pass through it. The grass of a cemetery may not be used as pasture, though in medieval times the practice prevailed of allowing firstborn animals to graze on it.[1]

A Jewish cemetery is known euphemistically as a "house of life" or an "eternal home." The former name is derived from the verse in the Book of Job (30:23): "I

know that Thou wilt cause me to dwell in the realm of death, in the house where all the living must convene." *
The latter is taken from Ecclesiastes (12:5), "Man goeth to his long home, and the mourners go about the streets."
A less familiar term—found on a funerary inscription of the Roman age and likewise in the poem chanted by Sephardic Jews when making circuits around the bier*—is "Abode (or, City) of Peace," an expression which finds its origin in Isaiah (32:18), "My people shall abide in an abode of peace, and in safe dwellings, and in quiet resting-places."

Tombstones are often embellished with emblems indicating the vocation or trade of the deceased. Outspread hands, for example, signify that he was a priest, since they symbolize the pronouncement of the priestly benediction.

It is customary to write the date of death (sometimes also that of birth) in the form of a Biblical verse, the Hebrew letters of which, when taken in their numerical values, add up to the number of the year, according to the traditional Jewish calendar.

At the end of the epitaph are usually inscribed the initial letters of the motto: "May his (her) soul be bound up in the bundle of the living." The phrase is taken from the passage in the First Book of Samuel (25:29) where Abigail says to David: "And a man rise up to pursue thee and to seek thy soul, the soul of my lord shall be bound up before Jehovah thy God in the bundle of the living." These words have been variously interpreted. The late Sir James Frazer, who devoted an entire essay to the subject, suggested that they might be explained in the light of the common primitive belief that the "soul" or life-

. . . . .

* The Hebrew for "house where all the living must convene" is *beth mo'ed* which alludes to the ancient term for a synagogue.
* See above, p. 145.

force of a man can be temporarily detached from his body and lodged in an inanimate object.[2] In that case, the meaning would be, of course, that in moments of peril God will snatch the soul of His servant from its corporeal frame and thereby deliver it from harm. There is, however, no clear evidence of this belief among the ancient Israelites. It is therefore far more probable that the expression is purely metaphorical and that all it really implies is that God will keep the soul of His servant like a treasure wrapped in a bundle or wallet; and as a matter of fact, a comparable expression occurs in an old Babylonian letter in which the writer says to the addressee: "May thy god and thy goddess keep thee like a wallet in their hands."[3] Nevertheless, whatever the Biblical writer may have intended, Jewish fancy has read into these words the more profound concept of an eternal timeless community in which the living and the dead are alike embraced. The "bundle of the living" is an immortal community of souls held like a treasure in the hand of God, and it is in this sense that the expression is used both on tombstones and in memorial prayers.

Jewish traditional teaching looks with disfavor—indeed, with abhorrence—upon the practice of erecting symbolic figures—guardian angels, weeping Niobes, and what not—over the graves of the departed. They are found, to be sure, in all too many Jewish cemeteries at the present day, and they were not unknown also to the Jewish communities of the Graeco-Roman period; but the clearer and more sensitive minds of all ages have always regarded them as "heathen abominations" foreign to both the spirit and the taste of Israel's faith. Indeed, among the Sephardim, and increasingly in new American Jewish cemeteries, the rule obtains that all tombstones must be laid flat, and in East European communities, the most that was usually permitted in the nature of a "monument" was a crude tentlike structure set up over the grave of a distinguished sage. In Judaism, too, simplicity is sacred.

6

COMMEMORATION

Jahrzeit and Yizkor

The anniversary of a death is known among Ashkenazic Jews by the German name of *Jahrzeit,* and among Sephardic Jews by the Spanish name of *Annos.* On this occasion, a lamp is burned in the home (often also in the synagogue) from sunset to sunset; the *Kaddish,* or Sanctification, is recited by the surviving sons; and among the Sephardim, the Requiem (*Hashkabah*) is repeated. If the anniversary occur on a Monday, Thursday, or Sabbath, or on any major or minor holy day when the Law is read in the morning service, one of the survivors is "called" to the rostrum during the reading, and he usually makes an offering to charity. Besides these individual ceremonies, however, there is also a public commemora-

tion of the dead at regular seasons during the year. This
is known as *Yizkor*.

The Yizkor service—so called because the memorial
prayer begins with the Hebrew word *yizkor,* which means
"may [God] remember"—forms a statutory part of the
public devotions in the synagogue on the eighth day of
Passover and Succoth (Booths), the second day of Sha-
vuoth (the Feast of Weeks), and on the Day of Atonement. It is recited by the cantor—usually attired in a long
white robe (*kittel*)—after the reading of the lessons from
the Law and the Prophets. The prayer consists of a petition to God for the repose of the souls of the departed
—especially of those who have died during the current
year—"under the wings of the Divine Presence, in the
exalted height reserved for the holy and pure." It is accompanied by an enumeration of the names of the recently
deceased and by a pledge on the part of their living descendants to make appropriate contributions to charity.
While the prayer is being recited, those whose parents
are still living usually withdraw from the body of the
worshipers.

Yizkor is observed in this form, however, only in con-
gregations which follow the so-called Polish rite. Other
Ashkenazic communities recite the prayer only on the
Sabbaths preceding the Feast of Weeks and the Fast of
Ab; while the Sephardim, or Spanish and Portuguese
Jews, content themselves with a collective enumeration
of the year's dead on the eve of Atonement,* and the
requiem prayer does not begin with the word *yizkor* but

. . . . .

* It has been suggested that the custom of commemorating the dead on
the Day of Atonement was derived from the fact that, in the morning
service, the lesson from the Law begins: "And the Lord spake unto
Moses *after the death* of the two sons of Aaron . . ." (Lev. 16:1).

is the same as is recited throughout a year of mourning
or on the anniversary of a death. Reform Jews also have
their own version of the ceremony, incorporated into the
morning service of Yom Kippur.

The history of the Yizkor service is profoundly interesting. It appears to have originated in Western Germany
in the twelfth century,* and its primary purpose was to
commemorate the Jewish martyrs slain during the First
and Second Crusades. The earliest reference that we have
to it occurs in the celebrated *Memorbuch* of Nuremberg
which, though begun only in 1296, contains a roster not
only of the local dead of the thirteenth and fourteenth
centuries, but also of those who met death "for the sanctification of God" and whose names were therefore recited
weekly in the Sabbath services. The list is prefaced by
reference to such general Jewish worthies as Gershon ben
Judah, the "Light of the Exile," and Rashi, and it is
introduced by a prayer which runs as follows: *"May God
remember* [yizkor] *the soul of N.N. along with the souls
of Abraham, Isaac, and Jacob. By virtue of this vow to*

. . . . .

* It has been claimed that the custom is really far older and goes back
at least to the second century B.C.E., an allusion to it being found in a
passage of the Second Book of Maccabees (12:44) where we are told
that when Judah the Maccabee and his followers picked up the bodies
of their fallen comrades after the defeat of Gorgias near Adullam, and
found that they had secretly been wearing images of heathen gods, the
survivors were ordered to contribute 2,000 drachmas each to the Temple
in Jerusalem. Says the writer of the account: "In this he acted quite
rightly and properly, bearing in mind the resurrection, for if he had not
expected the fallen to rise again, it would have been superfluous and
silly to pray for the dead—and having regard to the splendor of the
gracious reward which is reserved for those who fall asleep in godliness—
a holy and pious consideration. Hence he made propitiation for the dead,
that they might be released from sin." This, however, was a special case;
its purpose was to make restitution for idolatry by a gift to the Temple.
It is no evidence for an annual or periodic Yizkor ceremony.

charity may his soul be bound up in the bond of the living, together with the rest of the righteous who are in Paradise, amen." This prayer, we are informed, might also be recited in the vernacular, and it is carefully distinguished from the ordinary requiem (*hashkabah*) repeated by near relatives throughout a year of mourning or on the anniversary of a death.

Originally, it would seem, the recitation of the Yizkor prayer was not accompanied, as it is today, by vows to charity. The latter were, to be sure, commonly made by individual mourners who wished to commemorate departed ancestors, and the Midrashic work *Peskita Rabbati*, compiled by a Western writer in the ninth century, even goes so far as to say that they have the power of releasing the dead from hell (*Gehenna*). Such vows, however, had nothing to do with the collective Yizkor ceremony, and the two practices are kept sharply apart by the early authorities on the liturgy. The combination arose only at a later date in consequence of the fact that the commemoration of the year's dead, *with the accompaniment of vows,* happened to coincide, on the Day of Atonement, with the Yizkor service proper.

The custom of commemorating martyrs by reciting their names and praying for their repose was borrowed directly from the Christian Church. From the fourth century onwards it was the practice of the Church, during the celebration of the Mass, to offer a special prayer for local martyrs and deceased dignitaries, their names being read out from a diptych—that is, from two wooden boards folded together like the pages of a book. The prayer, which *followed* the recitation of the names (*oratio post nomina*), originally ran as follows: "To the souls of all these give rest, O sovereign Lord our God, in Thine holy tabernacle." Later this was developed into a longer petition which is still part of the service and which is known from its opening word as the Memento, viz.: "Remember also, O Lord, thy servants male and female who have preceded us with a token of their faith; and may they sleep in the sleep of peace. To ourselves, O Lord, and to [the souls of] all who are at rest in Christ we beseech Thee to grant a place of repose and peace, through that same Christ our Lord, amen."

The correspondence of this formula—apart, of course, from its purely Christian elements—with that of the Yizkor prayer and, in even more marked degree, with the requiem for the dead (*Hashkabah*) used in the Sephardic liturgy, is indeed remarkable. First: the names "Memento" and "Yizkor," both derived from the opening words of the prayer, are in fact identical. Second: just as the diptych lists begin with the names of generally venerated worthies of the Church, so too, as we have seen, does the Jewish *Memorbuch*. (Indeed, it is still customary in England to recite a *second* Yizkor commemorating deceased Chief Rabbis.) Third: the expressions used are virtually the same. In the Christian prayer, God is besought to grant to the souls of the deceased a place in His "holy tabernacle"; in the Jewish prayer, He is asked to grant them "abiding rest under the wings of the Divine Presence in the exalted place of the holy and pure"— where the word rendered "exalted place" really refers to a particular degree or level of heaven, and "the holy" (*kedoshim*) is the regular Hebrew term for "martyrs." In the Christian formula, God is entreated to grant that the martyrs "sleep in the sleep of peace"; while the Jewish requiem used by the Sephardim asks that the dead "may rest in peace upon their beds" and that "peace may accompany them." Finally, the Christian formula invokes on the departed the blessing of eternal repose "alongside all who

are at rest in Christ"; while the Jewish version entreats
that they abide "with all the righteous who are in Paradise."

Moreover, it is difficult to resist the suspicion that some
of the phrases used in the Jewish versions may have been
designed deliberately to provide a kind of counterpart to
Christian beliefs. Thus, for example, in the Sephardic
formula God is besought to grant the deceased a "keeping-
afar of transgression and a bringing-near of salvation,"
words which have a curiously un-Jewish ring and sound
like an adaptation of the Christian doctrine of absolution
and salvation at death. Similarly, when it is entreated
that the dead may rest in peace "along with all the righteous of His people Israel, who lie with him in the pleni-
tude of mercy and forgiveness," one can perhaps detect
a clever modification of the Christian doctrine of the communion of the saints, seeing that the word rendered "plen-
itude"—a somewhat curious expression in the Hebrew
—may also mean "communion, totality."

During recent years, the appeal of the Yizkor service
has come, especially in the United States, to exceed any
other element of the traditional liturgy in its hold, except,
perhaps, the Seder on Passover. Jews who are otherwise
remote from the synagogue or any other affiliation with
their ancestral faith make a point of closing their places
of business on "Yizkor days" and of attending divine
service. For this there are several reasons.

In the first place, the American Jew is often but one
generation removed from the more intensive Jewish at-
mosphere of an original East European home. The parents whom he commemorates in the Yizkor service represent a way of life which is frequently very vivid in his
memory and from which, under the pressure of his new

environment, he has steadily regressed. In calling them
to mind, therefore, he is performing an act not only of
filial piety but also—and perhaps more importantly—of
nostalgic recollection. Moreover, for most Jews there is,
besides, a sense of guilt toward the traditional pattern of
life which they have abandoned. In their hearts they feel
that the divorce from that life has been the result not of
intellectual conviction or of genuine enlightenment but
rather of a constant process of drifting, an easy assimila-
tion of other mores, a consequence of pressure rather than
of persuasion. No amount of participation in communal
affairs, in community centers and Zionist drives and "defense" activities and charitable appeals, can appease this
feeling or allay this unrest; albeit on a smaller, more individual scale, it is simply the age-long yearning of the
Jewish exile for the dust of Zion. It is the same instinct
that makes a Jew in a strange city halt automatically before Hebrew lettering in a shop window, even if it spells
nothing more than "kosher meat." In this sense, the Yizkor service is, indeed, an act in which the congregation
remembers its own past rather than one in which God
remembers the dead.

Secondly, the American Jew is, as a rule, far better off
economically than were his immigrant parents, who came
over steerage, toiled in sweatshops, and underwent endless poverty and privation in order to give their offspring
their "chance." The Yizkor services provide an outlet
for the feeling of pity and compassion that the average
successful American Jew must feel toward that earlier
generation which, so to speak, died in the wilderness so
that he and his children might enter and enjoy the Prom-
ised Land. Always at the back of his mind there is the
sense, by no means so keen elsewhere in the world, that
his present situation has been paid for in the blood, sweat,

and tears of an older generation; always, behind the fa-
çade of his own expensive office lurks the specter of grandfather with his peddler's pack and of father stitching
pants under a dim swinging lamp or picking cucumbers
out of a barrel of brine. The Yizkor services provide him
with an opportunity of acknowledging this debt of his
and of periodically "coming home."

In sum, what seems to give the Yizkor services their
current appeal is not so much a desire specifically to remember one's parents as a desire through such remembrance to recapture a part of one's self—to hear above
the traffic of the world the purling of an ancient rivulet.
However it may have begun, the Yizkor service is today
an intercession not for the souls of the dead but for those
of the living.

But while such all too human motivations as these are
the dominant themes of the ceremony today, from the
historical point of view Yizkor was informed by another,
rather more religious idea—namely, that the living can
"redeem" the dead or modify the judgment of God upon
them. The sages gave an interesting justification for this
belief. In the twenty-first chapter of the Book of Deuteronomy, which prescribes the procedure to be observed in
the case of homicide by an unknown hand, it is said that
if the corpse of the victim be discovered in an open field,
the elders of the nearest town are to take a heifer, break
its neck, and cast it into a neighboring stream. Then they
are to wash their hands in the flowing waters and declare:
"Our hands have not shed this blood, neither have our
eyes seen it. Forgive, O Lord, Thy people Israel whom
Thou hast redeemed." In this phrase, said the sages, the
words "Thy people Israel" refer to the living community
which performs the rite, while the words "whom Thou

hast redeemed" refer to the corpse on whose behalf it is performed, thereby indicating that the dead may indeed be redeemed before God by the actions of the living.

To our modern tastes, this may seem no more than primitive, outmoded superstition. But the sages were careful to point out that they were speaking in figurative terms and that what they really had in mind was not so much the idea of intercession before a heavenly tribunal as the "redemption" of a man's good name after his death. Those, they explained, who have wasted or abused their lives and left nothing of value behind them may yet be "redeemed" by the piety or learning which they have inculcated in their children or by the gifts and talents which they have fostered and developed in them. In this sense, they observed, a son may vindicate or acquit his father in the final judgment, for when the merits or good deeds of a son reflect the upbringing which his deceased father gave him, death is defied, and it is the father who actually deserves and performs them. That, they added, is why the commemoration of the dead must be accompanied by gifts to charity. Such gifts are not mere ransoms, for "no man can by any means redeem his brother, nor give to God a ransom for him" (Ps. 49:8); they are gifts made, albeit *through* their descendants, by the dead themselves, and this is what is really meant by the words of Scripture that "Charity delivereth from death" (Prov. 11:4).*

The Yizkor ceremony is informed also, if only subconsciously, by two other ideas which play a prominent part in the thinking of ancient peoples. The first of these is the idea that something has to be done by the living in

. . . . .

* The English Bible renders it "*Righteousness* delivereth from death," but it is well known that the Hebrew word *zedakah,* which originally meant "righteousness," came later to acquire the specific connotation of "charity, alms," and it is in this sense that the sages understood it.

order to insure the dead their repose; in all civilizations, an unquiet spirit is regarded as a menace, for it is apt to roam the earth and torment the living until it is "laid." This notion was extremely common in Semitic antiquity. Among the Babylonians, for example, the heir of the deceased was expected to discharge three principal duties toward him: he had to "pronounce his name," thus keeping it alive and in remembrance; he had to "pour out water" to slake the thirst of the departed in the netherworld; and he had to "offer food" so that, although physically withdrawn from the company of the living, the deceased might, so to speak, retain his place at the family board and thereby continue as a member of the family group. The same duties are likewise mentioned in an inscription set up by a king of Sama'l, in North Syria, in the eighth century B.C.E.; while a recently discovered Canaanite epic poem, some six hundred years earlier in date, specifies the "setting up of statues for departed ancestors" as a duty (besides that of laundering his clothes, repairing leaking roofs, and helping him home when he is in his cups!) which a dutiful son owes to his father. Similarly, too, we are told in the Second Book of Samuel (18:18) that because he had no son to keep his name in remembrance, Absalom set up a pillar to himself in his own lifetime, "and it is called the monument of Absalom unto this day."

Behind this idea lies something more than a mere fear of the poltergeist. The notion that the untended dead haunt the living in the form of spooks or specters is simply a symbolic way of saying that if the past be forgotten or ignored and the connection with it negligently dismissed, it will nevertheless rise up of its own accord and obtrude itself upon the present. Indeed, it is to be noted especially in this connection that in the thought of primitive peoples it is not merely the lack of burial that renders a spirit unquiet but the neglect of those rites which insure its continued incorporation in the family. If the past be interred and forgotten, its grave will be unquiet; only when it is fully integrated with the present will it cease to behave like a restless ghost.

The other ancient idea which comes into play in the Yizkor service is that the renewal of life which takes place at seasonal festivals involves not only the living generation but the whole continuity of which that generation is but the present and immediate phase; to use modern terms, it is not only the community of New Yorkers but also New York *per se,* as a continuous and ideal entity, that is then revived and renewed. In this wider continuity the past is also embraced. The primitive way of expressing this idea is to say that at seasonal festivals the dead return and rejoin the living. Instances of this belief are legion. In Babylon, for example, it was thought that the dead came up from the netherworld in connection with the annual wailing for Tammuz, the ousted god of fertility, in high summer, while in Egypt it was the custom at Siut to kindle lamps on the first and last days of the year in order to lead the dead back to their homes—a practice which survives in the Christian Hallowe'en on October 31, the eve of what was originally the New Year and what is now celebrated as All Saints' Day.* Similarly, the Romans prefaced their cycle of spring festivals with the Parentalia, or Feast of the Ancestral Dead; while at the present time the Zuñi of western New Mexico will not begin their summer dances until they have visited the sacred lake of the dead, just as Jews make a point of visiting cemeteries

. . . . .

* Note that November 2, the day *after* the old New Year, is observed by the church as All Souls' Day—likewise, in all probability, a transmutation of a pagan festival of the dead.

during the last month of the Hebrew year. The Siamese hold that the dead return at their New Year feast in April; while the ancient Celtic winter festival of Samhain included a feast of the dead; and among the Huzul of the Ukraine, honey is provided for deceased ancestors at Easter and Christmas, and God is besought to "let all the dead and lost return and drink with us."

To this time-honored idea the Jewish Yizkor service gives a new and arresting turn: *by the very act of remembrance,* oblivion and the limitations of the present are defied, death is made irrelevant, and a plane is established on which the dead do indeed meet and mingle with the living. The ceremony is transformed from a memorial of death into an affirmation of life.

It is in line with this more advanced conception that there is no reference in the Yizkor service to the resurrection of the dead. A sound Jewish instinct is aware that this doctrine is really superfluous, for what needs to be affirmed is not that the dead will someday arise from their graves but that even now they are indeed alive.†

From this it follows in turn that the Yizkor ceremony is in no sense a cult or worship of the dead. Indeed, it is highly doubtful whether worship of the dead really bulks so largely in any religion as former generations of students supposed, for what has been taken as evidence of this practice may be far better explained on a different basis. When, for example, food and drink are set out for the deceased, this is *not*—as usually thought—a sacrifice to them; it is simply a means of cementing their ties with

· · · · ·

† It may be suggested that it is such a *perpetual* quickening, rather than an *instantaneous* resurrection "at the end of days," that is really to be understood by the familiar Hebrew expression *tehiyyath ha-methim.* Such, at least, was the view of Maimonides and Judah Halevi, who took it to refer to the immortality of the soul.

the living by the convention of commensality—that is, of breaking bread together. Similarly, where it is held that the dead have an influence on the crops and must therefore be given the first portion of them (a custom prevalent in many parts of the world), this does not imply, as is frequently supposed, that they are regarded as active agents of vegetation, fertility, and increase; it means only that the periodic and seasonal renewal of life is considered to be something in which they too are involved and in the celebration of which they must therefore take part. What animates these ceremonies is, in a word, not an approach *to* the dead, far less a submissive attitude toward them— the essence of worship—but a feeling of wanting to be *with* them, of being part of a larger life in which death has finally no meaning and imposes no division.

Reform Judaism has given a new direction to the traditional Yizkor service, altering not only its form but also its meaning. In Reform Jewish congregations, Yizkor is recited only on the Day of Atonement, and the emphasis is placed not on the actual commemoration of the dead, or on the evocation of the past, but on the transience of human life and the vanity of earthly wishes. Although the Yizkor prayer is itself retained and the roster of the year's dead usually recited, the principal element of the service is the chanting of Scriptural verses dealing with the evanescent character of earthly existence as contrasted with the eternal mercy of God. These verses are worked into a kind of cento, beginning with Psalm 144:3-4 ("Lord, what is man that Thou regardest him, or the son of man that Thou takest account of him?"), proceeding to Psalm 90:6 ("In the morning he flourisheth and groweth up; in the evening he is cut down and withereth"), and leading up finally to the theme that since "when he dieth

he shall carry nothing away" (Ps. 49:18), his proper
duty is "to mark the perfect man and behold the upright"
in the assurance that "the Lord redeemeth the soul of
His servants, and none of them that take refuge in Him
shall be desolate" (Ps. 34:23). The recital of these verses
is followed by various responsive readings and by the
Twenty-third Psalm ("The Lord is my shepherd. . . .
Though I walk through the valley of the shadow of
death, I will fear no evil; for Thou art with me: Thy rod
and Thy staff, they comfort me"). Then, after sundry
meditations in prose and verse, expressing and exhorting
resignation to the inevitability of death, the service passes
to the actual commemoration of relatives and of the
martyrs of Israel throughout the ages. Finally, the entire
congregation recites the Kaddish in unison.

It may be questioned, however, whether this revision
of the traditional form really represents an advance in
religious thinking, for what it has done, in fact, is to shift
the emphasis from triumph to resignation. In the traditional form of the Yizkor service, the dominant note is
that there is a larger life in which there is no death; that
those who have passed from the earthly scene are nevertheless embraced in a wider communion of all generations
—the "bundle of life"; and that they survive also in their
children and their children's children. This it is that constitutes evident proof of the eternal mercy of God; this
is the true "reward in the world to come"; this it is that
finally vindicates and "redeems" the martyrs and that
compensates for the defeats and frustrations of individual
lives. The Reform version dulls these clarion notes. The
real message of the Yizkor service is not that in the midst
of life we are in death, but that in the midst of death we
are in life; that Memory is a living thing and makes alive.

VI

The Dietary Laws

CLEAN
AND UNCLEAN

*To make a distinction between the
unclean and the clean and between
the living thing that may be eaten and
the living thing that may not be eaten.*

LEVITICUS 11:47

Few Hebrew words are more familiar today, even to non-Jews, than the term *kosher,* applied to food permitted by the Law of Moses and prepared in accordance with traditional rabbinic specifications. Observance of *kashruth,* or the Dietary Laws, is and always has been one of the hallmarks of the so-called "orthodox" Jew, while even those who are lax about other institutions of the faith are often rigid and punctilious about eating only sanctioned food.

Back of the term *kosher*—which has passed, indeed, into the American vernacular—lies a long and fascinating story.

The basic dietary laws are set forth in the eleventh chapter of the Biblical Book of Leviticus and are subsequently repeated in the Book of Deuteronomy (14:3 ff.).

They consist in a list of "clean" and "unclean" animals the consumption of which is respectively permitted and forbidden. The list is arranged systematically by zoological categories, and in each case the distribution between "clean" and "unclean" rests on a broad general principle.

Only those *quadrupeds,* may be eaten that have a parted ("cloven") hoof and that regurgitate their food ("chew the cud"). Possession of the one characteristic without the other disqualifies them. Moreover, the camel, rock-badger, hare, and pig are expressly forbidden.

Only those *aquatic creatures* may be eaten that possess both fins and scales. Lobsters, crabs, oysters, shrimps and all other forms of shellfish are thus excluded; so too are eels.

Only those *flying insects* may be eaten that "have jointed legs above their feet, wherewith to leap upon the ground," *i.e.* only the so-called *saltatoria*—the locust, cricket, and grasshopper.

Reptiles and animals that "go upon their paws" are taboo as a class. These include specifically: the mouse, weasel, lizard, gecko, and chameleon. Even a dead reptile, if touched, conveys impurity.

All *carnivorous birds* and all fowl that live in swamps and marshes are automatically proscribed. This comprehends, on the one hand: the vulture, griffon, osprey, kite, falcon, raven, ostrich, nighthawk, sea-mew, owl, cormorant, and ibis; and on the other: the water hen, pelican, stork, heron, and hoopoe. The bat, which is oddly classed among fowl, is likewise regarded as unclean.

Some of the animals mentioned are, to be sure, difficult to identify, because their Hebrew names are vague and ambiguous, or generic rather than specific. It has been pointed out, for example, that the word usually rendered *eagle*—a forbidden bird—can really refer only to the *griffon-vulture,* since the former does not congregate around carrion nor have a "bald" neck, as is said elsewhere in the Bible (Job 39:30; Mic. 1:10) of the bird in question. Similarly, the term translated *kite* means properly no more than *screecher* and might thus apply to any one of several strident birds of prey. Again, what appears in the King James Version and in the Revised Version as the *chamois,* and in the ancient Greek translation as the *camelopard,* is more probably some kind of wild *mountain sheep,* for the chamois is not found outside of Central Europe, while the camelopard is confined to North Africa.

An intriguing case is that of the "unclean" bird called *dūchiphath,* which is mentioned beside the stork and heron and is therefore obviously some kind of water fowl. The ancient Greek and Latin translators rendered this as *hoopoe.* To the Syrians and the Aramaic-speaking Jews, however, the Hebrew name sounded uncommonly like the words *dū cêphâ,* "he of the rock," in their own language; they therefore pronounced the fowl in question to be the *mountain cock.* Moreover, to add to the confusion, the King James Version says it is the *lapwing,* and the Moffat Version says it is the *bittern;* while a modern German scholar has declared—literally—that "there ain't no sich animal" and that *dūchiphath* is simply a scribe's error for *kukuphath,* in turn to be identified with the Egyptian *kukupi,* the name of a bird which likewise eludes precise identification! The observant Jew who wishes to avoid eating *dūchiphath* is therefore placed in a singularly awkward predicament.

Sometimes, too, there were unexpected reasons why the ancient translators could not convey the true sense. One of the "unclean" quadrupeds, for instance, is called *arnebeth.* Now, we happen to know from other Semitic languages that this denotes the *hare,* but if we had to rely only on the ancient Greek (Septuagint) Version, we should be in something of a quandary, for the translators deliberately chose a rare and recondite word in place of the regular Greek term, *Lagōs,* for fear of offending the reigning sovereign, a descendant of Ptolemy Lagos!

In addition to specifying the "clean" and "unclean" animals, the Law of Moses also lays down the rule that the carcass of an animal which has died naturally may not be eaten (Lev. 11:39-40; Deut. 14:21); and it likewise taboos carrion (Ex. 22:30; Lev. 17:15; 22:8). The Hebrew word for the latter, viz. *ṭerephah* (literally, "ravened") came, in fact, to be used by extension to denote any "unkosher" food.

It is commonly asserted, and more commonly believed that the Hebrews were the only people ever to frame comprehensive dietary laws, and that the Jewish system of *kashruth* is therefore unique. This, however, is not the case. Such laws obtained also among the ancient Hindus. The famous Code of Manu,* for instance, likewise proscribes all carnivorous birds and all beasts that do not "part the hoof," and it likewise furnishes broad criteria for distinguishing between the clean and the unclean. Roundly forbidden are all fowl that feed by striking with their beaks, or scratching with their toes, or that dive for their food, or that live on fish. As in the Bible, certain birds and beasts are specified by name; thus the sparrow, woodpecker, parrot, and starling are expressly forbidden, while the rhinoceros, porcupine, hedgehog, iguana, and tortoise are expressly permitted, as are also all ani-

.....

* The Code has come down to us in a Buddhist verse version composed, apparently, in the first century C.E., but it claims to embody traditional laws first promulgated by the primeval hero, Manu, the "Hindu Noah." It is significant in this connection that in the Bible, basic dietary laws are likewise assigned to the age of Noah (Gen. 9:3-6), while the Sumerians attributed a code of law to the hero of the Flood.

mals that have teeth in one jaw only, with the exception of the camel.[1]

Similar prescriptions occur also in the compendia of ancient "Aryan" laws attributed to the sages Apastamba[2] and Vasishta.[3] The former says explicitly that single-hoofed animals, camels and pigs, may not be eaten; and although he too permits the rhinoceros, porcupine, iguana, and tortoise, he adds the interesting detail that, with these exceptions, all five-toed animals must be eschewed. The latter gives a list of forbidden fowl which agrees very closely with that in the Bible, viz.: the water hen, flamingo, crow, blue pigeon, osprey, crane, grey heron, vulture, falcon, ibis, cormorant, wagtail, village cock, parrot, and starling.

To the Biblical writers, as to their Hindu counterparts, the dietary laws were part and parcel of a general regimen of purity incumbent upon those who would serve as the apostles of God and as the exemplars of His rule and dispensation in the world of men. Their purpose was to ensure a cleanliness next to godliness (cf. Lev. 11:44-45; Deut. 14:2, 21), and it is significant that in each case they are followed immediately by precepts relating to purification, especially after childbirth. It is apparent, however, that the Biblical distinctions between clean and unclean do not rest in all cases upon objective criteria or correspond to actual fact. There is, for instance, no valid reason for supposing that animals which "part the hoof" and "chew the cud" are necessarily cleaner as a class than those which do not, even though some of them may be so.*

. . . . .

* On the other hand, it has been pointed out that fish which possess fins and scales usually swim in midstream or out in the sea and do not congregate, as do others, at the mouths of rivers where sewers empty and other impurity is to be found. It may be questioned, however, whether the ancient Israelites or their forerunners possessed such hygienic knowledge.

Similarly, it has been pointed out that "the uncleanness of swine is at its height when they are kept in sties and left dirty, but in Old Testament and New Testament time they seem to have been fed in herds out of doors. Compared with sheep and goats, they are fond of mud, but so are buffaloes in modern Palestine, which are not regarded with the same horror." Modern scholars therefore believe that the comprehensive dietary laws go back ultimately to a number of individual food taboos, of quite different origin and motivation, which had long been current among the Hebrew and which the priestly legislators of Israel were attempting at once to systematize and to sublimate.[4]

Such taboos are common enough in both ancient and primitive societies, and many of them in fact run parallel with the Biblical laws. Thus, to cite but a few examples, the Navahos and the Yakuts of North Turkey likewise eat no pork;[5] neither do the Guiana Indians[6] or the Laplanders.[7] The Iranians abstained from all fish that do not have fins and scales,[8] and the Romans would not offer them in sacrifice.[9] The pre-Mohammedan Arabs shared the Hebrew aversion to the chameleon (though they permitted the hare),[10] and the South Sea Islanders will not touch eel.[11]

As a rule, these prohibitions have nothing whatsoever to do with hygiene, but are inspired by quite other considerations. Often, for instance, an animal is proscribed because it is believed that by absorbing its flesh one might also absorb its less agreeable traits. Thus, the Loango of West Africa will not eat goat lest their skin likewise "scale," nor hare lest their hair moult and fall out.[12] The Sea-Dyaks of Borneo abstain from pork for fear of acquiring skin disease[13]—a notion which, incidentally, also underlies our own designation of such disease as *scrofula* from the Latin *scrofa,* "swine." The Caribs used formerly to eschew pork lest they got "pigs' eyes," and tortoises lest they became clumsy.[14] The Caroados of Brazil make a point of not eating meat from the humps of tapirs in order not to acquire the lecherousness characteristic of that animal.[15] The Kafirs of the Hindu Kush will not eat hare lest they grow timid;[16] while several South American Indian tribes (e.g. the Zaparo of the Upper Amazon) refrain from "heavy" meats as a precaution against becoming sluggish.[17] Taboos of this type, it may be added, are often imposed also upon pregnant women in order to prevent untoward animal characteristics from passing to their offspring.[18]

Animals are proscribed also on account of certain religious associations. Hindus, for example, will not eat meat because they regard all dumb beasts as earthly representatives—incarnations, as it were of the divine *baghavāti*. Egyptian priests, says Herodotus, abstained from fish because it was sacred,[19] and it has been suggested that their aversion to pork may have been inspired by the fact that the pig featured prominently in sacrifices to the god Osiris.[20] In modern times, members of the Russian Orthodox Church avoid eating dove on the grounds that in Christian belief it is the symbol of the Holy Spirit.[21]

Again there is the factor of *totemism*—that is, the belief that the corporate "soul" or life-essence of a community is bound up with a particular species of animal or plant. Peoples that profess this belief will not eat the animal or plant in question lest they thereby impair or destroy their being. Among the native tribes of Western Australia, for example, each clan adopts an animal or vegetable as its distinctive "crest" (*kabong*), and consumption of it is strictly taboo. Similarly, among the Tshi-speaking peoples of the Gold Coast, members of the Leopard Clan will not eat leopard, those of the Buffalo Clan will not eat buffalo, and so forth; while the Oraons on the plateau of Chota Nagpur in Bengal consider it an ineffable offense not only to eat but also to hunt or injure the totem animal.[22] It should be observed, however, that there is as yet no sound evidence that totemism ever existed among the Semitic peoples.*

Lastly, it has been claimed that avoidance of certain animals (*e.g.* the owl) as food was sometimes inspired by the belief that "the soul of our grandam might haply inhabit a bird"—that is, that such animals might be reincarnations of departed ancestors.[23] But here again, there is no clear evidence of the belief among the Semites.

"THE BLOOD IS THE LIFE"

Besides the catalogue of "clean" and "unclean" animals, the Law of Moses also contains other regulations concerning diet.

The most important of these is that blood must not be eaten (Lev. 3:17; 7:26; 17:10; Deut. 12:16)—a rule

. . . . .

* The classic argument has been that certain Old Testament characters bear animal names, e.g. Rachel (ewe), Shaphan (rock-badger), Huldah (weasel), etc. This, however, proves nothing, for such names could have been given out of affection or have expressed hopes that a newborn child would acquire the strength, cunning, dexterity, etc. of this or that animal. Compare, in our own day, such forms of endearment as "slick chick," "my little chickadee," "kitten," or such expressions as "wise old bird," "old warhorse," "silly goose," German *Backfisch,* French *poulette,* etc.

which was evidently of such high antiquity that it was popularly attributed to the age of Noah (Gen. 9:4). The reason given is that "the blood is the life," i.e. the seat of the vital essence, and this belief has interesting parallels in several parts of the world.

Homer, for instance, speaks alternatively of the blood and of the soul as issuing from a mortal wound (*Iliad* xvii, 86; xiv, 518); and Theophrastus assures us that the blood is the seat of the intelligence.[1] The ancient Germans, we are told, used to drink blood mixed with wine and honey in order to acquire vigor,[2] and a medieval chronicler relates of the Hungarians that they were wont to fortify themselves in battle by slashing the bodies of captives and sucking their blood.[3] Nor, indeed, are such practices confined to ancient times. Even at the present day, the wounded Somali sucks his blood in order to regain his strength;[4] while among the Caribs, a newborn boy is sprinkled with drops of his father's blood in order that his father's vitality and courage may be transmitted to him.[4a] Moreover, it is customary among huntsmen in Upper Austria to drink the blood of a newborn beast so as to gain what they call a "resolute breast."[5]

Other qualities also can be thus imbibed. It is recorded, for example, that when the Count of Montmorency was put to death at Toulouse in 1632, the troops drank his blood in order to fill their veins with his intrepid valor,[6] and the natives are said to have done likewise when the Jesuit missionary, Jean de Brebeuf, was martyred by the Iroquois in 1648.[7]

Conversely, witches and other workers of evil can be rendered innocuous if their blood be shed. There is an interesting allusion to this belief in Shakespeare's *Henry the Sixth*, where Talbot says to La Pucelle:

I'll have a bout with thee;
Devil or devil's dam, I'll conjure thee;
Blood will I draw on thee; thou are a witch.[8]

Similarly, in Cleveland's *Rebel Scot* occur the lines:

Scots are like witches; do but whet your pen,
Scratch till the blood come, they'll not hurt you then.

According to Hebrew law, it is a crime not only to eat blood but also to shed it unnecessarily. This is not merely an injunction against murder or homicide; it is directed specifically against the wanton or needless spilling of the "vital fluid," and this, too, has several arresting parallels in other civilizations. Thus, to cite but a few instances: the Warika and Damara of Africa insist that when an animal is slaughtered, as little as possible of its blood must be spilled,[9] and the same rule obtains among the Caffres.[10] In the Middle Ages, special precautions were taken to avoid shedding the blood of executed felons, and for this reason, stoning was commonly preferred as the means of carrying out capital sentences.[11]

The pre-Mohammedan Arabs gave a peculiar twist to the time-honored superstition. They too held fast to the belief that the qualities and properties of a man were latent in his blood, but they too, like the Hebrews, were forbidden to drink it. They therefore maintained that in certain cases the blood could, as it were, avenge itself if the law were breached. The blood of kings and nobles, they asserted, could requite those who drank it by causing hydrophobia and demoniacal possession![12]

Fat, too, may not be eaten (Lev. 7:22). The Hebrew word so translated, however, refers specifically to *internal fat* or *suet*—that is, to the fat of the omentum and of the organs in or near it, not to the fatty parts of an animal in general.

The reason for this prohibition, though it is not stated explicitly, is that in ancient times such fat was popularly regarded, like the blood, as the seat of the vital or sentient principle. In Psalm 17:10, for example, the expression *They have shut tight their midriff* is used to describe insensitive people; * while in Arabic, the same term is a virtual synonym for "heart, feeling."

The notion is by no means exclusively Semitic. It would appear that the Greeks likewise entertained the idea that the center of vitality lay in the diaphragm; † [13] while even today it is held by the aborigines of Australia that the "soul" reposes in the kidneys.[14] Indeed, so firmly entrenched is this idea in the mentality of primitive peoples that the Basutos seek to impart "new life" to a sick person by hanging around his neck the intestinal covering of a slaughtered animal! [15]

. . . . .

* The King James' Version and the Revised Version render inaccurately *They are inclosed in their own fat;* while the American Revised Standard Version contents itself with the paraphrase, *They close their hearts to pity.* Brady and Tate, misled by the King James' Version, translate: *O'ergrown with luxury, inclos'd in their own fat they lie!*

† The belief has an obvious physiological basis and is but the primitive counterpart of what we express today by such phrases as "having butterflies in the stomach," *i.e.* an apprehension of the fact that strong emotion are felt "in the belly."

"THE SINEW
THAT SHRINKS"

It is forbidden also to eat the so-called ischiatic nerve of an animal. This prohibition, however, is not contained in the formal dietary laws, nor is it even said to have been enjoined by Moses. It is represented rather as a time-honored institution dating back to remote antiquity, and it is explained in the Book of Genesis (32:25 ff.) by reference to an incident in Jacob's struggle with the "angel" *
at the Ford of Jabbok.

And when he [i.e. the angel] saw, that
he prevailed not . . . [we read] . . . he touched
the hollow of his thigh; and the hollow of
Jacob's thigh was strained, as he wrestled
with him . . . and he halted upon his thigh.
Therefore the children of Israel eat not the
sinew of the hip [literally, the ischiatic nerve]
which is upon the hollow of the thigh unto
this day.

This, of course, is simply a "just-so-story"—what scholars call an aetiological legend. The real reason for the ban was that the nerve in question connects with the thigh and the thigh was thought to be the seat of procreation and

. . . . .

* To speak of Jacob's adversary as an angel is simply a concession to common usage. The Bible calls him "a *man*" (Gen. 32:25). Actually, he was a demon; that is why, like all demons, he had to flee at break of day (*ibid.*, 27).

hence another of the vital centers of being. In several of the Semitic languages, the word for "thigh" is used by metonymy to denote "clan" or "progeny," and similar properties are attributed to it in the popular lore of the ancient Greeks on the one hand [1] and of the Chotaws and Cherokees on the other.[2]

It should be mentioned, however, that an alternative explanation of the Hebrew custom has also been advanced. Limping due to an affection of the ischiatic nerve is said to have been a not uncommon complaint among the early Arabs, and this fact has inspired the suggestion that the Israelites may have avoided eating the corresponding part of an animal's body out of a primitive fear that the affliction might be transmitted to them by magical attraction.[3] In support of this view it has been pointed out that the Cherokees refrain from eating the hamstrings of an animal because, when severed, they draw up into the flesh, and they are frightened lest the eater of them be thereby afflicted with a like condition and go lame.[4] Moreover, according to some scholars, the Hebrew term for "ischiatic nerve" means properly *shrinking sinew* * and therefore bespeaks a similar belief.

MEAT AND MILK

Yet a further provision of the dietary laws is that *meat and milk must not be eaten together*. Among observant Jews, a six-hour interval is required between the consumption of the one and of the other, and separate cooking

· · · · ·

* It is so translated in the ancient Greek (Septuagint) and Latin (Vulgate) Versions.

utensils, china and crockery must be used for each. If a "milk" plate accidentally come into contact with a "meat" plate, or vice versa, it must be broken, and if this happen in the case of a steel object (e.g. a knife, fork or spoon), the latter must be scalded, passed through fire, or plunged into the earth for a specified time.

The provision is an elaboration of the Biblical commandment: *Thou shalt not seethe a kid in its mother's milk.* The commandment occurs thrice in the Law of Moses, *viz.* in Exodus 23:19; 34:16 and in Deuteronomy 14:21. It is doubtful, however, whether it was intended originally to bear the comprehensive significance which has come to be attached to it. In both passages of the Book of Exodus, it is conjoined with laws governing seasonal offerings and the presentation of first fruits. At first blush, this might appear a *non sequitur.* The fact is, however, that in a Canaanite document of the fourteenth century B.C.E. evidently designed for a public—and, in all probability, a seasonal—rite there is a rubric which specifically enjoins that at a certain point in the proceedings, "young men are to seethe a kid in milk," [1] and it so happens that among the Arabs this is, even at the present day, a favorite method of cooking meat! [2] It would seem, therefore, that the Biblical law referred more immediately to this common seasonal ceremony, and that its real purpose was not so much to forbid the practice *per se* as simply to impose the merciful provision that the animal should not be cooked in the milk of its own dam. It would have been, in fact, of the same order as the commandment in Leviticus 22:28 which prohibits the sacrificial slaughter of a calf or a sheep and of its dam on the same day. The general principle had, of course, a wider application and was by no means confined to the case of seasonal offerings, and in the Book of Deuteronomy (14:21) it is this wider application that is stressed, the regulation being there included among formal dietary laws.

Here, too, alternative interpretations have been proposed. A medieval Karaite writer declares that the law was directed originally against an ancient practice of the pagans whereby "when they had gathered all the crops, they used to boil a kid in its mother's milk and then, as a magical rite, sprinkle the milk over trees, fields, gardens and orchards in order to render them more fruitful in the coming year." [3] There is, however, no evidence of this practice among the ancient Semites, and it is not improbable that our author was merely retrojecting into the remote past a usage current in his own day, for charms of the type which he describes are indeed attested in medieval European and Oriental folklore. [4]

Again, the late Sir James Frazer has suggested that the taboo was based originally on the widespread notion that the boiling of milk affects adversely the animal which produces it. [5] The practice would therefore have been expressly forbidden at the time of year when it was deemed expedient to do everything possible in order magically to ensure the productivity of the milch beasts during the ensuing twelve months. This, however, loses sight of the crucial point that what was in fact forbidden was not any boiling of an animal in milk but specifically the boiling of it in the milk of its own dam.

Many modern Western Jews regard the dietary laws as obsolete. Food, they point out, is now generally prepared, packaged, and sold under far more sanitary conditions than in the past; there are official rules and regulations governing its distribution, and the availability of refrigeration in most homes reduces still further the risk of impurity. Consequently, so they maintain, it is possible to fulfill the basic requirements of cleanliness without recourse to outmoded provisions.

Such an attitude, however, overlooks entirely the essential genius of Jewish traditional institutions which consists in the deliberate combination of archaic forms with progressive interpretations for the express purpose of illustrating and dramatizing the process of a Divinely directed evolution and the dynamic character of an eternal law.

VII

The Shield of David

THE SHIELD
OF DAVID

The Shield of David (Hebrew, *Magen David*)*—that
is, the hexagram formed by two inverted triangles—is today the universally recognized symbol of Judaism. It is
frequently emblazoned on the walls and windows of synagogues or on ritual implements and vessels. It is the central element of the Israeli flag. It surmounts the graves of
fallen Jewish soldiers, and is the official badge of the
Jewish military chaplain. In the Holy Land, the Red
Shield of David is the equivalent of the Red Cross elsewhere. This widespread use of the symbol is, however, of
comparatively recent date. Back of it lies a long and com-
plicated history, woven of many strands.

In order to unravel that history, the first thing to be

. . . . .

* Often called wrongly the *Star* of David.

observed is that the symbol itself is far older than its
name; the hexagram had been in use in both Jewish and
non-Jewish circles for several centuries before it was
styled the Shield of David.

The earliest known occurrence of it appears to be on a
scaraboid agate seal from Palestine dated by most authorities to the seventh century B.C. It there occurs after the
name of the owner, a certain Joshua son of Asayahu, but
its significance is obscure.[1] In all probability, it represents
a current magical symbol, for seals were often employed
as amulets and were therefore embellished with such
"signs of power." Moreover, the six-pointed star is indeed
found again in association with a portrait of the goddess
Astarte on a plaque discovered at Tel es-Safi (the Biblical Libnah),[2] and it figures also on several ancient Mesopotamian seals.[3] Whether, however, it has any connection
in such cases with the formal hexagram, or whether it was
there merely a stylized representation of a star, is still in
doubt.

In the Graeco-Roman period, the hexagram seems to
emerge more clearly as a Jewish symbol. It is a not infre-
quent adornment of the early synagogues of Galilee,[4] and
it is found along with the pentagram on the jamb of a
door at Marissa.[5] In the third century C.E., it appears on
a tombstone at Tarentum, in Southern Italy.[6]

What meaning the design may have held at this early
period we do not know. It has been suggested that, whatever its original significance may have been, to the Jews it
served as a symbol of the coming Messiah and bore direct
reference to the prophecy of Balaam (Num. 24:17),
There steppeth a star out of Jacob—words which were
indeed interpreted in Jewish tradition as alluding to the
advent of the Redeemer. This suggestion, however, is as
yet unproved.

The hexagram next comes into prominence in the Middle Ages, where it was widely employed, along with the inverted pentacle, as an emblem of magic. In Germany, it received the intriguing name of Drydenfuss, and was regarded as representing the footprint of a *trud* or *incubus*—a special kind of demon. It could serve alike to conjure demons or to keep them at bay,[7] and it is mentioned frequently in the magical charms attributed to the celebrated Doctor Faustus.[8] Sometimes its efficacy was further enhanced by its being combined with the sign of the Cross![9]

Nor, indeed, did such ideas die out with the passing of the Dark Ages. A curious tract published at Jena in 1716 concerning the Faustlike death of a young student of medicine and his companions on the previous Christmas Eve, relates that among his effects were found various magical objects including a small lead seal containing on one side two hexagrams divided by the word *Adonai* (Lord), and on the other, an indecipherable inscription with the motto, *Christus est veritas et vita* ("Christ is the Truth and the Life").[10] Moreover, even in modern times, a common German charm against dangers and hazards was to carry upon the person a small hexagonal amulet covered with the skin of a lamb that had been torn to pieces by lions or bears.[11] This was known specifically as a "David's shield," and the practice was justified by reference to the words of I Samuel (17:34), *Thy servant* (i.e. David) *smote both the lion and the bear, and this uncircumcised Philistine* (i.e. Goliath) *shall be as one of them, seeing he hath defied the armies of the living God!*

Just why the hexagram came to be used as a magical symbol is again a problem. Perhaps the most plausible answer yet advanced is that the design originated as a combination of the familiar alchemical symbols, $\triangle = $ *fire*, and

∇ = *water.* In Hebrew, these elements are called respectively *esh* and *mayim,* and it was fancifully supposed that together they composed the word *shamayim,* "heaven," a recognized paraphrase for God. On this hypothesis, the hexagram, when used in magic, was a *graphic* substitute for the Ineffable Name, just as Adonai (Lord) was a *verbal* one. In support of this view, it is pointed out that even in Christian magical writings, each of the four outer triangles of the hexagram is usually labeled with one of the Hebrew letters of the Tetragrammaton, viz. *YHWH* (Jehovah).* It is observed also that in alchemical symbolism these four triangles represent the four cardinal points, and therefore convey the notion of the universality and omnipresence of God.[12]

Not until the twelfth century do we hear of the hexagram as the Shield of David. The earliest instance of this name thus far discovered occurs in the Hebrew work, *Eshkol Hakofer,* an exposition of Karaite beliefs and practices by Judah Hadassi, and there it is said that the sign often precedes the writing of the names of angels— a clear reference to the use of it in magical spells.* [13]

Nobody knows for certain how and why this peculiar name came to be adopted. The most probable conjecture would seem to be that it was originally designed as a complement to the familiar *Seal of Solomon* which was a popular designation of the pentagram. In a legend recorded in the Koran, it is said that the seal in question

. . . . .

* Sometimes the alternative legend *AGLA* is employed, representing the initials of the Hebrew words, *Attah Gibbor Le'olam Adonai,* "Thou art mighty for ever, O Lord"—the beginning of the Second Blessing in the famous Eighteen Benedictions (*Shemoneh 'Esreh*) which form a prominent element of every Jewish service of prayer.

* Analogous would be the use of the cross before the names of angels and spirits in the "Faust-books" and similar collections of charms.

came down from heaven engraven with the all-powerful name of God. It was partly of brass, partly of iron. With the brass part, Solomon sealed his orders to the good spirits; with the iron, to the bad.† [14] This seal is mentioned frequently in ancient magical texts as an instrument of power efficacious in controlling or banning the princes of darkness. Indeed, in an early document of approximately the eighth century C.E., a demon is exorcized *by the seventy seals of Solomon and by the seals of the angels of the Most High*.[15] So commonplace, indeed, was this legend that the plant which is called botanically *Convollaria multiflora polygonata* (and which is also styled Lady's Seal) was known popularly as Solomon's Seal, "because," says the herbalist Gerarde, "it is marked in such a manner as to suggest Hebrew characters." [16]

Possibly we can go a step further, for the fact is that it was common practice in antiquity to name particularly powerful charms after Biblical or other heroes. A famous Hebrew book of spells, for instance, was entitled *The Key of Solomon*,[17] and another went under the name of *The Sword of Moses*.[18] Among the Greeks, a similar compilation (now lost) bore the title, *Sword of Dardanos*, in reference to a celebrated wizard,[19] and in magical incantations which are still current among the Mandeans of Iraq and Iran, we hear, in the same way, of the powerful "Lance" of a worthy named Qatros. On this analogy, the "Shield of David" would have seemed a peculiarly appropriate name for a magical sign.*

. . . . .

† On the use of iron to forfend demons, see above, pp. 9 ff.

* It is probably a mere accident that the epithet "Shield of David" is applied to God in one of the blessings which follow the Lesson from the Prophets in the service of the synagogue.

EPILOGUE

There is an old tradition that the word of God which issued from Mount Sinai was spoken simultaneously in all the languages of the earth. Jewish folkways are a living expression of the same basic truth—an inspired and consistent attempt to articulate the essential message of the Torah in all the idioms of men.

Just as their forefathers brought to the building of the Tabernacle something of all their worldly goods—their "blue and purple and scarlet and fine linen"—so, throughout their later generations, the Jews have drawn readily upon the spiritual and cultural resources of their environment to furnish a visible habitation of God in the wilderness of men.

In so doing, they have rolled away the reproach that

commonly attaches to the word "superstition." To the Jew, that which "stands over" from the past stands over not in evidence of decay but in promise of regeneration. A superstition, he affirms, is not merely a cultural "has-been"; it is also a cultural "maybe." Out of ruin and rubble, a new Temple may be upreared, and the latter glory of God's house may indeed be greater than the former. Judaism insists that a holy thing which has lost its appeal need not degenerate into the profane, as is all too often the case, but that the profane can always be transformed into the holy. For Judaism knows that the process of creation is continuous and that the breath of God may be breathed at all times into the dust of the earth and turn it into a living soul. And Judaism would agree with Saint Paul that, as often as not, "God hath chosen the foolish things of the world to confound the wise."

REFERENCES
AND NOTES

I. BLESSED EVENT

Be fruitful and multiply

1. Talmud, Kiddushin 30ᵇ.
2. R. Patai, *Talpioth* V (1953), 248, n. 38.
3. C. Brewster Randolph, "The Mandragora of the Ancients in Folklore and Medicine," *Proceedings of the American Association of Arts and Sciences*, No. 12 (1905), pp. 1 ff.; Josephus, *Bellum Judaicum*, vii, 6.3, says it expels demons.
4. A. Lang, *Custom and Myth* (1885), pp. 143-55.
5. Cf. G. Lammert, *Volksmedizin und medizin. Aberglaube in Bayern* (1869), p. 150.
6. Hesychius, s.v.
7. Pseudo—Albertus Magnus, *Buch der Versammlung* (1508).
8. *Standard Dictionary of Folklore* (1950), p. 1156.
9. A. de Gubernatis, *La mythologie des plantes* (1878-82), ii, pp. 367-69; J. G. Frazer, *The Fasti of Ovid* (1925), ii, pp. 158 ff.
10. ibidem.
11. *HN*, xxviii, 248.
12. J. Jüngling, *Die Tiere in d. deutsch. Volksmedizin* (1900), p. 54; M. Höfler, *Die volksmedizinische Organotherapie* (n.d.), p. 196.
13. A. Keller, *Antike Tierwelt* (1855), i, p. 216.
14. ibidem.

15. Patai, *op. cit.*, 243.

16. E. Brauer, *Ethnologie der jemenischen Juden* (1934), p. 194.

17. A. Reubeni, *Zion* (1940), p. 102.

18. Abraham ha-Rophê, *Shilṭe ha-Gibborim* (1612), p. 42a.

19. M. Gaster, *The Book of Prayer . . . according to the Custom of the Spanish and Portuguese Jews,* iii (1904), pp. 174 f.

20. Aelian, *De nat. animal.,* i, p. 35; Philostratus, *De vita Apoll.,* iii, p. 55; Levret, *Essai sur les accouchements* (1766), p. 52; Wm. Jones, *Credulities Past and Present* (1880), p. 388; J. Mantegazza, *Arch. per l'antropol.* XXVII (1897), p. 483, No. 15; C. J. S. Thompson, *The Hand of Destiny* (1932), p. 249; S. Seligmann, *Der böse Blick* (1910), pp. 215-17; W. B. McDaniel, *Birth and Infancy in Ancient Rome and Modern Italy* (1948), pp. 12-13; *Notes and Queries,* Sixth Series, iii (1880), pp. 327, 509; iv (1881), p. 297.

21. Plutarch, V, 95 Didot; Pliny, *HN,* xxx, 14; xxxvi, 39; Dioscorides, v, 161.

22. B. Meissner, *Babylonien und Assyrien,* i (1920), p. 390; *Archiv f. Gesch. Medizins* xiii, pp. 17 f., 26.

23. *Handwörterbuch deutsch. Abergl.,* v, pp. 133 f.; McDaniel, *loc. cit.;* Canziani, *Folk-Lore* xxxix (1928), p. 211.

24. Bede, *Historia eccles. gentis Angl.,* ed. Smith (1722), p. 740.

25. T. Nicols, *Arcula Gemmea* (1662), p. 184.

The Pangs of Eve

On the subject in general, see: M. Zobel, "Bräuche nach der Geburt eines Kindes," *Almanach des Schocken Verlags* (1939), pp. 98-104; Regina Lilienthal, "Das Kind bei den Juden," *Mitteilungen zur jüd. Volkskunde* 25-26 (1908), pp. 1-24, 41-53.

1. Sprenger, *Das Leben und die Lehre Mohammeds* (1861-65), i, p. 142; Perles, *Monatsschrift f. Ges. u. Wiss. Judentums* XIX, p. 428.

2. Seligmann. *Böse Blick,* ii, p. 8.

3. W. Crooke, *The Tribes and Castes of the North-Western Provinces and Oudh* (1896), iii, p. 307.

4. A. C. Kruit, *Bijdragen tot de Taal-Land an Völkerkunde von Nederlandsch Indie* (1901), pp. 157 ff.

5. E. W. Lane, *Arabian Society in the Middle Ages* (1883), p. 36.

6. J. A. Montgomery, *Aramaic Incantation Texts from Nippur* (1913), No. 2.

7. E. Clodd, *Tom Tit Tot* (1898), p. 35.

8. M. Cox, *Introduction to Folk-Lore* (1897), pp. 8, 16.

On the use of iron against demons, see further: I. Scheftelowitz, *Altpalästinensischer Bauernglaube* (1925), pp. 66 f.; E. Riess, Pauly-Wissowa, i, pp. 59 ff.; T. Höpfner, *Griech.-aeg. Offenbarungszauber* i (1921), §596; E. Clodd, *Tom Tit Tot* (1898), pp. 33-36; A. Abt, *Apologie des Apuleius* (1908), p. 86; W. Kroll, *Antiker Aberglaube* (1897), pp. 7 f.; J. G. Frazer, *Taboo and Perils of the Soul* (1911), p. 232; E. B. Tylor, *Primitive*

Culture, i (1897), p. 140; I. Goldziher, *Archiv für Religionswissenschaft*
X, pp. 41 ff. [Arabic]; *Notes and Queries*, First Series, iii (1861), p. 56
[Lancashire, England].

9. F. Liebrecht, *Zur Volkskunde* (1879), p. 321.
10. T. Keightley, *Fairy Mythology* (1850), p. 488.
11. Odyssey, xi, 48 (see Scholiast *in loc.*).
12. Keightley, *op. cit.*, p. 413.
13. L. Löw, *Die Lebensalter in der jüdischen Literatur* (1875), p. 77.
14. Keightley, *op. cit.*, p. 148.
15. Talmud Jer., Ket. i, 25a; Talmud Bab., Sanh. 32ᵇ.
16. Tertullian, *Adv. nat.*, ii, p. 11. For modern survivals in Greece, see
H. Wachsmuth, *Das alte Griechenland im neuen* (1864), p. 79.
17. Shayast la-Shayast, x, 4; xii, 11 = *Sacred Books of the East*, v, pp.
315, 312.
18. Hillebrandt, ERE, ii, 650ᵇ.
19. Liebrecht, *op. cit.*, p. 31.
On candles at childbirth, see further: E. Samter, *Geburt, Hochzeit und
Tod* (1911), pp. 67 ff.; H. Usener, *Kleine Schriften* (1913), iv, pp. 87, 91;
H. Ploss, D. *Weib* (1913), ii, p. 309 [Russia]; id., *Das Kind* (1911-12), i,
pp. 95 ff.
20. Crawley, *Mystic Rose*, ii, p. 103.
21. N. B. Dennys, *The Folklore of China* (1876), p. 13.
22. M. Granfland, *De Minahassa* (1869), i, p. 326.
23. Sartori, *op. cit.*, i, p. 31; Samter, *op. cit.*, pp. 90 ff., 110; Liebrecht,
op. cit., p. 360.
24. Tosefta, Shabbat vii, 1; Yalqut, §529; Talmud Bab., Shabbat 66ᵇ;
Scheftelowitz, *Zeitschrift f. alttestamentliche Wissenschaft* xli (1921), pp.
117 ff.; id., *Schlingen- und Netzmotif* (1912), pp. 32 ff.
25. *Enuma elish*, iv, 61.
26. G. Parrinder, *La religion en Afrique centrale* (1950), p. 134.
27. E. Crawley, *The Mystic Rose*, Second ed., (1927), i, p. 333.
28. *Globus* lxxxix, p. 60.
29. *Folk-Lore* ix (1898), p. 79.
30. Talmud Bab., Shabbat 129ᵇ.
31. Wiesner, *Scholien*, ii, p. 248.
32. *De sanitate tenenda*, i, p. 7.
33. Samter, *op. cit.*, p. 152, n. 6.
34. W. H. Rivers, *The Todas* (1906), pp. 263 ff.
35. E. W. Lane, *Arabian Society in the Middle Ages* (1883), p. 188.
36. A. Wuttke, *Deutscher Volksaberglaube*, Second ed. (1900), p. 91;
Mogk, ERE, ii, 633ᵃ; J. Grimm, *Deutsche Mythologie*, Second ed. (1844),
ii, p. 999.
37. *Globus*, LXXXIX, p. 582.
38. C. Bock, *Temples and Elephants* (1884), p. 260.
39. *Notes and Queries*, Sixth series, iii (1881), pp. 73 f.
40. *Manchester Guardian Weekly*, March 22, 1947.
41. R. B. Beck, *Honey and Health* (1938); W. Roscher, *Nektar und Am-
brosia* (1883); Robert-Toknow, *De apium mellisque apud veteres signifi-*

catione symbolica et mythologica (1893); T. H. Gaster, *Thespis* (1950), pp. 201, 364.

42. J. Wellhausen, *Skizzen* (1884), iii, p. 154; id., *Reste des arabischen Heidentums* (1887), p. 173; W. Robertson Smith, *Journal of Philology* XIV, p. 185; T. Noeldeke, *Zeitschrift d. Deutsch. morgenländische Gesellschaft* XLIX, p. 514; Lane, *Lexicon*, 659a; Dozy, *Supplement*, ii, p. 332; Mishkat, ii, p. 315.

43. Beck, *op. cit.*, pp. 222 f.

44. *Argonautica*, iv, 1136.

45. Beck, *loc. cit.*

46. *ibidem.*

47. Translated in *Ancient Near Eastern Texts* . . . , ed. Pritchard (1950), p. 328.

48. Piṯ̄ê Teshûbah on Shulḥan 'Aruch, Yoreh De'ah, 179.9; Maimonides, *Hilchoth "Akum,"* xi, 12.

49. M. Cox, *Introduction to Folklore*, p. 231.

50. G. Bassi, *Archivo*, 14 (1895), p. 219.

A Time to be Born

1. Cf. Talmud Bab., *Shabbat* 156ª; A. Cohen, *Everyman's Talmud* (1949), p. 281.

The Wiles of Lilith

1. M. Gaster, "Two Thousand Years of the Child Stealing Witch," *Folk-Lore* 1900: 129-62; T. H. Gaster, "A Canaanite Magical Text," *Orientalia* XI (1942), pp. 41-79; I. Zoller, "Lilith," *Filologische Schriften*, II (1929), pp. 121-42; J. Montgomery, "The Lilith Legend," *The Museum Journal* XLI, pp. 62-65 [popular].

ASSYRO-BABYLONIAN PARALLELS: C. Frank, *Bab. Beschwörungsreliefs* (1900); id., *Lamashtu, Pazuzu und andre Dämonen*, MVAorG 14/2 (1941); D. Myhrman, *Labartu [Lamashtu] -Texte* (1901); F. Thureau-Dangin, "Rituels et amulettes contre Labartu [Lamashtu]," *Revue d'assyriologie* XVIII (1921), pp. 161-98.

ARABIC PARALLEL: H. A. Winkler, *Salomo und die Karina* (1931).

EUROPEAN PARALLELS: G. Kittredge, *Witchcraft in Old and New England* (1929), pp. 224 f.; 532, nn. 104-108; Hoffmann-Krayer, *Zeitschrift für Volkskunde* 25, p. 121, n. 3; A. H. Krappe, *Balor with the Evil Eye* (1927), pp. 87 ff.

2. *Ancient Near Eastern Texts* . . . , ed. Pritchard (1950), p. 328.

3. J. Brand, *Observations on the Popular Antiquities of Great Britain*, ed. H. Ellis (1849), ii, p. 68 ff.

4. Frank, *Beschwörungsreliefs*, p. 78.

5. S. G. Oliphant, *Transactions Amer. Philos. Assoc.* XLIV (1913), pp. 127 ff.; Kirby Smith on Tibullus I, v. 52; Oppenheim, *Wiener Studien*

XXX (1908), pp. 158 ff. For survival in modern Greece, cf. W. Klinger, *Philologus* LXVI (1907), pp. 344 f. Analogous is the Scottish *whaap,* "curlew" (or "bittern"?) as a name for the hobgoblin; Tennant, *Notes and Queries* (1865), p. 334.

6. C. Doughty, *Travels in Arabia Deserta* (1888), i, p. 53.

7. *Handwörterbuch d. deutsch. Abergl.*, viii, p. 356.

8. C. H. Gordon, *The Living Past* (1941), pp. 203, 213 f. It was customary in antiquity to shoot arrows over the roof in order to protect pregnant women: Pliny, *HN*, xxviii, 33; E. Riess, *Rhein. Mus.* II' (1894), pp. 188 f.; O. Gruppe, *Griech. Mythologie* (1906), p. 859, n.1.

9. T. H. Gaster, *Orientalia* XI (1942), pp. 41-79.

10. Aristophanes, *Thesmoph.*, 417; Plato, *Phaedo,* 77E. The name Mormo was commonly used by English nurses to scare children: *Notes and Queries,* Fifth Series, xi (1879), p. 427; xii (1879), p. 18.

11. Bergerac, *Satyrical Characters and Handsome Descriptions in Letters translated out of the French by a Person of Honour* (1658), p. 45.

11a. In Aramaic charms, she is often called "the Strangleress," and so too among the ancient Hittites: T. H. Gaster, *Studi e Materiali di Storia delle Religioni* 25 (1951-52), pp. 154-57. In modern Greece, when a child dies suddenly, it is said, "the Lamia has strangled it": W. Hyde, *Greek Religion and its Survivals* (1923), p. 177.

12. Diodorus, xx, p. 41; Photius, *Lexicon,* s.v. ΛΑΜΙΑ. See also S. G. Oliphant, *Trans. Amer. Philosoph. Assoc.*, XLIV (1913), pp. 127 ff.

13. Sappho, fragment 94 Wharton. C. Frank, *Zeitschrift für Assyriologie,* XXIV (1910), pp. 161-65, would trace the name to the Assyro-Babylonian *gallu,* a kind of demon. More, probably, however, it is connected with the term *ghoul,* which derives from an Arabic word meaning "vampire, bloodsucker." A curious survival of this name may perhaps be recognized in the following passage of the famous English booklet, *Robin Goodfellow: his mad pranks and merry jests* (1628): "When mortals keep their beds, I walk abroad, and for my pranks am called by the name of Gull. I with a feigned voice do often deceive many men, to their great amazement. Many times I get on men and women, and so lie on their stomachs, that I cause them great pain, for which they call me by the name of Hag or Nightmare. 'Tis I that do steal children, and in the place of them leave changelings." Here, of course, the ancient name has been fancifully connected with the English *gull,* i.e. cheat.

14. *Alphabetum Siracidis,* B = Eisenstein, *Oṣar Midrashim* (1915), i, pp. 46-47.

15. E. Littmann, "The Princeton Ethiopic Magic Scroll," *Princeton Univ. Bulletin,* 15/i (1903), pp. 31-42; C. Fries, *Actes du Huitième Congrès Intern. des Orientalistes,* Sect. i B (1893), pp. 53-70, boldly identifies Werzeliya with Saint Ursula and Sisneyos with Socinius.

See also: R. Basset, *Les apocryphes éthiopiens,* iv (1894). An Arabic version is also known: A. Mai, *Script. Vet. Nova Collectio* (Rome, 1821), iv, p. 314. For an excellent account of the various versions, see Worrel, ERE, iii, p. 399-40.

16. (Mrs.) J. S. Wingate, *Folk-Lore* XLI (1930), pp. 169 ff.

17. L. Allatius, *De templis Graecorum recentioribus* (1645), pp. 126 ff.

18. M. Gaster, *Folk-Lore* XI (1900), pp. 129 ff.

19. Thos. Blundevill, *The Four Chiefest Offices belonging to Horseman-ship,* quoted in *Notes and Queries,* Sixth Series, i (1880), p. 54. The same charm is found in Phineas Fletcher's *Monsieur Thomas,* Act IV, Scene 6, except that the last line there reads, "She must not stir from him (Qy. "him disturb"?) that night." It is quoted also in Reginald Scot's *Discovery of Witchcraft* (1584). Cf. T. F. Thistleton-Dyer, *The Folk-Lore of Shake-speare* (1883), pp. 266 f.

20. Act III, Scene iv.

21. Hesiod, *Theogony,* p. 267.

22. R. Reizenstein, *Poimandres* (1904), pp. 295 ff.; C. von Lemm, *Koptische Miscellen* (1907).

23. Brand-Ellis, ii, pp. 76 f.

24. There is an interesting parallel to this among the Huichol of Mexico. "The shamans," we are told, "think themselves able to catch a certain class of deities in votive bowls, and when thus caught, the gods, they believe, assume the shape of small stones"; C. Lumholz, *Unknown Mexico* (1902), ii, pp. 196 f.

25. J. A. Montgomery, *Aramaic Incantation Texts from Nippur* (1913), Nos. 8 and 17. (Our text is composite.)

Days of Peril

1. E. Rohde, *Psyche* (1897), p. 360, n.l. Cf. Censorinus, *De die natali,* ii 17.

2. H. Wachsmuth, *Das alte Griechenland im neuen* (1864), pp. 73 ff.

3. Stanley Lane-Pool, ERE, ii, 660[a].

4. J. Modi, ERE, ii, 660[a].

5. D. C. Graham, "Customs of the Chi'ang," *Journal of the West China Border Research Society* XIV (1941), p. 83.

6. G. Maspero. *Contes populaires de l'Égypte ancienne* (1882), pp. 36 ff.

7. P. Sartori, *Sitte und Brauch,* i (1910), p. 29.

8. Vita Adami, chap. ix; Löw, *Lebensalter,* pp. 78 ff.

9. Talmud Bab., Niddah 31[b]; Nahmanides on Lev. 12: 1-5.

10. *Notes and Queries,* Third Series, viii (1865), p. 500; ix (1866), pp. 49 f.

11. It was compiled for English Jews by Chief Rabbi Nathan Marcus Adler (1803-90). The text will be found in S. Singer's *Authorized Daily Prayerbook.*

Names and Nicknames

On the subject in general, see J. Z. Lauterbach, "The Naming of Chil-dren in Jewish Folklore, Ritual and Practise," *Yearbook of the Central Conference of American Rabbis* XLII (1932), pp. 316-60.

1. *e.g.* in the case of Jacob's children (Gen. 29-30).

2. On the *tenth* day: Euripides, *Electra* 1126; Aristophanes, *Birds* 494, 922 f.; on the *seventh* day: Aristotle, *Hist. animal.*, vii, p. 12.

3. Plutarch, *Quaest. rom.*, p. 102.

4. J. Forbes, *Eleven Years in Ceylon* (1840), i, p. 326.

5. M. Parkyns, *Life in Abyssinia* (1853), i, p. 301. Cf. Crawley, *The Mystic Rose*, Second ed. (1927), ii, p. 196.

6. E. P. Im Thurm, *Among the Indians of Guiana* (1883), p. 220.

7. E. Clodd, *Tom Tit Tot* (1898), p. 91 [from W. Sussex, England].

8. A. Bastian, *Siam*, p. 219, quoted in Andree, *op. cit.*, (1879), i, p. 177; *Zeitschrift d. Gesell. für Erdkunde zu Berlin* I (1866), p. 386.

9. Th. Bent quoted in Clodd, *op. cit.*, p. 94.

10. G. B. Gray, *Studies in Hebrew Proper Names* (1896), p. 2 ff. Significant in this connection is the incident related in Luke 1: 59.

11. *Folk-Lore Journal* VI (1888), p. 49.

12. Sartori, *op. cit.*, i, p. 40.

13. *Notes and Queries*, Fourth Series, xi (1873), p. 341.

14. *Denham Tracts*, ii, p. 49.

15. *e.g.* Assyro-Babylonian *shumu*.

16. A. Landau, "Hollekreisch," *Zeitschrift d. Vereins für Volkskunde* IX (1899), pp. 72-77; M. Güdemann, *Geschichte d. Erziehungwesens . . . d. abendländischen Juden* (1880-88), iii, pp. 104-08.

17. A. Dieterich, *Mutter Erde* (1905), pp. 7 ff.; E. Goldmann, "Cartam levare," *Mitt. d. Instituts für österreich. Geschichtsforschung* XXXV (1914), pp. 1 ff. [radical critique of Dieterich]; E. Samter, *Geburt, Hochzeit und Tod* (1912), pp. 2 ff.; B. Struck, "Niederlegen und Aufheben der Kinder von der Erde," *Archiv für Religionswissenschaft* X (1907), p. 158; J. Grimm, *Deutsche Rechtsaltertümer*, Fourth ed. (1899), i, p. 627; M. Delcourt, *Stérilités mysterieuses et naissances maléfiques dans l'antiquité classique* (1938), pp. 31 ff.

18. Temesváry, *Volksbräuche und Aberglauben in der Geburtshilfe in Ungarn* (1900), p. 127.

19. F. Drechsler, *Schlesiens volkstümliche Überlieferungen*, ed. Vogt, xi, 1, p. 183.

20. *Schweiz. Archiv für Volkskunde* VIII (1904), p. 267.

21. Plautus, *Amph.*, p. 501; Terence, *Andria*, p. 219. The technical expression was *tollere*.

22. *Globus*, LXXXIX, p. 60.

23. *Notes and Queries*, Fifth Series, x (1878), pp. 205, 255, 276.

24. F. Nork, *Die Sitten und Gebräuche der Deutschen . . .* [= Das Kloster, XII] (1849), pp. 153 f.

25. Dieterich, *op. cit.*, pp. 18 f.

The Tree of Life

1. Talmud Bab., Gittin 57ᵃ; Talm. Jer., 'Erubin 4, 27ᵇ. See also: *Aruch Completum*, ed. Kohut, iv, p. 209; Scheftelowitz, *Altpal. Bauernglaube* (1925), p. 26.

On the custom in general, see: R. Andree, *Ethnographische Parallelen und Vergleiche,* ii (1889), pp. 21 ff.; W. Mannhardt, *Wald- und Feldkulte,* Second ed. (1904), i, pp. 49 ff.; Ploss, *Das Kind* (1911-12), i, pp. 71 ff.; Scheftelowitz, *op. cit.,* pp. 25-27; J. G. Frazer, *The Golden Bough,* vii/2 (Balder), pp. 159-68; id., *The Fasti of Ovid* (1929), ii, pp. 402 ff.; R. Kohler, *Kleine Schriften,* ed. Bolte (1898), i, p. 179; G. Kittredge, "Arthur and Gorlagon," *Harvard Notes in Philology and Literature* VII (1903), p. 171, n.1; A. Porteous, *Forest Folklore, Mythology and Romance* (1928), pp. 155-60, 182; C. Bötticher, *Der Baumkultus der Hellenen* (1856), p. 156 [ancient Greece]; E. Riess, *Rhein. Mus.* XII (1894), 186 [Greece and Rome]. Cf. also: Artemidorus, *Oneirocr.,* ii, 10; Josephus, *Contra Apionem,* ii, 25.

2. E. S. McCartney, "Folklore Heirlooms," *Papers of the Michigan Academy of Science, Arts and Letters* XVI (1931), pp. 115-117.

3. W. R. Smith, *Religion of the Semites* (1927), p. 189.

4. P. Sartori, *Sitte und Brauch* (1910-14), i, p. 26 f.

5. *ibidem.*

6-9. H. Ploss, *Das Kind* (1911-12), i, p. 63.

10. *Archiv für Religionsgeschichte* X (1913), p. 475.

11. Ploss, *loc. cit.*

12. H. V. Stevens and A. Grundwedel, *Materialen zur Kenntniss d. wilden Stämme auf d. Halbinsel Malaka* (1894), pp. 113, 117.

13. The tale is told in the celebrated D'Orbiney Papyrus, now in the British Museum.

14. J. Sibree, "Malagasay Folk-Tales," *Folk-Lore Journal* II (1884), pp. 52, 130.

15. W. A. Clouston, *Popular Tales and Fictions* (1887), i, pp. 170 f.

16. M. Cox, *Introduction to Folk-Lore,* pp. 222-23.

17. Suetonius, *Vespas.,* V, 2.

18. Ael. Lamprid., *Alex. Sev.,* XIII, 7.

19. Gudrunarquifa, ii, 40.

20. *Die Woche,* 31 August 1901, p. 3.

21. J. Roscoe, *The Baganda* (1911), p. 202.·

22. *Archiv tradiz. popul.* IV (1885), p. 296. Parallels are noted in E. Cosquin, *Contes populaires de Lorraine,* i, pp. lxii ff., 173.

II. CHILDHOOD

The Covenant of Abraham

On the subject in general, see: A. J. Glassberg, *Die Beschneidung, in ihrer geschichtlichen, ethnographischen, religiösen und medizinischen Bedeutung* (1896); M. Pogorelsky, *Die rituelle Beschneidungszeremonie der Israeliten: Geschichte, Technik, und Bedeutung dieser Operation* (1888); M. M. Harsu, *Anuar pentru Israeliti* XIV (1891), pp. 25-50 [Roumanian]; S. Kohn, *Oth Berith* (1903) [Hebrew].

1. Herodotus, ii, 36.

2. Stele of Uha (23rd cent. B.C.E.) ; *Ancient Near Eastern Texts* (1950), p. 326.

3. Tomb of Khonsu (XXIst Dynasty) : Klebs, *Reliefs,* i, fig. 10; S. A. B. Mercer, *The Religion of Ancient Egypt* (1949), p. 359.

4. Herodotus, ii, 37, 104.

5. R. Andree, *Ethnographische Parallelen und Vergleiche,* ii (1889), pp. 166-212 [the classic comparative study]; H. Fehlinger, *Sexual Life of Primitive Peoples* tr. Herbert (1931), pp. 103 ff.; F. Bryk, *Die Beschneidung bei Mann und Weib* (1931); W. Thesiger, *Geographic Journal* (London), April 1948.

6. E. Petitot, *Les grands esqimaux* (1887), p. 293.

7. Andree, *op. cit.,* pp. 170 f.

8. Fehlinger, *op. cit.,* pp. 104 f.

9. *ibidem.*

10. *ibidem.*

11. M. Merker, *Die Masai* (1925), pp. 60 f.

12. A summary of the various theories will be found in Andree, *op. cit.*

13. i.e., *shadi* (a Persian word).

14. Andree, *op. cit.*

15. Fehlinger, *op. cit.,* pp. 116 f.

16. G. Buschan, *Die Sitte der Völker* (1914-15), iii, p. 40.

17. Wm. Robertson Smith, *The Religion of the Semites,* ch. viii.

18. *Midrash Yelamedenu,* Levit. *Sav,* §14. In the Grace After Meals, thanks are rendered to God "for Thy covenant which Thou hast *sealed* in our flesh"; while the officiant's benediction at the circumcision ceremony refers to "the covenant which God set in our forefather's flesh and whereby He hath *sealed* his descendants with the sign of the holy covenant."

18a. Code of Hammurabi, §§226 ff.

19. R. P. Dougherty, *The Shirkûtu of Babylonian Deities* (1923), pp. 81-87. Similarly, the Egyptians tattooed bound captives with the name of a god or of the divine king: Breasted, *Ancient Records of Egypt,* iii, §414; iv, §405. See on this: F. Dölger, *Antike und Christentum,* ii (1930), pp. 100-106; L. Keimer, *Mémoires de l'Institut d'Égypte,* vol. 53.; C. Schuster, "Modern Parallels for Ancient Egyptian Tattooing," *Sudan Notes and Records,* XXIX (1948), pp. 71-77; S. Tardiau, "Le tatouage sacré et la religion dionysiaque," *Aegyptus,* XXXIX (1950), pp. 56-66.

20. E. Norden, *Die Geburt des Kindes* (1924), p. 28, n.4.

21. Lucian, *De Dea Syria,* chap. 59.

22. Tertullian, *De praescr. heret.,* 40; *Corpus Inscriptionum Latinarum,* p. 586; F. Cumont, *Les mystères de Mithra,* Second ed. (1902), p. 131.

23. H. Hepding, *Attis* (1903), p. 162 f.

24. Wolters, *Hermes* XXXVIII (1903), pp. 268 ff.; A. Rapp, *Die Beziehungen des Dionysuskultus zu Thrakien und Kleinasien* (1882), p. 25.

25. G. Anrich, *Das antike Mysterienwesen in seinem Einfluss auf das Christentum* (1894), pp. 120 f. It is so designated also by the Mandaeans of Iraq and Iran: Scheftelowitz, *Monatsschrift für Ges. und Wiss. des Judentums* LXXIII (1929), p. 216.

26. Hepding, *op. cit.*, p. 163, n.2.

27. T. Trede, *Das Heidentum in der römischen Kirche* (1889-91), iv, p. 324.

28. O. H. Parry, *Six Months in a Syrian Monastery* (1895), p. 63.

29. Herodotus, ii, 113.

30. Assyrian Version, Tablet II, iv 20 f. = *Ancient Near Eastern Texts* . . . , p. 81.

30a. It was formally abolished by the Reform Conference of 1892, but opinion on the subject has changed.

31. L. Zunz, *Gesammelte Schriften* (1875), ii, p. 199.

31a. Joseph Karo, *Shulhan 'Aruch, Yoreh De'ah*, §§360-66.

32. The Karaites and the Sephardim of Palestine regularly perform the rite in the synagogue.

33. Löw, *Lebensalter*, p. 384; Kohut, *Aruch Completum*, vi, p. 83 f.

34. Sartori, *op. cit.*, i, p. 37.

35. *ibidem.*

36. Sartori, *loc. cit.*

37. Sartori, *op. cit.*, i, p. 36, n.26.

38. E. Hull, *Folklore of the British Isles* (1928), p. 193.

39. *Zeitschrift des Vereins für Volkskunde* I, p. 184; Sartori, *loc. cit.*

40. Brand-Ellis, ii, pp. 77 f.

41. *Urquell* VI, p. 146 [Pomeranica]; *Zeitschr. d. Ver. f. rheinische und westfälische Volkskunde* II, p. 179.

42. I. Holzer, "Aus dem Leben der alten Judengemeinde zu Worms," *Zeitschrift für Geschichte der Juden in Deutschland* V (1934).

43. E. Brauer, *Ethnologie der jemenitischen Juden* (1934), p. 194.

44. Servius on Vergil, *Eclogues*, iv, 62; Tertullian, *De an.*, 39. In the Attis-cult, the expression "spread thrones" (*stronuein thronous*) was the technical term for serving the mystic meal. It is the equivalent of the Latin *lectisternium;* Hepding, *Attis* (1903), pp. 136 ff.

On Elijah's chair, see: Bergmann, "Der Stuhl und der Kelch des Elijah," *Monatsschrift für Ges. u. Wiss. Judentums*, LXXI (1927).

45. Karo, *Shulhan Aruch, Yoreh De'ah*, §170.17; 178.3 gloss; H. J. D. Azulai, *Birke Joseph* (1774-76) on Yoreh De'ah, §170.17; M. Schul, *Superstitions et coutumes populaires du judaisme contemporaine* (1882), p. 6.

46. Varrus, quoted by Servius on Vergil, *Aeneid*, x, 76; G. Wissowa, *Religion und Kultus d. Römer* (1932), p. 357, n.1.

47. Talmud Bab., Nedarim 56ᵃ.

Coming of Age

On the subject in general, see: I. Rivkind, *Le-Oth u-le-Zikaron* (1942) [Hebrew]; H. Balfour, "The Rite of Confirmation in the Jewish and in the Christian Church," *Lutheran Church Review* (April, 1899).

III. BETROTHAL

Troth and Ring

1. L. M. Epstein, *The Jewish Marriage Contract* (1927), pp. 16 f.
2. *The Espousals of Nikkal* (= C. H. Gordon, *Ugaritic Handbook* [1940], No. 77), 34-37.
3. Epstein, *op. cit.*, pp. 22 f.
4. The ring is not mentioned in the Talmud, but there is an allusion to it in a document of the Gaonic age, c. viith-viiith cent: A. Harkavy, *Teshuboth Hageonim* (1887), §65. On the subject in general, see: A. Langbank, *Bikkurim,* I (1864), pp. 114 f. [Hebrew].
5. The notion is prettily expressed in Herrick's *Hesperides:*

And as this round
Is nowhere found
    To flaw or else to sever,
So let our love
As endless prove
    And pure as gold for ever.

6. I. Abrahams, *Jewish Life in the Middle Ages,* Second ed. (1932), p. 199.
7. *ibid.,* p. 197. On the other hand, it is significant that in Iceland the ring was usually large enough to pass the palm of the hand through it. Indeed, the bridegroom passed four fingers and his palm through it to receive the hand of the bride: H. C. Trumbull, *The Blood Covenant* (1893), p. 71.
8. Pliny, *HN,* xxxiii, 12. |(The oft-quoted passage, Juvenal, vi, 25 is inconclusive.) So, too, in early Christian usage: Tertullian, *Apolog.,* 6. On the history of the wedding ring, see: J. Grimm, *Deutsche Rechtsaltertümer,* i, pp. 244 ff., 596 ff.; Sartori, *Sitte und Brauch,* i, pp. 87 f.; Brand-Ellis, ii, pp. 100 ff.
9. R. Chambers, *Book of Days* (1886), i, p. 719.

Exchange of Gifts

1. Sartori, *Sitte und Brauch,* i, p. 56; H. N. Hutchinson, *Marriage Customs in Many Lands* (1897), pp. 235, 244.
2. F. A. Larson, *Larson, Duke of Mongolia* (1930), pp. 135 ff.
3. Tacitus, *Germania,* 18.
4. H. Granquist, *Marriage Conditions in a Palestinian Village,* ii (1935), pp. 66 f.
5. E. Westermarck, *Marriage Ceremonies in Morocco* (1914), pp. 263, 293 ff., 324, 331.
6. A. Büchler, *Israel Lewy Festschrift* (1911), p. 112; L. Ginzberg, *Revue des Études Juives* LXVIII, p. 149; Wm. Robertson Smith, *Kinship and Marriage in Early Arabia* (1883), pp. 87, 269.

7. Ibn Hisham, ed. Wüstenfeld, p. 763.

8. J. L. Burckhardt, *Bedouins and Wáhábys* (1832), p. 213.

9. Hutchinson, *Marriage Customs,* p. 119.

10. *ibid.,* pp. 243 f.

11. A. Van Selms, "The Best Man and the Bride—from Sumer to St. John," *Journal of Near Eastern Studies* IX (1950), pp. 68-75.

12. A. T. d'Abbadie, *Dictionnaire de la langue amariñña* (1881), s.v.; C. Levias, *Freidus Volume* (1929), p. 417.

Spinnholz

1. Dio Cassius, xlviii, 44; lix, 12; lxiii, 13; Plautus, *Aul.,* ii 2; iii 5; Cicero, *Ad. Qu. Cur.,* ii, 6.

2. Northbrook, *Treatise on Dicing* (1579), p. 35, quoted in Brand-Ellis, ii, p. 113. At Roman weddings, the *puer Camillus* carried the bride's spinning apparatus before her in a basket: Varro, i, viii, 34; Plutarch, *Quaest. Rom.,* 31; W. A. Becker, *Gallus,* tr. Metcalfe, Seventh ed. (1882), pp. 160 f. On the spindle as a symbol of womanhood, see: Grimm, *Deutsche Mythologie,* Third ed. (1854), p. 390.

IV. MARRIAGE

A Time to Embrace

1. I. Scheftelowitz, *Altpalästinensischer Bauernglaube* (1925), p. 137, n.1.

2. E. Westermarck, *Pagan Survivals in Mohammedan Civilization* (1933), p. 114.

3. Tacitus, *Germania,* 11; Caesar, *Bellum Gallicum,* I, 50; J. Grimm, *Teutonic Mythology,* tr. Stallybrass (1880), pp. 713 ff.

4. P. Sartori, *Sitte und Brauch,* i, p. 60, n. 4.

5. Ketuboth 81a.

6. Grimm, *Deutsche Mythol.,* Second ed., p. 662.

7. R. Andree, *Ethnographische Parallelen und Vergleiche,* i (1878), p. 1.

8. *Ausland,* 1840, p. 1075.

9. Ovid, *Fasti,* v, 487 ff.

10. Ovid, *Fasti,* iii, 393; Porphyrion on Horace, *Epistles,* ii, 209 (p. 343 Meyer).

11. Sartori, *op. cit.,* i, p. 60.

12. D. L. and L. B. Thomas, *Kentucky Superstitions* (1920), p. 64, No. 620. On the subject in general, see: H. Gaidoz, "Le mariage en mai," *Mélusine* VII (1894), pp. 105-11; J. G. Frazer on Ovid, *Fasti* v, 487; Landsberger, *Jüdische Zeitschrift für Wissenschaft und Leben* VII (Breslau 1869), pp. 91-93; I. Levi, *Mélusine* VIII (1896), pp. 93-94.

13. T. H. Gaster, *Thespis,* Second ed., pp. 27-28.

14. P. Toschi, *Il Folklore* (1952), p. 46.

Bride and Groom

1. In Sumerian, the bride is called E.GI, literally, "house-confined."
2. J. L. Burckhardt, *op. cit.*, p. 153; A. Musil, *Arabia Petraea* iii (1908), p. 206.
3. D. Livingstone, *Missionary Travels and Researches in South Africa* (1857), p. 412. So too in Somaliland: Hutchinson, *op. cit.*, p. 95.
4. A. Parkinson, *30 Jahre in der Südsee* (1907), p. 178.
5. F. Schönwerth, *Aus der Oberpfalz, Sitten und Sagen* (1857-59), i, pp. 60 f.
6. G. Lees, *The Witness of the Wilderness* (1909), p. 123; H. Jaussen, *Coutumes des arabes au pays de Moab* (1908), p. 54; A. Musil, *Arabia Petraea,* iii (1908), p. 152.
7. Jennings-Bradley, *Quarterly Statement of the Palestine Exploration Fund* XXXVII (1907), pp. 24 ff.
8. E. Westermarck, *History of Human Marriage* (1921), ii, p. 529.
9. Crawley, *op. cit.*, ii, p. 48.

Bride's Adorning

1. Crawley, ERE, v, pp. 40-72.
2. J. D. Eisenstein, *Oṣar Dinim u-Minhagim* (1928), p. 145.
3. Ovid, *Fasti,* iv, 619; Tibullus, ii, 1.16.
4. Cicero, *Leg.*, ii, 18, 45.
5. T. H. Gaster, *Folk-Lore,* XLIX (1938), p. 367 f.
6. D. Leslie, *Among the Zulus and Amatongas* (1875), p. 116.
7. R. H. Codrington, *The Melanesians* (1891), p. 148.
8. H. S. Sanderson, *Journal of the Anthropological Institute,* XXIV (1895), p. 305.
9. E. W. Lane, *Manners and Customs of the Modern Egyptians,* Minerva Library ed. (1890), pp. 151 ff.
10. A. Leared, *Morocco and the Moors* (1876), pp. 36-38.
11. Dulac, *Contes arabes,* p. 63, n.3 (Socin).
12. E. W. Lane, *Manners and Customs of the Modern Egyptians,* Minerva Library ed. (1890), p. 156.
13. Lobel, *Hochzeitsgebräuche in der Türkei* (1897), p. 39; Granquist, *op. cit.*, ii, p. 116, n.1.
14. Abrahams, *op. cit.*, p. 221. But in several parts of Germany, the bridegroom used to wear a high hat throughout the day, except, of course, while he was in church: Sartori, *Sitte und Brauch,* i, p. 79, n.6. The Jews may have thus been giving a new twist to a standard Gentile usage.
15. W. Crooke, *Punjab Notes and Queries* (1884-85), ii, p. 182, n.960.

Tresses and Wigs

On the subject in general, see: N. Brüll, "Die Haarbedeckung bei jüdischen Frauen," *Jahrbücher für Geschichte und Literatur,* VIII (1887), pp. 51-52; *Notes and Queries, Sixth Series,* i (1880), pp. 458, 485; ii (1880), p. 294; iv (1881), p. 76; vi (1882), p. 438.

1. Talmud Bab., 'Erubin 18ᵃ.
2. *King John,* Act III, Scene i.
3. Sartori, *op. cit.,* i, p. 79; Meinhold, *Die deutschen Frauen in d. Mittelalter,* Second ed. (1882), i, p. 386; Grimm, *Deutsche Rechtsaltertümer,* i, pp. 612 f.
4. G. F. Klemm, *Allgemeine Cultur-Geschichte der Menschheit* (1843-52), iii, p. 53.
5. Sozomen, v, 10.7; E. Samter, *Familienfeste der Griechen und Römer* (1901), pp. 64 ff.; S. Eitrem, *Opferritus und Voropfer der Griechen und Römer* (1915), p. 350, n.2.
6. Samter, *loc. cit.*
7. R. Chambers, *Book of Days* (1886), i, p. 721.
8. F. Nork, *Die Sitten und Gebräuche der Deutschen und ihrer Nachbarvölker* (= Das Kloster), xii (1849), p. 163.
9. Hutchinson, *Marriage Customs,* p. 275.
10. *Notes and Queries,* Third Series, ii (1862), p. 67.
11. J. Shooter, *The Kaffirs of Natal and the Zulu Country* (1857), p. 75.
12. A. B. Cook, *Zeus,* i (1923), p. 68.

Swords and Daggers

1. E. Westermarck, *History of Human Marriage* (1925), ii, pp. 499 ff.; Granquist, *op. cit.,* ii, p. 60; G. Dalman, *Palästinischer Diwan* (1908), pp. 133, 147; P. Haupt, *The Book of Canticles* (1907), p. 23, n.15.
2. J. Abercromby, "Marriage Customs of the Mordvins," *Folk-Lore,* i (1890), p. 445.
3. J. Doolittle, *Social Life of the Chinese* (1867), i, p. 95.
4. H. Oldenberg, *Die Religion des Vedas* (1894), p. 271.
5. Rev. J. P. Fasler, quoted in *Notes and Queries,* Sixth Series, ii (1880), p. 245.
6. M. Abeghian, *Der Armenische Volksglaube* (1899), p. 91.
7. Sartori, *Sitte und Brauch,* i, p. 83.
8. Granquist, *op. cit.,* ii, pp. 115, 117.
9. C. F. Conder, *Heth and Moab* (1885), p. 293; Jaussen, *Moab,* p. 53; Bauer, *Volksleben im Lande der Bibel,* Second ed. (1903), p. 108.
10. R. Chambers, *The Book of Days* (1886), i, p. 721.
11. Maimonides, *Ḥiddushim,* p. 512; I. Abrahams, *Jewish Life in the Middle Ages,* Second ed. (1932), p. 209.

Torches

1. E. W. Lane, *Manners and Customs of the Modern Egyptians,* Minerva Library ed. (1890), p. 154.
2. *The Poem of Dawn and Sunset* (= Gordon, *Ugaritic Handbook* [1940], No. 52), lines 35-36.

3. Catullus, lxi, p. 15; Vergil, *Aeneid,* iv, p. 18.
4. Moses Premsla, *Maṭṭeh Mosheh* (Frankfort, 1720), viii, 3.
5. *Revue des Études Juives,* XXIV, 289; C. Roth in I. Abrahams, *op. cit.,* p. 226.

The Wedding Ceremony

a. Huppah: *The Bridal Canopy*

1. Talmud Bab., Sotah 49[b].
2. *Sepher Ha-Manhig* (Warsaw, 1885), p. 109 f.; Löw, *Lebensalter,* p. 188. Note that the Greek word *pastos,* denoting a bridal baldachin, is explained by the lexicographer Hesychius as "a bower adorned with pictures (*oikos gegrammenos*)". It was portable, for cf. the title *pastophoroi,* "carriers of the *pastos,*" applied to certain officials of the Attis-cult: Hepding, *Attis,* pp. 193 f.
3. Xenophon, *Ephes.* A. viii, 2. Cf. also: Theocritus, xviii, 3; Rhetores Graeci, x, 271; Scholiast on Iliad, ii, 701.
4. Hutchinson, *Marriage Customs,* 5 f.
5. Crawley, *Mystic Rose,* Third ed., i, p. 51.
6. *ibidem.*
6a. Hutchinson, *op. cit.,* p. 210.
7. *ibid.,* p. 194.
8. *ibid.,* p. 172.
9. Brand-Ellis, ii, pp. 141 f.

b. Ketubah: *The Marriage Contract*

1. L. Epstein, *The Jewish Marriage Contract* (1927), pp. 40 ff.
2. *id.,* pp. 26 ff.; E. Kraeling, *The Brooklyn Museum Aramaic Papyri* (1953), Nos. 2, 7, 14.
3. Reproduced in *Jewish Encyclopaedia,* iv, p. 475. Cf. also M. Gaster, *The Ketubah* (1923), pp. 49 ff.

d. *The Cup of Betrothal*

1. Gaius, *Institutionum juris civilis commentarii,* I, 112.
2. A. Wuttke, *Der Deutsche Aberglaube der Gegenwart* (1900), p. 560.
3. L. von Schroeder, *Die Hochzeitsgebräuche der Esten* (1888), p. 84.
4. *ibid.,* pp. 82, 84.
5. Crawley, *Mystic Rose,* Second ed., ii, p. 124.
6. E. T. Dalton, *Descriptive Ethnology of Bengal* (1872), p. 193; H. H. Ridley, *Tribes and Customs of Bengal* (1891), ii, p. 8.
7. L. W. Küchler, *Transactions of the Asiatic Society of Japan,* XIII (1883), p. 115.

e. *Smashing the Glass*

1. Westermarck, *op. cit.,* ii, p. 459; H. Bächtold, *Die Gebräuche bei Verlobung und Hochzeit* (1914), pp. 105 ff.; J. Z. Lauterbach, "Breaking a Glass at Weddings," *Hebrew Union College Annual,* II (1925).

2. Hutchinson, *op. cit.,* p. 242.
3. *ibid.,* p. 230.
4. *ibid.,* p. 237.
5. *ibid.,* p. 227.
6. R. Chambers, *Book of Days,* i, p. 239.
7. T. H. Gaster, *Thespis,* Second ed., p. 82.
8. *New York World-Telegram,* August 16, 1943.

f. *Rice, Nuts and Confetti*

1. Talmud Bab., Berachoth 50ᵇ; Mishnah, Semahoth, viii. Cf. W. A. Becker, *Charicles,* tr. Metcalfe, Third ed. (1911), p. 487; Scholiast on Aristophanes, *Plutus,* p. 768; Samter, *Geburt* . . . , pp. 172 ff.; Wester-marck, *Marriage,* ii, p. 470; Crawley, *Mystic Rose,* Second ed., ii, pp. 38 f.; V. Cajkanovic, "De nucibus in Romanorum nuptiis usurpatis," *Prizoli za Knjizevnost; Jezik, Istorija i Folklor* (Belgrade), XVII/i (1937), pp. 94 ff.
2. Granquist, *op. cit.,* ii, p. 79; A. Betts, "The Symbolic Use of Corn at Weddings," *The Westminster Review* 128 (1912), pp. 542 ff.; J. G. Frazer, *Totemism and Exogamy* (1910), ii, p. 260; I. Scheftelowitz, *Altpalästinensisher Bauernglaube,* (1925), pp. 86 f.; *Notes and Queries,* Fourth series, xii (1873), pp. 327, 438.
3. Crawley, *op. cit.,* ii, p. 80.

g. *Insult and Ribaldry*

1. J. Shooter, *The Kaffirs of Natal and the Zulu Country* (1857), p. 74.
2. Maya Dás, *Punjab Notes and Queries* 2 (1884-5), p. 184, n.976.
3. Robinson Ellis on Catullus, lxi 127; Kirby Smith on Tibullus, I, iv. 73-74.
4. Catullus, lxi, 127 ff.
5. F. M. Cornford, *The Origin of Attic Comedy,* Second ed. (1934), p. 50.
6. Talmud Bab., Ketub. 17ᵃ; Yalqut Shime'oni on Job, §917.

h. *Round and Round*

1. Gaster, *Thespis,* Second ed., pp. 93 f.
2. Tor Irstam, *The King of Ganda* (1944), p.
3. R. O. Winstedt, *Journal of the Royal Asiatic Society,* 1945, pp. 139 f.
4. W. Warde Fowler, *The Roman Festivals of the Period of the Republic* (1899), p. 319.
5. Brand-Ellis, i, pp. 197 f.; Gaster, *op. cit.,* p. 194.
6. Hutchinson, *op. cit.,* p. 241.
7. *ib.,* p. 195.

An Ancient Hebrew Wedding

1. Granquist, *op. cit.*, ii, pp. 136 f.; Crawley, *op. cit.*, ii, p. 50.
2. Granquist, *op. cit.*, ii, pp. 38 f.
3. Textual matters need not be discussed here. They are treated fully in the standard critical commentaries. Two original emendations should, however, be mentioned: (*a*) at the end of v. 8, we read *MᵃḤᵉGoRêKa* for *MᵉḤᵃBᵉRēKa*, joining to v. 9; (*b*) in v. 14, we vocalize *KᵉLê KᵉBōDaH* for the traditional *KoL KᵉBūDaH*.

"Children Under the Mantle"

1. Hommel, *Jurisprudentia numismatibus illustrata* (1763), pp. 214-18; Du Cange, iii, p. 114c, s.v. *pallio cooperire.*
2. Grimm, *Rechtsaltertümer,* i, p. 220 (*filii mantellati*); F. Nork, *Die Sitten und Gebräuche der Deutschen* [= Das Kloster, xii], (1849), p. 170; Liebrecht, *op. cit.,* p. 432.

V. DEATH

The Last Journey

1. Mishnah, *Sanhedrin,* vi, 4; Maimonides, *Hilchoth Ebel,* iv, 8; Karo, Shulhan Aruch, *Yoreh Deʻah,* §537.1.
2. N. Brüll, *Jahrbücher,* I (1874), p. 51.
3. Testament of R. Judah the Pious, in *Sepher Hasidim* (Lemberg 1863).
4. Kohler, *Jewish Encyclopaedia,* iii, p. 436.
5. J. Trachtenberg, *Jewish Magic and Superstition* (1939), p. 301, n.50; ib., pp. 170 f. (where literature is cited).
6. Mishnah, *Ket.* iv, 4. Cf. Josephus, *Bellum Judaicum* iii, 9 §5.
7. Isaac Lofretz, *Sepher Maṭʻamim* (Warsaw 1889).
8. M. Gaster, ed., *The Book of Prayer . . . according to the Custom of the Spanish and Portuguese Jews,* i (1901), pp. 197 f. The translation is by the present writer.
9. M. Gaster, in *Livre d'hommage à la mem.ʾre du Dr. Samuel Poznánski* (1927), p. 401.
10. Tur, Yorah Deʻah, §375; J. D. Eisenstein, *Oṣar Lʾᵏim u-Minhagim* (1923), p. 355.
11. Obadiah Bertinoro, on Mishnah, Baba Bathra, viii, 7.

A Time to Mourn

1. The Jewish Encyclopaedia, *s.v.* Cochin.
2. J. D. Eisenstein, *Oṣar Dinim u-Minhagim* (1928), p. 5 [Hebrew].

3. Often, however, *white* gloves are used; *Handw. d. deutsch. Abergl.,* iii, col: 1409 f.

The Folklore of Death

On the subject in general, see: A. P. Bender, "Beliefs, rites and customs of the Jews connected with death, burial and mourning . . . ," *Jewish Quarterly Review, Old Series,* VI (1894-95), pp. 317-47, 667-71; VII (1895-96), pp. 101-18, 259-69; A. Marmorstein, "Some rites of mourning in Judaism," *Studi e materiali di storia dell religioni* X, pp. 80-94; J. Rabbinowitz, *Der Totenkultus bei den Juden* (Frankfort, 1889); E. Bendann, *Death Customs: an analytical study of burial rites* (1930); B. Puckle, *Funeral Customs: their origin and development* (n.d.).

a. *Removal of Feather Pillows*

1. *Timon of Athens,* Act IV, Scene iii.
2. J. Harland and T. Wilkinson, *Lancashire Folk-lore* (1869), p. 268; *Notes and Queries, Choice Notes: Folk-Lore,* pp. 43, 44, 90; A. R. Wright, *English Folklore* (1928), p. 20.
3. *Notes and Queries,* Sixth Series, iii (1881), p. 165.
4. Sartori, *Sitte und Brauch,* i (1910), p. 126, n.6.
5. F. Liebrecht, *Zur Volkskunde* (1879), p. 331.
6. *Folklore of the Northern Counties,* Folk-Lore Society (1895), p. 60.
7. *Urquell,* Neue Folge, II, p. 209.
8. C. Questel, *De pulvinari morientibus non subtrahendo* (Jena 1698).
9. ERE, iv, p. 451a.

b. *Opening Windows*

On the subject in general, see: F. Liebrecht, *Zur Volkskunde* (1879), pp. 371 f.; Samter, *Geburt . . . ,* pp. 28 ff.; H. Höhn, *Sitte und Brauch bei Tod und Begräbniss* (1913), p. 316; Sartori, *Sitte und Brauch,* i, p. 128, n.1; Negelin, *Zeitschrift für Volkskunde* XI, p. 267; P. Toschi, *Il Folklore* (1952), p. 57.

10. *King John,* Act V, Scene viii.
11-16. M. Cox, *Introduction to Folklore* (1897), p. 65.
17. R. Kühnau, *Schlesische Sagen,* i (1910), p. 171.
18. *Globus,* LXVII, 357 f.
19. *ibidem.*
20. G. Meier, *Archiv für Orientforschung,* XII (1938), pp. 241 f.
21. J. Grimm, *Teutonic Mythology,* tr. Stallybrass (1880), p. 1189.

c. *Closing the Eyes*

22. Babrius, xciii, 35.
23. Pliny, *HN,* ii, 145. Cf. Crusius, *Rhein. Museum,* XLVI, p. 319.
24. Pliny, *HN,* xxviii, 64; Servius on Vergil, *Aeneid,* iv, 244; Grimm-Stallybrass, p. 1181; E. B. Tylor, *Primitive Culture* (1920 ed.), i, p. 431;

Kirby Smith, "Pupilla Duplex," *Studies in honor of Basil L. Gildersleeve* (1902), pp. 287-300.

25. *Iliad*, xi, 453.

26. *Odyssey*, xi, 426; cf. also xxiv, 296.

d. Closing the Mouth

27. Herodas, iii, 4, with Headlam-Knox's note. Cf. also: Dio Chrysostomus, i, 678; Meleager, *Anthol. Pal.*, v. 197; Seneca, *Epist.*, xxx, 14.

28. Vergil, *Aeneid*, iv, p. 684.

29. *Verr.*, v, p. 45.

30. Tylor, *Primitive Culture*, i, p. 391.

31. Harland-Wilkinson, *Lancashire Folklore*, p. 210.

On the subject in general, see: Rohde, *Psyche*, p. 23; E. Riess, *Classical Review* X, (1896), p. 409; T. J. Duncan, "Transfer of the Soul at Death," *Classical Journal*, XXV (1929), pp. 230-34; R. B. Onians, *The Origins of European Thought about the Body, etc.* (1951), p. 128.

32. *Zeitschrift für Volkskunde* VIII, p. 122.

33. W. Caland, *Altindische Toten- und Bestatungsgebräuche* (1896), p. 11.

34. B. Maisler, *Archiv für Orientforschung* XI (1936), pp. 239 f.

35. M. Dunand, *Kemi*, 1931, pp. 133, 151 f.

e. Rending of garments

On the subject in general, see: M. Jastrow, *Journal of the American Oriental Society*, XXI, pp. 23-29; Ch. Roehrensee, in Ugolini, *Thesaurus* (1765), xxix, cols. 1053-66.

36. Canaanite: I Aqhat (= Gordon, *Ugaritic Handbook* [1940], p. 179), 36, 46. Roman: Suetonius, *Caes.*, 23; *Nero*, 42; Statius, *Theb.*, iii, 125; Livy, xxxiv, 7.

f. Graveclothes free of knots

On the subject in general, see: J. G. Frazer, *The Golden Bough*, one-vol. edition, pp. 238-44.

g. Laying the Dead upon the Floor

37. Caland, *op. cit.*, p. 8.

38. Servius on Vergil, *Aeneid*, xii, 395.

39. Aelfric, *Anglo-Saxon Homilies*, ed. B. Thorpe (1841), i, p. 623.

40. A. Dieterich, *Mutter Erde* (1913), pp. 25 ff.

41. *ibidem*.

42. *Notes and Queries*, Sixth Series, ii (1880), pp. 87, 214; Mooney, "Funeral Customs of Ireland," *Proc. Amer. Philos. Soc.*, XXV, p. 226 [but wrongly explained].

43. Dieterich, *loc. cit.;* Sartori, *Sitte und Brauch*, i, p. 134; Rieder, *Zeitschrift für Kulturgeschichte* I, pp. 59 ff., 97 ff.; Stolz, *Zeitschr. f. österreich. Volkskunde* XII, fasc. 4-5; Rohde, *Psyche*, p. 204.

43a. Sartori, *Neue Jahrb. f. d. klass. Altertum* XV, pp. 36 ff.

43b. E. Goldmann, *Cartam levare* (1914) ; M. Eliade, *Traité d'histoire des religions* (1949), pp. 217 ff.

43c. Monseur, *Revue de l'histoire des religions*, 1906, pp. 299 ff.

43d. W. Schulenberg, *Wendische Volkskunde* (1880), 110.

h. *Washing and perfuming the corpse*

43e. E. Ebeling, *Tod und Leben* . . . (1931), p. 69; E. Dhorme, *Revue d'assyriologie* XXXVIII, p. 61.

43f. Mishnah, *Sem.*, viii. The practice was known also to the early Arabs (Wellhausen, *Reste*, Second ed., p. 178) and in ancient Christianity (Varronius, *Annal.*, an. 310).

44. Cornelius Agrippa, *De occulta philosophia*, i, p. 43.

45. Lohnmeyer, "Der göttliche Geruch," *Sitzb. d. Heidelberg. Akad.* (1919) ; K. Schwenk, *Philologus*, XVII (1861), p. 451.

46. T. H. Gaster, *Thespis*, Second ed., p. 236.

47. Homeric Hymns, iii, 231.

48. *Aeneid*, i, 403.

i. *White for the Dead*

49. Plutarch, *De aud. poet.*, 8; Pausanias, iv, 13.1.

50. Sartori, *op. cit.*, i, p. 133, n.15.

51. *ibidem.*

j. *Lamps*

On the subject in general, see: Abbé Lecler, *Etudes sur les lanternes des morts* (Limoges, 1882) ; J. G. Frazer, *Journal of the Anthropological Institute* XV (1886), pp. 90 ff.

52. A. E. Cowley, ed., *The Samaritan Liturgy* (1913), p. 883.

53. H. Jennings, *Die Rosenkreuzer* (1912), i, p. 11.

53a. *Articles to be enquired of within the Archdeaconry of York by the Churchwardens and Sworn Men* (163-) includes the curious item: "Whether at the death of any, there be any superstitious burning of candles in the day, after it be light"; Brand-Ellis, ii, p. 234, n.1.

k. *Interment without Coffin*

54. Sartori, *Sitte und Brauch*, i, p. 135, n.26.

55. *ibid.*, i, p. 150, n.6.

56. *ibidem.*

57. F. Nork, *Die Sitten und Gebräuche der Deutschen, etc.* (1849), p. 453.

58. *Notes and Queries*, Sixth Series, i (1880), p. 173.

l. *Earth of the Holy Land*

59. *Notes and Queries*, Sixth Series, i (1880), p. 122.

On the Christian belief that consecrated earth aids resurrection, see U. Wasmandorff, *Die religiöse Motive der Totenbestattung* (1884), pp. 17 f.

m. *Objects in the Coffin*

60. W. W. Hyde, *Greek Religion and its Survivals* (1923), pp. 209 f.; Sartori, *op. cit.,* I, p. 136, n.38; *Notes and Queries,* Sixth Series, v (1882), pp. 186, 294.

On the subject in general, see: *Archiv für Religionswissenschaft* II, pp. 205 ff.

61. ERE iv, 486a.

n. *"Passports" for the Dead*

62. *i.e.* the various amulets which modern scholars have put together as the so-called "Book of the Dead."

63. Nork, *Sitten,* p. 471.

64. *Notes and Queries, Fifth Series,* xii (1879), pp. 148, 239, 478; Sixth Series, i (1880), p. 122.

o. *Speedy Burial*

65. Xenophon, *Memorabilia* i, 2.53. Cf. also Eustathius on Iliad viii, 410.

66. A. R. Wright, *English Folklore* (1928), p. 20.

p. *Pallbearers walk barefoot*

67. Callimachus, *Hymn to Demeter,* 124 (with Ezekiel Spanheim's note).

68. Bion, i, 20.

69. Suetonius, *Augustus,* 100. Cf. ERE, iv, 506a.

70. Tertullian, *Apol.,* 40.

q. *Pouring out Water*

71. J. C. Lawson, *Modern Greek Folklore and Ancient Greek Religion* (1910), p. 521.

72. B. Janiewitsch, *Archiv für Religionswissenschaft* XIII (1910), p. 627.

73. Sartori, *Sitte und Brauch,* i, p. 129, n.4.

74. E. Ebeling, *Tod und Leben* . . . , (1931), p. 37, n.1.

75. S. A. Cook in W. Robertson Smith, *Religion of the Semites,* Third ed. (1927), p. 580. For parallels, see: T. H. Gaster, *Thespis,* Second ed., p. 204.

76. *Journal of the Palestine Oriental Society* IV (1924), p. 27. The explanation here cited is that of O. Gruppe, *Griech. Mythologie* (1906), p. 831; C. Pascal, *Rivista di filologia classica,* XL (1912), pp. 441 f.

r. *Overturning Chairs and Breaking Pots*

On the custom in general, see: J. G. Frazer, *Folklore in the Old Testament* (1919), iii, pp. 321 ff.

76a. Sartori, *op. cit.,* i, p. 137, n.20.

77. Hyde, *op. cit.,* p. 202.

s. *Halting of the Cortege*

78. Sartori, *op. cit.,* i, p. 148, n.26.

79. *Am Urquell,* Neue Folge, II, p. 205.

80. M. Parkyns, *Life in Abyssinia* (1853), ii, pp. 53 ff.

81. *Das Bayerische Inn-Oberland* V, p. 57.

82. Sartori, *op. cit.*, i, p. 143, n.22.

83. *Notes and Queries*, Fourth Series, vii (1871), pp. 298 f. (The dirge is printed *in extenso*.)

83a. Pennant's MS., quoted by Brand-Ellis, ii, 285n. [Skivog].

t. *Circuits around the Dead*

On the subject in general, see: J. G. Frazer, *The Golden Bough,* iii, pp. 423 f.

84. K 164, 5; E. Dhorme, *Revue d'assyriologie* XXXVIII (1941), p. 63.

85. I. Goldziher, *Muhammed. Studien* (1889), i, p. 246.

86. *Sacred Books of the East,* xvii (1882), p. 299.

87. *Iliad,* xxiii, 12-13.

88. Cf. E. F. Knuchel, *Die Umwandlung in Kult, Magie und Rechtsbrauch* (1919), pp. 43 f.

89. J. G. Kohl, *Petersburg in Bildern und Skizzen* (1841), i, pp. 280 f.

90. A. Kirchhoff, *Forschungen zur deutschen Landes- und Volkskunde* (1895), p. 61; L. Strackerjan, *Aberglaube und Sagen aus dem Herzogtum Oldenburg,* Second ed. (1909), ii, p. 218.

91. *Folk-Lore* XV, p. 88.

92. *Folk-Lore* XVIII, p. 88.

u. *Earth on the Coffin*

On the subject in general, see: ERE, iv, 437; *Zeitschrift für Ethnologie* 30, p. 354; H. Höhn, *Sitte und Brauch bei Tod,* etc. (1913), p. 246; C. Jensen, *Die nordfriesischen Inseln Sylt, Föhr, etc.* (1891), p. 394; Brand-Ellis, ii, p. 284.

93. *British Government Report on Trade, Commerce and Navigation of Saigon and Cochin China,* 1882 (quoted in *Notes and Queries,* Sixth Series, viii [1882], p. 44.)

94. E. Thurston, *Ethnographic Notes in Southern India* (1906), p. 106.

95. E. H. Meyer, *Badisches Volksleben in 19 Jhrt.* (1900), p. 594; Sartori, *op. cit.*, i, p. 50, n.8.

95a. J. Goar, *Euchologion* (1647), p. 538.

v. *Mourners wash their hands*

96. W. W. Hyde, *op. cit.,* p. 203.

97. H. Oldenberg, *Die Religion des Vedas* (1894), pp. 577 f.

98. *Globus,* XCII, p. 88; *Zeitschrift für Volkskunde* XVIII, pp. 368 ff.

99. R. Rattray, *Some Folk-lore Stories and Songs in Chinyanja* (1907), p. 94.

100. ERE iv, 434 b.

w. *Plucking of grass*
     Casting dust over the shoulder

101. M. Seligmann, *Die magischen Heil- und Schutzmittel aus der unbelebten Natur* (1927), pp. 148 ff., Samter, *op. cit.,* pp. 153-54.

102. A. Wuttke, *Der Deutsche Volksaberglaube der Gegenwart* (1900), pp. 93-145.
103. J. D. Eisenstein, *Oṣar Dinim u-Minhagim* (1928), p. 354 [Hebrew].

x. *Funeral meats*

104. Varro, *Non.*, i, 235; Servius on Vergil, *Aeneid*, v, 92; *Archiv für Religionswissenschaft* XI, pp. 530-46.
105. H. Höhn, *Sitte und Gebrauch bei Tod und Begräbniss* (1913), p. 333.
106. *Am Urquell* VI, pp. 26.
107. E. L. Rochholz, *Deutscher Glaube und Brauch im Spiegel der heidnischen Vorzeit* (1867), i, p. 319.
108. P. Sartori, *Die Speisung der Toten* (1903), p. 11.
109. Ovid, *Fasti* v, 438 ff.
110. J. G. Frazer, *The Fasti of Ovid* (1929), ii, pp. 448, 450.
111. Pliny, *HN*, xviii, 12, 30.
112. Sartori, *op. cit.*, ii, p. 262. The meal is set out on the grave.
113. Sartori, *Sitte und Brauch*, iii, p. 262, n.16.

The House of Life

1. A. H. Godbey, "The Decad of the Dead," *The Methodist Quarterly Review*, April 1925.
1a. E. R. Goodenough, *Symbols*, ii, p. 113.
2. *Folk-Lore in the Old Testament*, one-vol. edition, pp. 283-91.
3. P. Kraus, *Altbabylonische Briefe*, Part I (1931), pp. 49 f. = VAT 703, Obv. 11-12.

Commemoration:

Jahrzeit *and* Yizkor

On the subject in general, see: I. Lévi, *Revue des Études Juives* XXXIX (1894), pp. 43 ff.; S. Reinach, *ib.*, XLI (1900), pp. 161 ff.

VI. THE DIETARY LAWS

On the subject in general, see: H. Schurtz, *Die Speiseverbote* (1893); A. Wiener, *Die jüdischen Speisegesetze* (1893); G. Sommer, *Biblische Abhandlungen* (1846), pp. 271-362; R. Andree, *Ethnographische Parallelen und Vergleiche*, i (1878), pp. 114-27.

Clean and Unclean

1. V, 7. 11-20 = *Sacred Books of the East*, XXV, pp. 171 ff.
2. I, 5. 29-39 = *ibid.*, ii, p. 64.

3. XIV, 38-48 = *ibid.*, xiv, p. 74.
4. A. Lods, *Israël* (1930), pp. 286 f.; W. Nowack, *Lehrbuch d. Hebräischen Archäologie* (1894), i, pp. 116-19; S. R. Driver, *Commentary* (ICC) *on Deuteronomy*, p. 164.
5. E. Westermarck, *The Origin and Development of the Moral Ideas* (1906-08), ii, pp. 326 ff.; Stephens, *The American Anthropologist* VI (1893), p. 357.
6. Westermarck, *ibid.*
7. *Ibidem.*
8. Bertholet, Commentary on Lev. xi.
9. *ibidem.*
10. *'Iqd*, ed. Cairo (1305 Hej.), ii, 101.
11. T. Waitz, *Anthropologie der Naturvölker* (1860-77), V, ii, p. 147.
12. A. Bastian, *Die deutsche Expedition an der Loango-Küste* (1874-75), i, p. 185.
13. F. H. v. Kittlitz, *Denkwürdigkeiten einer Reise* (1858), iii, p. 103.
14. Waitz, *op. cit.*, iii, p. 384.
15. Bastian, *loc. cit.*
16. T. Hahn, *Tsuni-Goam* (1881), p. 106.
17. J. Adair, *American Indians* (1775), pp. 130 f.; J. G. Frazer, *The Golden Bough*, Second ed., ii, pp. 353 ff.
18. F. de Azara, *Voyages dans l'Amerique Meridionale* (1809), ii, p. 77.
19. Herodotus, ii, 36.
20. But see W. R. Dawson, *Journal of the Royal Asiatic Society* (1928), pp. 597-608, where it is shown that the attitude of the Egyptians toward the pig was by no means consistent.
21. G. Erman, *Reise um die Erde* (1833), i, p. 184.
22. S. Chandra Roy, *Oraons of Chōtā Nāgpur* (1915), pp. 324 ff.
23. Among the early Arabs, for example, deceased ancestors were often thought to be reincarnated as owls: Wellhausen, *Reste*, p. 157.

"The Blood is the Life"

1. *De sens.*, X, 23 f. On this concept, see: E. Rohde, *Psyche* (1921), iii, p. 176; W. Wundt, *Elements of Folk Psychology*, tr. Schaub (1916), pp. 208 ff.; O. Gruppe, *Griech. Mythologie* (1906), p. 728, n.5; J. Wellhausen, *Reste des arabischen Heidentums* (1897), p. 217; G. Jacob, *Altarabische Parallelen zum Alten Testament* (1897), pp. 9 f.
2. Hovorka-Kronfeld, *Vergleichende Volksmedizin* (1908-09), i, p. 79.
3. *ibid.*, p. 80.
4. P. Paulitschke, *Ethnographie Nordost-Afrikas*, i (1896), p. 186.
4a. H. Spencer, *Principles of Sociology* (1876-82), i, p. 116.
5. Hvorka-Kronfeld, *op. cit.*, ii, p. 29.
6. Chateaubriand, *Mémoire d'outre tombe*, iii, p. 120.
7. F. Parkman, *The Jesuits in North America in the Seventeenth Century*, Twentieth ed. (1885), p. 389.

8. Brand-Ellis, iii, pp. 15-16; Seligmann, *Böse Blick,* ii, p. 218; *Am Urquell* III (1892), p. 1. [Sweden].

9. J. G. Frazer, *The Golden Bough,* i, pp. 554 f., 357.

10. Col. Maclean, *A Compendium of Kafir Laws and Customs* (1866), p. 81.

11. F. B. Jevons, *Introduction to the History of Religion* (1896), p. 73 f.; Frazer, *Golden Bough,* iii, pp. 243 ff.; J. L. Saalschutz, *Das Mosaische Recht* (1846), p. 457, n.580.

12. G. Freytag, *Hamasa,* ii, p. 583; Wellhausen, *Reste,* Second ed., p. 182; W. R. Smith, *Religion of the Semites,* p. 369.

13. A. Platt, *Journal of Philology,* xix (1890), p. 46; R. B. Onians, *Origins of European Thought about the Body,* etc. (1951), [but to be read with caution]; Kirby Smith on Tibullus I, 3, 76 (liver).

14. E. Crawley, *The Idea of the Soul* (1909), p. 235.

15. E. Casalis, *The Basutos* (1861), as quoted in W. R. Smith, *Religion of the Semites,* Second ed., p. 381.

"The Sinew that Shrinks"

1. Onians, *op. cit.,* pp. 184-85; W. R. Smith, *Rel. Sem.,* Second ed., pp. 380 f.; id., *Kinship and Marriage . . .* (1865), p. 38.

2. Frazer, *Golden Bough,* viii, pp. 264 ff.

3. W. Robertson Smith, *The Religion of the Semites,* Third ed. (1927), p. 380, n.1; J. Skinner, *Genesis* (1910), p. 410 f.

4. J. G. Frazer, *Folk-Lore in the Old Testament,* one-vol. ed., p. 257.

Meat and Milk

1. *The Poem of Dawn and Sunset* (= C. H. Gordon, *Ugaritic Handbook* [1940] No. 52), line 15.

2. Cf. T. H. Gaster, *Thespis.*

3. The passage is cited in J. Spencer, *De legibus Hebraeorum* (1686), i, p. 271.

4. Gaster, *Thespis, loc. cit.*

5. *Folk-Lore in the Old Testament* (1919), iii, pp. 111-64.

VII. THE SHIELD OF DAVID

On the subject in general, see: T. Nussenblatt, "Magen David," *Yivo Bleter* XIII (1939), pp. 460-76 [Yiddish].

1. C. C. Torrey, *Journal of the American Oriental Society* XXIX (1908), pp. 193 ff. Torrey thought that the seal was of Roman date, but this view has not been endorsed by subsequent opinion; see: M. Lidzbarski, *Ephemeris für semitische Epigraphik* (1902-15), ii, p. 145; D. Diringer, *Le*

iscrizioni anticho-ebraiche palestinesi (1934), p. 187 (where further literature is cited).

2. *BMEP*, Pl. 67, No. 155.

3. e.g. W. H. Ward, *Seal Cylinders of Western Asia* (1910), Nos. 360, 413, 550.

4. H. Kohl and C. Watzinger, *Antike Synagogen in Galiläa* (1916), p. 30, figs. 55-57; S. A. Cook, *The Religion of Ancient Palestine in the Light of Archaeology* (1930), pp. 213 f.; H. G. May, *The Biblical Archaeologist* VII/i (1944), p. 19.

5. J. R. Peters and H. Thiersch, *Painted Tombs in the Necropolis of Marissa* (1905), p. 60. Cook, *op. cit.*, p. 60, says the hexagram is "very rare."

6. H. M. Adler, *Jewish Quarterly Review*, Old Series, 14, p. 11.

7. See on this: J. A. Fabricius, *Codex pseudepigraphus Veteris Testamenti*, i (1713), pp. 1007 f.; ii (1723), pp. 143 f.; J. C. Dannhauer, *Catechismusmilch* (1657), v, pp. 884 f.; Dom Angelo Gabriello Anguiscola, *Della hebraica medaglia detta Magen David dichiaratione* [placed on the Index in 1621!]; Jacoby, *Handwörterbuch d. deutsch. Aberglaubens*, ii, pp. 180 f.

8. Examples will be found in J. Scheible, *Das Kloster*, v (1847).

9. e.g. in the "twentieth citation" in *Doctor Faustens dreyfacher Hoellenzwang* (Passau, 1704).

10. *Wahre Erlösung der Jenaischen Christusnachts-Tragödie* (Jena, 1716), reprinted in Scheible's *Das Kloster*, V (1847), p. 1055.

11. *Am Urquell*, Neue Folge, I, p. 6; A. J. Storfer, *Marias jungfrauliche Mutterschaft* (1914), p. 160.

12. F. von Oefele, ERE, xii, 55^b.

13. *Eshkol Hakofer* (Eupatoria 1836), ch. 242.

13a. The word "seal" is often used in magical texts as a parallel to "bind"; e.g. J. A. Montgomery, *Aramaic Incantation Texts from Nippur* (1913), No. 19, line 15: "With the bonds on earth and with the seals in heaven."

14. Koran, xxi. 80, 81; xxvii. 16, 17; xxxiv. 11, 12; xxxviii. 33, 35, 37.

15. H. Hyvernat, *Zeitschrift für Keilschriftforschung* II (1885), p. 113. The Seal of Solomon is likewise mentioned in a Mandaean charm: Lidzbarski, *Ephemeris* . . . , ii, p. 105.

16. *Notes and Queries*, Sixth Series, viii (1883), pp. 289 ff.

17. Published by H. Gollancz (London, 1903).

18. Published by M. Gaster (London, 1896). A charm of the Graeco-Roman age mentions a compilation known as *The Diadem of Moses;* E. R. Goodenough, *Symbols*, ii, p. 195. This name probably plays on the familiar words of the Standing Prayer (*'Amidah*) of the Sabbath Morning Service: "A diadem of splendor didst Thou bestow upon him (Moses) when he stood before Thee on Mount Sinai."

19. E. Drioton in *Lefort Volume* (Louvain, 1947), p. 489. Dardanos the magician is mentioned by Pliny, *HN*, xxx, 11 and by Apuleius, *Apolog.*, 40.

INDEX

"Abode of Peace," 179
Abraham, Covenant of, 44 *ff.*
Abravanel, Isaac, on segregation after childbirth, 31
Abyssinians, and Child-stealing Witch, 22
Aelfric, on placing corpse on floor, 163
Aello, harpy, 25
aetites (eaglestone) 7 *f.*
Albertus Magnus, on vervain, 5
Alchemical symbols, 219 *f.*
Amen-em-ope, maxims of, xiv
Anna, miracles of, 15
Annos, 182
annulus pronubus, 88
Apastamba, dietary laws of, 203
Aphrodite of the Mandrake, 4
Apollonius Rhodius, on honey, 14
Apple tree, sap of, 3
Aquatic creatures, taboos about, 200
Aristotle, on human fetus, 31

Arnebeth (hare), 201 *f.*
Arrows, shot at weddings, 108
Ashes, at weddings, 104

Babel, Tower of, xiii
Bacchus, vine of, transmogrified, xvi
Baptism, averting demons at, 60 *f.*
Barefoot, pallbearers go, 143, 170
Bar mitzvah, 66 *f.*
Beans, given to the dead, 176 *f.*
"Beating the bounds," 125
Benno of Osnabruck, 163
Berchta, 159
Betrothal, 79 *ff.;* cup of, 118
Birds of carrion, 200
Black in mourning, 154
Blessings, seven, at wedding, 116 *f.*
Blinds, drawn at death, 159
Blood, precautions about spilling, 208; drinking of, in non-Jewish usage, 207; forbidden as food,

206 *ff.;* menstrual, 4; as seat of soul, 207; of witches, 207 *f.*
"Bond of Life," 179 *f.*
Branding, of slaves and votaries, 51 *f.*
Bowls, use of in magic, 27
Breath, last, 161
Bridal couple, rolled in mat, 113; treated as royalty, 128; stroking of, 4
Bride, hair of, shorn or unkempt, 105; seclusion of, 100 *f.;* kept screened, 103
Bride-price, 82
Burial, 142 *ff.;* coffinless, 140; deferred, 142; speedy, 169

Calvin, John, on honey, 14
Camelopard, 201
Canaanite charm against Lilith, 19; myths, xiv
Candelifera, 11
Candle, at childbirth, 11 *f.*
Canopy, bridal. *See Huppah*
Carcass, taboos about, 202
Care-cloth, 113
Carrion, forbidden as food, 202
Casket. *See* Coffin
Catullus, on ribald songs, 123
Cemetery, 178 *f.;* grass in, 178
Chairs, overturned at death, 171
Chameleon, forbidden as food, 204
Chamois, 201
Charon, obol for, 168
Cherubim, xv
Childbirth, "uncleanness" of, 29 *f.*
"Children under the Mantle," 133
Child-stealing Witch, 18 *ff.*
Cicero, on kissing the dead, 161; on white, 103
Circe, drug of, 4
Circuitous route, at funeral, 144
Circuits, around bier, 144; around bridal couple, 125; around corpse, 173
Circumambulation, 125
Circumcision, 44 *ff.;* among non-Jews, 46 *f.;* pre-nuptial, 47, 101; service at, 56 *ff.*
Circumcision door, 62
Cleveland, Robert, on witches' blood, 208

Clothes, new at wedding, 102
Cock, eaten to induce male offspring, 4
Coffin, "bumped" at funeral, 172; burial without, 167; objects placed in, 167 *f.;* plank removed from, 140, 167; tipped at funeral, 172
Coins, placed on coffin, 168
Commemoration of the dead, 182 *ff.*
Commensality, 119
Conception, magical recipes for, 3 *ff.*
Confarreatio, 119
Confirmation. *See* Bar mitzvah
Corpse, perfuming of, 164; washing of, 164
Covenant, wedding symbolizes, 126 *f.*
Cuisine, of Jews, xii
Cup of betrothal, 118
Cyprian, St., scroll of, 23

Daggers, at weddings, 107
Dardanos, Sword of, book of magic, 11, 221
David, shield of, 217 *f.*
Days, auspicious for birth, 16; auspicious for marriage, 96
Dead, placed on floor, 163; carried out feet foremost, 143; garments of, 138; kissing of, 161; mouth of, closed with sherds, 162; orientation of, in burial, 147; redeemed by the living, 189; return at seasonal festivals, 192
Dietary laws, 199 *ff.;* Hindu, 202
Dionysus, lips of smeared with honey, 14
Diptych, 185
Dirge, Corfiote, 147; Sephardic, 144
Disguise, at weddings, 104
Dissertation (*derashah*), at Bar mitzvah ceremony, 69
Distaff, at weddings, 89
Divorce, of Lilith, 27 *f.*
Door, special, at baptism, 61
Dove, in Christianity, 157
Dow-purse, 84
Drinking together, 118 *f.*
Drydenfuss, 219
Dūchiphath, unclean bird, 201

Dust, cast over shoulder at funerals, 175 *f.*

Eagle, 200
Eaglestone, 7 *f.*
Earth, strewn on coffin, 147, 173; Palestinian, in coffin, 140, 167
Eating together, by bridal couple, 119
Eddas, on life-tree, 41
Egg, used in cleansing corpses, 138
Eggs, in funeral meats, 176
Eel, tabooed, 204
Elephantine, marriage contracts from, 115
Elijah, Chair of, 63; and Lilith, 21, 26; patron of circumcision, 63
Epitaphs, 178
Erdmutter, 38
Eve, locks of, trimmed by God, 105
Eye, seat of soul, 160
Eyes, closing of, at death, 159

Fare, for dead, 168
Fat, internal. *See* Suet
Fatima, hand of, 6
Faustus, Doctor, and hexagram, 219
Fescennine verses, 123
Fish, taboos about, 204
Feather-bed, dying may not lie on, 157
Flint knife, in circumcision, 55
Flood, story of, xiii
Floor, dead placed on, 163
Foods, forbidden, 204
Foreskin, swallowed as charm, 4
Francis of Assisi, 163
Frazer, James, on boiling milk, 213
Friday, weddings on, 96
Fumigation, to avert demons, 165
Funeral, 144 *ff.;* cortege halted, 144, 172; return from, 148
Funus, 166

Gad, Phoenician god of luck, 64; table (couch) of, 64
Galen, on "salting" of newborn, 13
Garments of the dead, 138; husband's, at childbirth, 12
Gello, 20
Ghatti, 15
Ghosts, laying of, 191

Gifts, exchange of, at betrothal, 86
Girdle, bridal, 87 *f.*
Glass smashed at wedding, 119 *f.*
Gloves, black, worn by mourners, 155
Goel, 133
Goethe, on Lilith, 19
Grace after Meals, at circumcision, 63; in house of mourning, 152
Grass plucked at funerals, 148, 175
Graveclothes, 139; of murdered person, 140
Greetings, during mourning, 150

Hair, of bride, unkempt (shorn), 104; cut at puberty, 67, 106; cut at wedding, 105; as life-index, 106
Hallowe'en, 192
Hammer, in coffin, 169
Hand, amulets, 6
Hands, washed at funeral, 174
Hare, 4 *f.;* sacred to Aphrodite, 5
Hashkabah (requiem), 153, 182
Hatan (bridegroom), 101; original meaning of, 48
Hebrâ Kadîshâ (burial society), 138
Heidmann, demonic being, 159
Hermes, transmogrified, xvi
Hermesiel, xvi
Herodotus, on circumcision, 46
Herondas, on "soul on lips," 160
Hexagram, 218
Heywood, John, on unkempt bride, 105
Hippocrates, on purification after childbirth, 31
H-n-k, 14
Holle, Frau, 37
Hollekreisch, 36
Honey, at childbirth, 14, 129
Horseshoe, 10
"House of Life" (cemetery), 178
Huppah (bridal canopy), 111 *ff.*

Ibn Ezra, Abraham, on segregation after childbirth, 31
Insects, flying, 200
Insults, at weddings, 122 *f.*
Iron, averts demons, 9 *f.*
Ischiatic nerve, 210 *f.*

Jacob at Jabbok, 210
Jahrzeit, 182
Jerome, St., on "salting" of the newborn, 13
Joshua ben Levi, 17
Judah Hadassi, on Shield of David, 220

Kaddish, 147, 182
Kallah (bride,) 99
Kashruth (dietary purity), 199 *ff.*
Ketubah (marriage contract), 113; decoration of, 115
Key of Solomon, book of magic, 221
Kid, seething of, in mother's milk, 212
Kiddushin (betrothal), 84, 127
Kimpezettl, 21 *ff.*
Kissing, of dead, 161
Kittel, 139
Knife, averts demons, 11; circumcision, 5, 55; at weddings, 108
Knots, forbidden in graveclothes, 164; untied, 105, 164
"Know," in sexual sense, 104

Lamashtu, 20
Lamia, 20
Lamp, in mourning, 150; in tombs, 166
Lampoons, at weddings, 122
Languages, of Jews, xii
lectus, after childbirth, 64
Lent, marriage during, 99
Lentils, as food of mourners, 177
Leviathan, myth of, xiii
Lifting of child, at naming ceremony, 37; as sign of paternity, 37
Lights, at baptism, 61; at childbirth, 11; for the dead, 166
Lilith, 18 *ff.*; names of, 22, 25
Lips, soul on, 160
Lupercalia, 125

Magen David, 217 *f.*
Mandrake, 3 *f.*
Mannikin, in eye, superstition about, 160
"Mantle, Children under the," 133
Manu, Code of, 202
March, marriages in, 97
Mare, pregnant, in magic, 4

Marriage, best times for, 95; contract, 113
Martyrs, Commemoration of, 186
May, weddings in, 97
Meat and milk, 211 *ff.*
Meats, funeral, 176
Memento, in Christian Mass, 186
Memorbuch of Nuremberg, 184
Menorah, at weddings, 110
Mensa, after childbirth, 64
Mesh'al (cresset), 109
Metempsychosis, 206
Milk and meat, 211 *ff.*; sprinkled over fields, 213
Moon, and weddings, 95
Mormolukeion, 19
Mortification, periods of, 98
Moses, Sword of, book of magic, 11, 221
Mourners' meal, 148
Mourning, customs of, 149 *ff.*
Mourning garb at weddings, 104
Mouth, closed at death, 160
Muzzle, for the dead, 162

Nahmanides, on segregation after childbirth, 31
Names, 33 *ff.*; concealed at birth, 34
Nökhe, Danish river-sprite, 11
North, abode of demons, 120
Nudipedalia, 170
Nuts, at weddings, 122

Oil, smearing newborn with, 14
Okypete, harpy, 25
Omer-period, weddings in, 98
Onoskelis, 19
Oratio post nomina, 185

Pallium, held over bridal couple, 113
Passports, for the dead, 169
Pentacle, 219
Pentagram, 218
Perfuming of corpse, 164
Pesikta Rabbati, on commemoration of the dead, 185
Pillow, removed from the dying, 137, 157
Platoke (headgear), 106

Pliny, on beans, 177; on eaglestone, 7; on hare, 5; on vervain, 5
Plutarch, on eaglestone, 7
Poker, use of, in churning butter, 10
Pope, Alexander, on kissing the dead, 161
Pork, taboos about, 204
Pots, symbolical breaking of, 120; broken at death, 171
Pregnant women, touching of, 4
Purification, after childbirth, 29 *ff.;* of Women, Order of, 32
Purim, non-Jewish analogies to, xvi

Qatros, Mandaean hero, 11, 221
Quadrupeds, taboos about, 200

Red, averts demons, 13; child painted, 13
Rending of garments, 154, 162
Reptiles, taboos about, 200
Requiem, 182
Rice, at weddings, 121 *f.*
Ring, betrothal, 83 *f.*
Rose water, 6
Royalty, bridal couple treated as, 128
Ruby, 6

Sacramentum, Roman rite of betrothal, 84
Salt, averts demons, 13 *f.*
Samaritan dirge, 166
Sargenes (graveclothes), 139
Scent, exuded by deities, 165
Scroll of Law, at childbirth, 15
"Seal," baptism as, 51; circumcision as, 51
Sealing of slaves and votaries, 51
Sechswöchnerin, 30
"Seeing the face" of the bride, 103
Segregation, after childbirth, 29 *ff.*
Shafashift (Amharic), "bridal cloth," 88
Shakespeare, on bride's tresses, 105; on Lilith, 25; on opening windows at death, 158; on snatching pillow from the dying, 157; on witches' blood, 207
Shawls, thrown over bride, 113
Sheitel (wig), 105

Shelley, on kissing the dead, 161
Shield of David, 217 *f.*
Shir ha-Ma'alos, 26
Shiv'ah, 149
Shofar, blown at funeral, 143
Shosbin, 87
Shusuppu (Akkadian), "dyed cloth," 87
Siddhi Kur, Kalmuk legend of, 40
"Sinew that shrinks," 210 *f.*
Sisinnius, Saint, and Lilith, 22 *f.*
Smashing of glass, at wedding, 119
Solomon, seal of, 220
Song of Songs, at weddings, 114
Spear, averts demons, 11; bachelor's, at Roman weddings, 106
Spinnholz, 88 *f.*
Sponsalia, 88 *f.*
Spreading of garments, symbolism of, 86
Springs, newborn extracted from, 38
Star, six-pointed, 218
Steel, averts demons, 10
"Stone of birth," 6
Strix, 25
Suet, consumption of, forbidden, 208 *f.*
Suetonius, on barefoot mourners, 170
Sword, at childbirth, 10; averts demons, 11
Sword of Dardanos, book of magic, xvii, 11, 221
Sword of Moses, book of magic, xvii, 11, 221
Swords, at weddings, 107 *f.*

Taeda (torch)-"marriage," 109
Taharah, 138
Tallith, bridegroom's, 86 *f.;* corpse wrapped in, 139
Tattooing, 51
Tetragrammaton, 220
Thalamos (marriage bower), 112
Thigh, as seat of life, 211
Thirst, of the dead, 171
Thirty Days, period of mourning, 149
Threads, tying with, 12 *f.*
Tombstones, 179
Torches, wedding, 110

Totemism, and food taboos, 205
Tree, as life-token, 40; planted at birth, 39; of sovereignty, 41
Trendl, Chanukah, xvi
Trowel, buried with the dead, 141
Trud, 219
Tuesday, auspicious for weddings, 97

Umbrella, held over bride, 113
Unleavened Bread, Feast of, xv
Unveiling, of bride, 104
Upstairs, newborn child carried, 38

Vasistha, dietary laws of, 203
Veil, bridal, 103
Vergil, on kissing the dead, 161; on scent exuded by deities, 165
Vervain, 3 ff.
Vitalis, Saint, and Lilith, 25

Wachnacht, 62
Wailers, at funerals, 143
Washing of corpse, 164; of hands at funeral, 147, 174
Water, impassable by demons, 171; poured out, at death, 143, 171;

of priestly lavation, 6; of taharah, magical properties of, 4, 138; bowl of, under Chair of Elijah, 5
Weddings, forbidden seasons for, 98
Wednesday, auspicious for weddings, 96
Werzeliya, Child-stealing Witch, 23
Wheat, at weddings, 121
White, ceremonial color, 103; dead clothed in, 165; worn by bride, 102; worn in mourning, 154
Willow, 6
Windows, demons climb through, 159; opened, at death, 158
Witch, Child-stealing, 18 ff.
Withold, Saint, and Lilith, 25
Wolf, Child-stealing Witch as, 19
Wortmann, 87

Yizkor, 183 ff.

Zemzem, water of, 5
Zidduk Ha-Din, 153
Zunz, Leopold, on circumcision, 53